VISUAL QUICKSTART GUIDE

Cubase SX

for Macintosh and Windows

Thad Brown

 **Peachpit Press**

Visual QuickStart Guide
Cubase SX for Macintosh and Windows
Thad Brown

Peachpit Press
1249 Eighth Street
Berkeley, CA 94710
510/524-2178
800/283-9444
510/524-2221 (fax)
Find us on the World Wide Web at: http://www.peachpit.com
Peachpit Press is a division of Pearson Education

Editor: Cary Norsworthy
Production Editor: Lisa Brazieal
Copyeditor: Judy Ziajka
Compositor: Christi Payne
Indexer: Joy Dean Lee
Cover Production: Nathalie Valette

Notice of rights

Notice of liability

Trademarks

ISBN 0-321-16218-8

9 8 7 6 5 4 3 2 1

Printed and bound in the United States of America

Dedication

For my parents, who from my earliest memories taught me to love words and music in equal measure.

Acknowledgements

Good editors are as hard to find as good drummers, and for this book I had two of them. Rebecca Gulick started with me on this book (and hired me for my first ever Peachpit gig), and without her the entire project might never have made it airborne. Cary Norsworthy picked up where Rebecca left off, and her impact on this project is incalculable. If this book helps you—particularly if you are new to computer music—you should thank Cary. Thanks also to Greg Ondo and David Leishman for technical advice, Judy Ziajka for working over my copy, and to Christi Payne and Lisa Brazieal for making it look good in layout.

Many people aided me in writing this book. Rusty Cutchin, my editor at Home Recording Magazine, gave me both work and time off when I needed it. Thanks to Jimmy and Dottie Moore for helping me keep the rent paid and DSL turned on, and to Eric Dickerson, Kirsten Drymiller, and Tia Martinson for the same. Vielen Dank to Stephan M. Sprenger and the rest of the crazy Germans at Prosoniq who taught me volumes about software. Stephen St. Croix, Edmund Pirali, Andy Cactusfire, Brian Tankersley, Morgan Pettinato and the entire PARIS community taught me a great deal about sonics, software, and trusting my own ears. Thanks also to Mary Tyler for getting new music to those ears, year after year, disc after disc.

Levin Pfeufer earns special appreciation for the multiple, shape-shifting roles he played helping me with this book. He not only did the groovy illustrations, he also taught me survival InDesign skills and kept me fully loaded with dancehall mixes from the Canal Street Selector. Big up Lev.

Writing is a rather solitary task. For their very real contribution I would like to thank Scientist, Thievery Corporation, Grant Green, Neil Young, King Tubby, Jimi Hendrix, Sean Paul, the Flaming Lips, Augustus Pablo, Scratch Perry, the Meters, and Stan Getz. I spent the hours writing this book alone, but I was always in exquisite company.

TABLE OF CONTENTS

Chapter 11: The Cubase Mixer 241

Chapter 12: Audio Effect Plug-ins 291

INSTALLING & CONFIGURING CUBASE SX

As recently as a few years ago, only very brave and very experienced people would attempt to set up a computer as a serious music-recording platform. Beginners would spend days or weeks slogging to get hardware and software to work together, while power users would spend incredible amounts of time tweaking their computer configurations to squeeze a tiny bit of extra performance from a machine.

Most parts of this book apply equally to most users, because Cubase works about the same for everyone. However, in this chapter, we'll cover hardware and software setup and configuration—which involve many variables—and specific details will differ from user to user. This is one of the unfortunate realities of getting multiple pieces of fairly complex audio hardware working together.

While it's certainly easier to set up a digital recording studio now than it was a few years ago, smart Cubase SX users will still want to learn more about how the program is installed and configured. In this chapter, you will discover how to install the Cubase SX hardware and software, learn a bit about tweaks and tricks to get solid audio performance, find out about the types of audio cards and MIDI interfaces that Cubase SX supports, and learn about monitoring as you record.

Installing Cubase SX

The Cubase SX box contains the basic documentation, the installation CDs, a USB hardware copy-protection dongle, and various other pieces of paper relating to product registration, special offers, and sound files (**Figure 1.1**).

The USB hardware dongle prevents unauthorized use of the Cubase program. Over the years, software companies have used various tools to prevent software piracy. The USB dongle (like all anti-piracy tools) has its strengths and weaknesses. The good news about the dongle is that you can move it easily from machine to machine, so if you have both laptop and desktop systems, you can install Cubase SX on both machines and just plug the dongle into the one you are using at the moment. The bad news, of course, is that the dongle can break or be lost, and you can't run the program without it.

On both the PC and Mac versions of Cubase SX, you should run the installer on the CD-ROM without the dongle attached. However, once the program is installed on your hard drive, it won't run unless you have the USB dongle attached, and it will prompt you to attach the dongle if you've forgotten.

As of this writing, Steinberg released a downloadable 1.06 update for both the Mac and PC versions of Cubase SX. To access any update, visit the Download section of http://www.steinberg.net.

Figure 1.1 In addition to the software CD and documentation, the Cubase box contains a USB dongle. The program will not work without it.

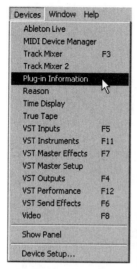

Figure 1.2 Click to open the panel to configure and manage Cubase plug-ins.

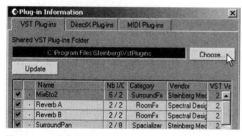

Figure 1.3 Click the Choose button to set a new plug-ins folder.

Figure 1.4 Selecting a folder for shared plug-ins

What Goes Where?

If you accept the default installation options, and you're using a PC, Cubase will be installed in C:\Program Files\Steinberg\Cubase SX, and this is where you will find most of the Cubase-related files you will ever need to see. If you want, you can install Cubase in a different directory, but I strongly recommend sticking to the defaults. This will reduce the risk of problems if you use Cubase in conjunction with other applications.

If you use a Mac, some of the files are scattered on your system, but the main application will be stored in \Applications\Cubase SX. (A quick search on "Cubase SX" will reveal other file locations.) I recommend adding the Cubase application to the dock by dragging it there.

PC users have an additional file-location option. Because you may have many applications using many different audio plug-ins and software instruments, to keep your files organized, you can set one folder as the place where all of these plug-ins reside. (On the Mac, third-party plug-ins are located in Users/(name)/Library/Audio/Plug-Ins/VST.)

To set up a plug-ins folder on a PC:

1. From the Devices menu, select Plug-in Information (**Figure 1.2**).

   At the top of the window that opens, the file path appears in the Shared VST Plug-ins Folder field.

2. Click the Choose button to the right of the path name (**Figure 1.3**).

3. In the Select directory file navigation box that opens, select the folder you want to use for common plug-ins (**Figure 1.4**).

4. Click OK in the dialog box to save your setting and close the dialog box. Close the Plug-in Information panel as well.

Audio Versus MIDI

Recorded audio and MIDI are fundamentally different. Each is the best option in particular situations, and neither is universally better.

The goal of recorded audio is to capture and store a sound for future playback with as much fidelity to the original sound as possible. Over the years, audio has been recorded on wax discs, magnetic tape, cassettes, hard-disk recorders, digital tape decks, and computers. When live music is digitized, the analog sound path includes a microphone or line-level sound generator (voice or acoustic or electric instrument); it also can include an external sound modifier (such as a hardware reverb unit), and it generally is routed through a mixer. The sound can be converted to digital data either inside or outside the computer and then stored as bits on your hard drive.

Whatever the source, the whole point of an audio recording is to store the sound and play it back so that it sounds as much like the original as possible. Audio recordings by nature capture the tempo, duration, pitch, and timbre of whatever is being recorded. In a nondigital process, it is comparatively difficult to change any of these values in a significant way after a recording is finished.

MIDI, in contrast, does not record acoustic events, but instead records data and instructions from a musical performance, most often from a keyboard. This data is not limited to a particular instrument, sound, tempo, or duration. When a sequencer like Cubase records MIDI data, it actually records something like this: "at bar 34, beat 2, play an A# that lasts until bar 34, beat 3." Normal MIDI recording also records the velocity of MIDI notes (how hard the key is struck), how much pressure is applied to a key as it is held down (the aftertouch), and how quickly the note is released.

Because MIDI records data, it provides a level of flexibility that recorded audio does not have. For example, if you record the audio output of a synthesizer playing a piano sound and store that in Cubase, you will pretty much have to use that sound as it is recorded. However, if instead you record only the MIDI generated by your performance into Cubase, you can then send this MIDI data to any other MIDI device to trigger the sound of a clavinet, organ, drums, flute, or whatever you dream up.

Because MIDI is recorded purely in reference to tempo and is easily transposed, a MIDI recording will automatically and transparently follow changes to the tempo and key of a project. After recording your MIDI performance, you can seamlessly change its characteristics; if you decide that the track sounds better five beats per minute faster or that a singer needs an arrangement that's three semitones lower, you can speed up the track or transpose it via a few clicks, with no loss in sound quality.

Neither MIDI nor recorded audio is "better," and both are used in almost every kind of music production. The smart musician uses each in its place, and a big part of what makes Cubase SX so powerful is that it has extremely advanced audio recording and editing capabilities in the same window as a top-quality MIDI sequencer. It's all there, and you should use as much of it as you can.

Recording Essentials

Cubase enables you to perform the entire process of music production with a computer—you can record, play, mix, process, add effects, and master audio in pretty much any way you can imagine. However, you will almost certainly need more than just the application and a computer to make music. Here is a list of equipment you may need for your Cubase studio:

◆ **Sound card** or **audio interface:** To record audio, you need a way to get it into the computer. Most, but not all, PCs ship with some kind of SoundBlaster-style sound card, and most, but not all, Macs have at least 1/8-inch minijacks for audio output (and sometimes for input). You almost certainly will want to upgrade either to a higher-quality audio interface. The upgrade may be an internal PCI card or an external converter that routes data to a FireWire or USB port on the computer (**Figure 1.5**).

◆ **MIDI interface:** If you plan to do any work with external synthesizers or samplers, or if you plan to record MIDI data to Cubase, you will need an interface to connect your MIDI hardware to your computer. Most MIDI interfaces these days use USB for the connection.

◆ **Monitoring setup:** Audio people refer to listening to a track or a mix as *monitoring*, so speakers are referred to as monitors. Most monitoring is done with near-field monitors: two speakers located a few feet away and pointed right at the spot where you sit when you mix. Headphones are not great for monitoring mixes, but they are indispensable for recording live musicians.

◆ **External mixer:** An external mixer will be handy if you plan to work with a large number of microphones or electric instruments or with external synths and samplers, all playing at the same time, or if you just want some extra inputs and convenience. Even small 12-input models that cost only a few hundred dollars can help a lot.

Of course, if you intend to record live instruments or hardware synths and samplers, you will need microphones, cables, and microphone preamps. There are many books written specifically about those topics, along with newsgroups and Web sites bursting with people ready to share their opinions and experiences.

Figure 1.5 Some of the equipment you will likely use with your computer and Cubase

Audio Interfaces and Drivers

Both Macs and PCs have system-level drivers for audio cards. They work fairly well for most people, but they don't always meet the needs of high-end users. If you are using Cubase SX, you're probably a high-end user, and you will want to get a card with an ASIO driver for use with Cubase. There are only three kinds of sound-card drivers you will run into when using Cubase, and if at all possible, you want to use the ASIO driver for your card.

◆ **ASIO** stands for Audio Stream In/Out, and it's the driver model created by Steinberg many years ago. At that time, system-level audio drivers were severely limited in the number of channels of audio they could play and record simultaneously, and they were also limited in the sound quality of those channels.

◆ **DirectSound**, or **WDM**, is the newest type of driver created by Microsoft for Windows multimedia. WDM drivers are quite good these days (earlier versions of DirectSound drivers were sometimes a horror show), but Cubase SX still works best with ASIO drivers, and you should use them if possible.

◆ **Core Audio** is the new system-level multimedia specification for Mac OS X. As this book is written, the first Core Audio sound card drivers are being released. Like the most recent PC DirectSound drivers, Core Audio is a big step up from Apple's previous Sound Manager system, but Cubase does not support Core Audio cards (at least not yet), and even if it ever does, ASIO will likely still be the preferred tool for working with Cubase on a Mac.

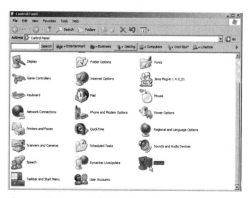

Figure 1.6 You open the Windows System control panel by double-clicking this icon.

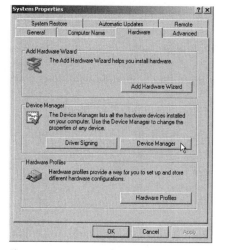

Figure 1.7 Opening the Device Manager from the Hardware tab

Figure 1.8 The Device Manager has a list of all installed hardware, including audio and MIDI interfaces.

Checking the Windows XP Sound Card

After you have physically installed your sound card, but before you set it up for use in Cubase, it's a good idea to check that it is installed properly so that Windows sees it. The easiest way to do this is through the Device Manager.

To confirm a working sound card in Windows XP:

1. From the Start menu, select Settings > Control Panel.

2. Double-click System (**Figure 1.6**) to open the System Properties panel.

3. Click the Hardware tab to display it.

4. In the Device Manager section of the Hardware tab, click the Device Manager button (**Figure 1.7**).

5. Click the small + symbol next to Sound, Video and Game Controllers to expand the list.

   Your sound card should be listed here (**Figure 1.8**). If it is not, or if it is covered with a red X, then there is a problem with the installation, and you should check the documentation that came with your sound card or try reinstalling it.

✔ Tips

- If you are using a PCMCIA card on a laptop, you may need to look under that item in Device Manager.

- If you are using a FireWire or USB interface, you may need to look in those sections of the Device Manager.

What Makes a Good Sound Card?

Choosing the right sound card for your needs can make your recording and mixing experience a delight, and choosing the wrong one can pretty much ensure that you'll hate turning on your music computer. There are three questions you need to answer before you choose a sound card.

First, how many inputs and outputs do you need? Note that the question is not how many could you possibly ever use if your band gets a major label record deal. If that happens, you can buy another sound card. In day-to-day use, though, how many inputs and outputs (usually called I/O) will you really need? If you are recording full bands, 8 inputs is the absolute minimum, and realistically you should shoot for at least 16. If you mostly sequence and overdub on your own, 4 or 8 I/Os may be plenty. If you are a DJ or samplehead, 4 I/Os, or even a stereo setup, may be enough.

The second question you need to ask is whether you should get a PCI card, USB, or FireWire audio interface. PCI cards have long been the high-end approach to audio interfaces. The PCI bus in a computer can handle many tracks of audio and MIDI, and the PCI specification has been around forever. The downside of PCI cards is that they are comparatively hard to install (you'll have to open up the computer case) and inconvenient to move to another computer.

USB (which stands for universal serial bus) audio interfaces are plugged into the USB ports that come on every computer built in the past few years. USB hardware is very convenient; it's easy to use and easy to move to another computer. You can even hot plug (plug the interface in with the computer already on) a USB audio interface. The problem with USB is that because of the low bandwidth of the bus itself, you will almost always be limited to stereo input and output plus MIDI. That may be enough for you, and if it is, then you can buy a nice USB interface for very little money.

FireWire is, in many ways, similar to USB; you can hot plug FireWire audio interfaces, and they are very convenient and easy to work with. FireWire, though, has a huge bandwidth advantage over USB and can manage many more tracks at very low latencies. FireWire has worked well on Macs for awhile, and Windows XP has high-quality support built in for FireWire devices. FireWire audio, though, has lagged a bit on Windows machines because of drivers. Two companies with significant experience in the PC audio interface world, MIDIMAN and Ego Systems, will probably have made FireWire a more viable option for the PC by the time you read this.

You also need to find out whether the sound card that fits your needs will work reliably with your computer. The sad fact is that not every computer works with every sound card, and the doubly sad fact is that the only way to really find out what works with what is to do research on your own. Spend some time on the Web in newsgroups and forums where Cubase users talk about their hardware setups and find out whether other people with a computer setup like yours have been happy using the sound card you are thinking of using. (Steinberg hosts a site for users to share their experiences—both good and bad—at www.steinberg.net/en/ps/support/forums.) Many hardware manufacturers also host mailing lists or newsgroups related to their hardware. I use an RME sound card, and the RME newsgroup has helped me keep my system working well.

continues on next page

Checking the Mac OS X Sound Card

You can easily check Mac OS X to verify that your sound card is properly installed and that the operating system has loaded the proper drivers to use it. Your exact setup will not likely be like mine, but it should be fairly close. The following example will work if your audio interface has a control panel in the Mac OS X System Preferences panel; not all will, and if your card does not, there are two places to look. First, check the documentation that came with the audio interface for further information. Second, use the OS X Audio MIDI Setup utility, which is described in relation to MIDI interfaces on page 15 in the section "Checking a Mac OS X MIDI Interface." The Audio MIDI Setup utility can be used to view and configure both audio and MIDI hardware.

What Makes a Good Sound Card? *(continued)*

The third question to consider is whether you have any specific and unique needs. Do you need digital I/O? Do you need microphone preamps or some kind of on-board synthesis or sampling capability? Do you collaborate with someone else who has a particular system that would be good for you to mirror? No two computer audio users are alike, and your setup may have a few quirks that influence your choice of sound card.

Once you've answered these three questions, you'll know the key options to look for in a sound card. Before you buy, check a variety of local dealers and online music retailers' sites to find the specs of cards that will fit your needs. It's also a good idea to check the return and exchange policies of the vendor from which you buy your gear.

To confirm a working sound card in Mac OS X:

1. In the dock, click the System Preferences icon (**Figure 1.9**).

2. In the System Preferences panel that opens, look for the control panel for your sound card (**Figure 1.10**). There's a good chance it will be in the Other section at the bottom of the panel, as in Figure 1.10, which shows the USB audio interface.

3. Click the icon for your sound card to open its control panel (**Figure 1.11**). Try changing any parameter to be sure that the operating system and the hardware are communicating.

Figure 1.9 Click to open the Mac OS System Preferences in the dock.

Figure 1.10 Some of the preferences, including a USB audio interface at the bottom of the window

Figure 1.11 The OS X control panel for one particular audio interface

Figure 1.12 Every digital audio system, including a computer, needs some time to perform analog-to-digital and digital-to-analog conversion.

What's a Millisecond?

It's possible to be *too* concerned about latency. The generally quoted speed of sound is 1,100 feet per second. That changes with temperature, humidity, and altitude, but it's the standard reference. With 1,000 milliseconds in a second, this means that sound travels pretty close to one foot every millisecond. In other words, if you move your speakers a foot away from the listening position, you introduce about a millisecond of latency into your system.

This is not to say that latency doesn't matter; it does, and for some people, it's a crucial factor. If you plan to record with software synths, samplers, or previously recorded tracks, for instance, you need to be much more concerned about the latency between what you hear and what you play. DJs and sampleheads probably don't need to worry much at all, because they are accustomed to working with external mixing, cueing, and monitoring. If you are having problems with sound card latency, read the sections at the end of this chapter about external monitoring, or consider investing in a new sound card.

Latency Defined

If you have done any work with audio on computers before, you have probably heard the term *latency*. If you haven't heard it yet, you'll be hearing it often now. A dictionary definition of latency is "the time that elapses between a stimulus and the response to it." In the computer world, latency generally refers to the time that elapses between the request for an action and the completion of the action.

For computer audio users, though, latency usually refers to sound card latency: the time the sound card takes to convert what you're recording into digital data and move the data to your hard drive, or the time needed to convert the stored data back to analog audio for output (**Figure 1.12**). Audio latency is of critical importance. If you are playing along with previously recorded material and there's a half-second lag between what you hear and what you record, your new material will not play back in time with the old.

Latency is affected by a huge number of factors, including the speed of the computer, the quality of its chipset, the limitations of the sound card or hardware, and the amount of time a signal takes to pass among these components. But the most important factor in achieving low-latency, high-reliability audio recording is a good software driver, because it can help you combat timing differences.

Setting Latency

Naturally, you want the lowest latency settings possible for your sound card. The only way to find the best settings is trial and error: setting the latency value lower and lower until the computer introduces clicks and pops and dropouts or excessive static into the audio. Keep in mind that there is also an insurmountable trade-off between lower latency and higher CPU use. These days, you can usually use the most aggressive latency settings because CPUs are so powerful, but if you seem to be surprisingly short on CPU bandwidth, consider bumping up your latency setting by a few milliseconds.

To set the latency for your sound card:

1. From the Devices menu in Cubase, select Device Setup.

2. In the panel that opens, select VST Multitrack (**Figure 1.13**).

3. Click the Control Panel button (**Figure 1.14**).
   The window for configuring your sound card settings opens (**Figure 1.15**).

4. Set the sound card latency in the sound card control panel and click OK to close the panel.

5. Click OK in the Cubase Device Setup panel to commit the changes to your Cubase setup.

✔ Tip

■ Not every audio interface will respond correctly and open from the VST Multitrack section of the Device Setup panel. You may have to exit Cubase and configure the card with its own control panel. If the steps described here don't work, check the documentation that came with your sound card.

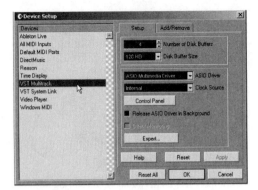

Figure 1.13 Selecting VST Multitrack in the Devices panel

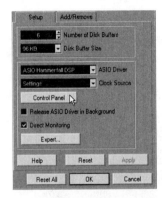

Figure 1.14 Click to open the control panel for the currently selected audio interface.

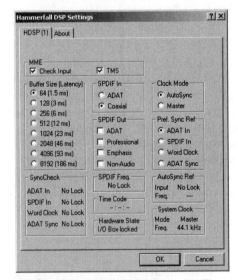

Figure 1.15 The control panel is set to 1.5 milliseconds of latency. The control panel for your card will probably be different, but it should have options for setting latency.

Figure 1.16 The Hardware tab of the Sounds and Audio Devices panel

Figure 1.17 To check system-level MIDI, select the sound card or interface and click Properties.

Checking the Windows XP MIDI Interface

A few pages back, you learned how to be sure that your sound card is working under Windows and is available for use with Cubase SX. Similarly, with MIDI interfaces, you want to be sure the interface is installed and available in Windows before you configure it in Cubase.

To confirm a working MIDI interface in Windows XP:

1. From the Start menu, select Settings > Control Panel.

2. In the Control Panel, double-click Sound and Audio Devices.

3. In the Sound and Audio Devices Properties Panel, click the Hardware tab to display it (**Figure 1.16**).

4. In the list of installed hardware, you should see the MIDI interface, or the name of your sound card. Select it and then click Properties (**Figure 1.17**).

continues on next page

5. In the panel that opens, click the Properties tab.

6. Click the small plus (+) sign to the left of the MIDI Devices and Instruments option to expand the list and see the installed MIDI interfaces (**Figure 1.18**).

7. If your MIDI interface is listed here, click Cancel to close the Properties window and then click Cancel to close the Sound and Audio Devices panel. All is well.

✔ Tip

■ If your MIDI interface is not visible in these panels, something is wrong at the system level. Try reinstalling the interface, or check the documentation that came with the interface to see what you may need to do to get everything working correctly.

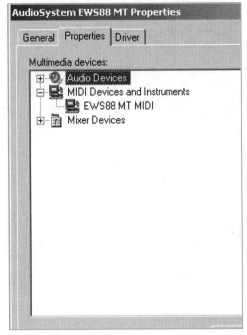

Figure 1.18 This list shows active, working MIDI.

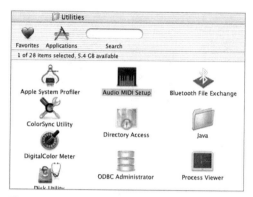

Figure 1.19 The Audio MIDI Setup utility is in the Utilities folder of the OS X Applications folder.

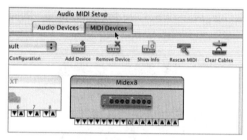

Figure 1.20 The MIDI Devices tab shows all installed MIDI interfaces—in this case, a Steinberg MidiEx8.

Checking the Mac OS X MIDI Interface

Every MIDI device you use on a Mac needs to be recognized at the system level, so it's a good idea to check that the operating system sees the hardware before trying to use it in Cubase. To do this, you use the very convenient Mac OS X Audio MIDI Setup utility.

To confirm a working MIDI interface in Mac OS X:

1. Open the Mac OS X Finder and click Applications on the top toolbar.

2. Double-click the Utilities folder to open it.

3. Double-click the icon for the Audio MIDI Setup utility (**Figure 1.19**).

4. In the Audio MIDI Setup window, click the MIDI Devices tab (**Figure 1.20**).

    All installed MIDI devices will be visible in this window. If your MIDI interface is not shown here, you need to consult its documentation regarding installation procedures and check the company's Web site to make sure you have the correct driver installed.

✔ Tip

■ When you have a moment, check out the other options (for both audio and MIDI hardware) that can be configured with the Audio MIDI Setup utility. You will find this utility very useful in your music production work on your Mac.

What Is Monitoring?

When musicians talk with recording engineers about monitoring, they generally mean being able to hear a mix of a previously recorded song so they can play along with it. On stage, though, monitors are the speakers sitting on the floor in front the band. Singers would have a mix with lots of their own vocals in those monitors so they could hear themselves above the rest of the band.

When recording in a studio, roughly similar procedures apply. The musicians usually monitor through headphones to hear themselves without creating extra noise in the recording space. The person in charge of the mixing board and who runs the recording session monitors through speakers in the control room (**Figure 1.21**).

When you start recording with Cubase, you will also need some means of monitoring. If you record other musicians, you may need headphone amplifiers and an outboard mixer just for monitoring (**Figure 1.22**). If you record only yourself playing instruments or singing, you may need only headphones. (**Figure 1.23**) No matter what method you use, though, you will have to make some decisions about monitoring, and they all involve problems with latency. Monitoring is complicated because every digital system has latency, which means that some traditional monitoring systems may not work well. The following few pages provide examples of three ways to monitor: monitoring through Cubase, through an external mixer, and using ASIO direct monitoring. Each example assumes that you are playing a bass line to go with a drum loop. (To simplify matters, we'll also assume that you're using a sound card for your sound conversion.)

Figure 1.21 You can monitor with headphones, speakers, or either of the two depending on the situation.

Figure 1.22 External monitoring avoids latency problems but involves more effort in routing audio. You probably will use some kind of external monitoring most of the time.

Figure 1.23 Monitoring through Cubase is simple and convenient but may create problems if your audio interface has high latency.

Monitoring Through Cubase SX

The simplest way to monitor is through Cubase, but it's the method with the most potential latency problems. For example, as your drum loop plays, you play along on your bass. The signal goes from the bass through a preamp to shape the tone and raise the level, and then to the sound card on your computer. The sound card converts the analog signal to digital data, and Cubase records what you play. Cubase also plays back what you are playing through the main outputs so you can hear it.

Let's say the lowest latency at which your sound card will work reliably is 18 milliseconds. This means that when you pluck the bass string, it takes 18 milliseconds for the sound card to get the digital signal into Cubase, and then 18 more milliseconds to get the sound back to the outputs from which you are monitoring it. In other words, you will hear yourself playing the bass 36 milliseconds later than if you were just playing live through an amplifier. That might not seem like much, but in practice it's way too high for a good performance, because the two sounds will play back at slightly different times.

What this means is that you should monitor this way only if you have a very high-quality sound card that operates at very low latency (less than 10 milliseconds). As this is written, the very best sound cards can operate with latency as low as 1.5 milliseconds.

Monitoring Using an External Mixer

One of the more common ways to get around the latency problem is to use an external hardware mixer to route and monitor signals. In the scenario in the preceding section, outputs from Cubase and the computer or sound card would be plugged into the hardware mixer and would play back the drum loop. Your bass would be plugged into a preamp to boost the level and shape the tone, and it would also be plugged into the mixer. As you play along with the drum loop, the bass would be routed to one of the inputs of your sound card, which would convert the audio signal to digital data for Cubase to record. You would monitor the bass only with the hardware mixer while Cubase records it.

The obvious advantage here is that there is no latency at all. The downside is that you can't hear any Cubase EQ or effects on the track you're recording, and it takes a little more effort to set things up. In general, I recommend that people use external monitoring if at all possible.

External monitoring is also often accomplished using the software mixer that came with your sound card. This will vary from system to system and card to card, but look at the documentation that came with your sound card. You may have a software mixer with a control panel that lets you route inputs on your sound card directly to another output for monitoring while Cubase records the track.

The setup for external monitoring can take a bit of effort, but zero-latency monitoring makes it worth the trouble. I use a combination of an external mixer and the very full-featured software mixer that came with my sound card.

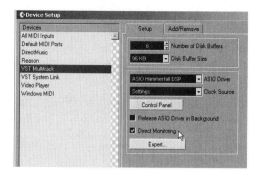

Figure 1.24 Click the check box to turn ASIO Direct Monitoring on or off.

Monitoring Using ASIO Direct Monitoring

Cubase includes an enhanced external monitoring function called ASIO direct monitoring. In practice, it offers the same features as a sound card control panel for routing sound card inputs to outputs for monitoring purposes, but it is integrated into Cubase.

Not all ASIO cards support ASIO direct monitoring, and those that do provide varying degrees of control. Some simply route hardware inputs to another output, while others include options for volume and pan to give you more choices for monitoring. The only way to be sure what you can do with ASIO direct monitoring is to try it.

To use ASIO direct monitoring:

1. From the Devices menu, select Device Setup.

2. In the Device Setup panel that opens, select VST Multitrack.

3. With VST Multitrack displayed at the right of the panel, click Direct Monitoring to activate it.

A check mark appears in the box on the left when Direct Monitoring is on (**Figure 1.24**). If this option is dimmed, your sound card does not support ASIO direct monitoring

4. Click OK to exit the Device Setup panel.

The features offered by your sound card in direct monitoring mode will vary depending on the card. Check the documentation that came with the card to get more information about these options.

Your Setup

Getting all of your hardware and software components talking to each other is usually the most difficult and frustrating part of making music with computers. Every setup is different, so every troubleshooting situation is different. If you are having problems, the first place to look is the documentation that came with your hardware, to ensure that you've hooked up all your cables and set all your switches correctly. Then check the system-level setup on your computer. If your audio interface isn't working in Cubase, try just playing back a CD through your interface. If you can't get MIDI input, import a MIDI file into Cubase and try playing it to determine whether you're getting MIDI output. You can also use the tutorial files that come with the application to test these systems.

You'll find a lot more information about selecting inputs and outputs and getting sound and MIDI in and out of Cubase in Chapter 4, "Recording Audio," and Chapter 5, "Recording MIDI." And don't forget those Cubase-related Web sites; if you have a question, they may have the specific answer you need. For starters, Steinberg Cubase forum is on the Web at http://forum.cubase.net.

Hardware Suggestions

I am always wary of giving broad endorsement of any particular make or model of audio and MIDI hardware for two reasons. First, no two systems are the same, and no two users are the same. A breakbeat mixer user on an Athlon box running XP has different hardware needs than an OS X user recording a live jazz trio. The second reason I am wary is that hardware and software change so quickly. At the same time, I want to offer something about the topic, so here are a few suggestions as this book goes to press.

For audio interfaces, I use, adore, and pay full price for equipment from RME Audio (www.rme-audio.com). The company writes fantastic drivers, makes innovative hardware, and does a great job with support. RME products are also pretty expensive, but in this case, they're more expensive for a reason. (As of this writing, RME has Mac OS X beta drivers for most of their products.)

For PC users, I also recommend Aardvark sound cards (www.aardvark-pro.com), and if you're tracking a lot of instruments, I recommend the Q10 in particular. It has great-sounding built-in microphone preamps and is a great choice for people recording their own bands. Aardvark is working on Mac OS X drivers, but their availability, quality, and stability are as yet impossible to test.

Both PC and Mac users should also look at the excellent, low-cost audio interfaces from MIDIMAN (www.midiman.com), which makes PCI, FireWire, and USB interfaces with drivers for both Macs and PCs.

Cubase SX on both Macs and PCs supports system-level multichannel MIDI interfaces, so in theory, any interface with correctly installed drivers will work. If you are serious about MIDI, though, I recommend one of the MidEx MIDI interfaces from Steinberg. These use proprietary Steinberg technology to get around many of the timing problems that can crop up when using MIDI. If you don't want a MidEx, Mark of the Unicorn makes excellent MIDI interfaces for Macs, and MIDIMAN makes cross-platform MIDI hardware as well.

TOURING THE CUBASE SX INTERFACE

2

Cubase SX offers many ways to record, view, edit, and mix audio and MIDI. The interface gives Cubase SX a sleek, polished, user-configurable way to work with all parts of a music project (**Figure 2.1**). Learning how to exploit all of these windows and views will give you incredible power over your music and creativity. If you are completely new to Cubase SX, the variety can be a bit overwhelming at first, but everything is organized in a logical way, and in only a little time you will be working quickly and capably with Cubase SX.

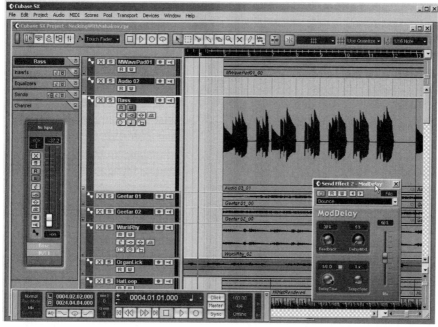

Figure 2.1
The Cubase
SX interface

Cubase SX concentrates power in its main Project window, which can be used for deep audio editing, lots of MIDI editing, automation editing, and full-mix editing for any one selected track. It is possible to create an entire song without ever leaving the Project window. The smart SX user, however, will learn where the other windows offer better or more convenient ways to edit and mix audio. As a general rule, the other editors, such as the MIDI Key editor, the Mixer, and the Audio Sample editor, are more specialized views that include more exact and finely grained tools for modifying audio and MIDI files.

In addition to the Project window, major innovations over Cubase SX's predecessor, Cubase VST, include new buttons that let you more easily accomplish many of the jobs and actions that were menu items in Cubase VST. With these useful buttons, you can use the program for hours without even looking at a menu. In addition, most Cubase SX windows include powerful context menus so that whenever a button won't do the job, one of these menus usually will. You access context menus by right-clicking (Windows) or Control-clicking (Mac). To see how much can be done with these menus, check out the context menu for an audio part in the Project window shown in **Figure 2.2**.

In this chapter, you will learn about the Project window and the other windows used in Cubase SX. You will also find important shortcuts and tricks to give you more control over your views and the way that you edit in Cubase SX. Cubase SX allows you to make choices about how you use the program, and this chapter will give you the skills you need to best set up and use the program to create your own music.

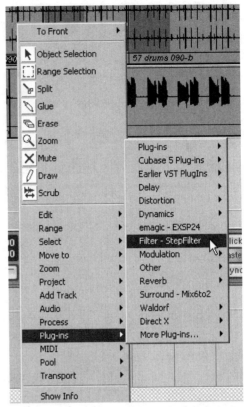

Figure 2.2 Options on the context menu that opens when you right-click or Command-click an audio part in the Project window

The Transport Bar

The Transport bar (**Figure 2.3**) lets you control playback, recording, and fast forwarding and rewinding for your project—but it also does much more than this. You will find the Transport bar mentioned in many places in this book precisely because it can be used to do so much.

Record mode selector: You can control the way that MIDI data is recorded.

Left and right locator settings: You use the left and right locators for looping and punch recording of audio and MIDI. You can set the locators here or in the Timeline of the Project window.

Pre-roll and post-roll settings: When you start recording, Cubase SX starts recording before the current position to allow musicians to get a feel for the place in the song. The duration of this pre-roll, and the post-roll after recording stops, is set here.

Time display: This display shows the current playback position in selectable time formats.

continues on next page

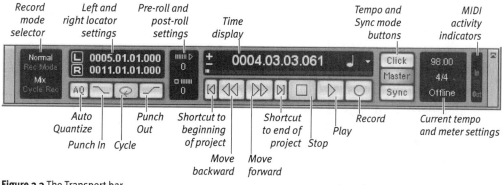

Figure 2.3 The Transport bar

THE TRANSPORT BAR

Tempo and Sync mode buttons: These buttons control a few slightly related parameters. If the Click button is selected, Cubase will generate an audio click as a tempo reference. The program can get tempo information from an internal tempo track if Master is selected and will synchronize to an external timecode if Sync is selected.

Tempo and meter settings: These show the current tempo and meter for a project. They can be edited manually here in the Transport by double-clicking and entering new values.

MIDI activity indicators: The red In light indicates incoming MIDI data, and the green Out light indicates that MIDI data is being sent out from the program. These indicators are invaluable when troubleshooting MIDI problems.

Transport controls: These standard buttons control playback, recording, stopping, and fast-winding of audio. The smaller buttons with a single arrow and a bracket are shortcuts to the very beginning or end of the project.

Loop, Autopunch, and Autoquantize buttons: These buttons let you configure Cubase SX to loop, automatically start or stop recording, and quantize incoming MIDI data if necessary.

✔ Tip

■ The Transport bar is the easiest place to configure the way that Cubase displays time. Cubase can show time in bars+ beats, various frame rates (if you use sound for video), seconds, and samples. Click to the right of the time display to open a menu and choose the way that time is displayed in Cubase (**Figure 2.4**). This setting also changes the way time is shown in the rest of your project.

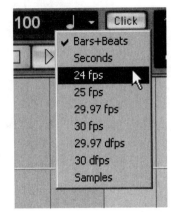

Figure 2.4 This menu sets the way that Cubase shows time throughout a project.

The Project Window

The Project window (**Figure 2.5**) is where you will spend the most time when using Cubase SX, because the complete view offered in this window makes it the best place to work. The Project window almost warrants its own book, but you will get a good start at understanding this critical part of Cubase SX in the next few pages. Each part of the Project window is described briefly here and then in greater detail on the following pages. Still, you should mark Chapter 3, "The Project Window," of the *Cubase SX Operation Manual* for reading at a later time.

Toolbar: You can use this collection of buttons to show and hide parts of the Project window, show windows, and change the tools used to edit in the Event display. The toolbar also includes buttons for basic transport control and automation setup.

continues on next page

Figure labels: Overview line, Info line, Toolbar, Ruler, Snap and Grid Settings, Track inspector, Track list, Event display

Figure 2.5 The Cubase SX Project window

THE PROJECT WINDOW

Overview line: The Overview line shows a minimal view of all events in a project and can be used for rough navigation of a project.

Info line: When a MIDI or audio event is selected in the Event display, its properties are displayed here. Often parameters for an event can be edited here as well.

Ruler: The ruler is a graphical timeline reference for the Event display. The ruler can display time in multiple formats and also shows the left and right locators.

Track inspector: The Track inspector displays parameters for the track selected in the track list. It organizes an incredible amount of information about audio and MIDI tracks in an easily accessible place. It can be used to show and change audio track record and playback settings, insert effects, send effects, and EQ settings, and even display a full channel strip, which includes buttons for changing settings and opening edit windows.

Track list: Every track in a project is shown in the track list. Many track-specific parameters in the Track inspector and Mixer can be set here as well, and the track list also shows and hides automation for audio tracks and MIDI continuous controller (CC) data for MIDI tracks.

Event display: All audio and MIDI events in a project appear in the Event display, along with any recorded automation and CC data for that track. Events can be edited directly in the Project window, which is structured like a timeline, or in specialized editor windows.

Snap and Grid settings: Located at the right end of the toolbar, the Snap and Grid settings are so important to Cubase SX that they are discussed separately in this chapter.

The Project Window Toolbar

The Cubase SX toolbar (**Figure 2.6**) serves multiple, sometimes seemingly unrelated, purposes. The toolbar consists of four general groups of settings. Much more about these buttons is included in other parts of this book and in the operation manual that comes with Cubase SX.

View Filter section: These buttons are used to show and hide the main windows in a project. The Track inspector, Overview line, and Info line can be displayed or hidden here. Two commonly used windows, the Mixer and the Pool, can also be opened with these buttons.

Automation mode: This menu determines how Cubase records and plays automation. Much about automation is covered later in this book.

Mini Transport bar: Record, Play, Stop, and Loop can all be controlled with these buttons. Often they are enough to enable you to hide the Transport bar.

Project Window tools: These buttons control cursor and editing actions. These tools change their functions and act differently depending on whether an audio or MIDI event is active, and are covered extensively in the audio and MIDI editing sections of this book. Here is a list of the most common functions of the Project Window tools.

Object Selection, or **Arrow Tool:** Most often used to select and resize events parts. Clicking and holding in this tool will open a contextual menu that changes what actions Cubase takes when resizing an event.

Range Tool: Used to select all tracks or parts across a particular range of a project. Very useful when making larger edits or when moving something like the entire chorus to a different part of the song.

Scissors Tool: Enables you to cut events at a grid line that you specify.

continues on next page

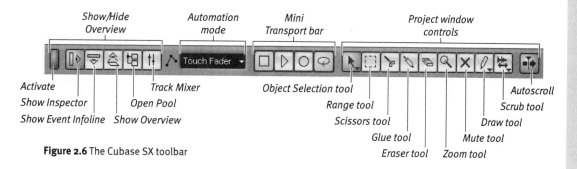

Figure 2.6 The Cubase SX toolbar

Glue Tool: Fuses two parts or events into one new part or event.

Eraser Tool: The Eraser is used to remove parts and events in the Project window. Essentially a shortcut to selecting something and then pressing the Delete or Backspace key, the Eraser also is used to remove specific notes or data in other editors.

Zoom: This tool is used to zoom in to view a smaller amount of the Project window in more detail. You can also select the Zoom tool and click and drag a box over the area of a project you wish to view. This will zoom both the vertical and horizontal area selected to take the full project window space.

Mute: Clicking on a part or an event with the Mute tool will prevent it from playing back.

Draw: The Draw tool is used extensively in other editors like the audio sample editor and the key editor, but also is used in the Project window. Most commonly in the Project window, the Draw tool is used to manually draw automation and MIDI CC data.

Scrub: In the days when analog tape dominated recording, tape was "scrubbed" slowly back and forth over tape heads to find exact places to make edits. Selecting the scrub tools allows you to digitally scrub over any part or event, and the scrub tool even mimics the sound of tape being dragged slowly or quickly over tape heads.

Figure 2.7 The main section of a Track inspector for an audio track

Figure 2.8 The same Track inspector with the Channel tab selected, showing the full channel for that audio track

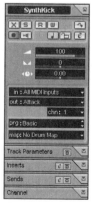

Figure 2.9 A Track inspector for a MIDI track

The Project Window Track Inspector

The Track inspector is one of the most powerful features in Cubase SX. The Track inspector shows practically every parameter for a single track in a project and it's where you need to select your input and output settings for each track. The track that is shown in the Track inspector window is determined by which track is selected in the track list, and parameters vary depending on whether an audio track or a MIDI track is selected.

The Track inspector (**Figure 2.7**) shows many of the important audio track settings available in other menus and windows, as well as some settings available only in the Track inspector. The main tab of the Track inspector provides buttons for the most common settings, such as solo, mute, record-enable, pan, and hardware routing. If one of the other tabs is selected, the inspector displays a completely different set of parameters for the same track. For example, if the Channel tab is selected (**Figure 2.8**), the full channel strip from the Mixer window is displayed. Other tabs show insert effects, send effects, and EQ settings for the track.

The main tab in the Track inspector for a MIDI track (**Figure 2.9**) shows commonly used MIDI parameters. Selecting one of the other tabs displays additional track parameters, MIDI insert effects, MIDI send effects, or a MIDI channel strip.

✔ Tip

- Track types not covered here, such as Group tracks, Folder tracks, and Video tracks, also have their own Track inspector windows.

The Project Window Track List

The track list is a list of every track in a project, regardless of whether it contains any events to play back. The listing of a MIDI track on the track list will look different from the listing for an audio track.

The listing for an audio track (**Figure 2.10**) shows the track name, record-enable and monitor settings, and track solo/mute and automation status. It also includes buttons to indicate whether send and insert effects are activated or bypassed. The listing for an audio track also shows buttons for additional track parameters and a small signal-level meter.

The listing for a MIDI track (**Figure 2.11**) shows many similar parameters, such as the track name, solo/mute and automation status, and record-enable and monitor settings. Some MIDI-only parameters, such as input and output channels, are also displayed.

It is often convenient to change the size of the track information in the track list.

To change the visual size of a track in the track list:

1. Move the mouse pointer to the vertical or horizontal edge of a track.

2. When the pointer changes to a double arrow, drag the edge of the track list (**Figure 2.12**).

3. When the track information is the size you want, release the mouse.

✔ Tip

- To resize all tracks simultaneously, hold down the Ctrl key (Windows) or the Command key (Mac) as you move the mouse pointer to the track edges and proceed as if resizing a single track. All tracks in the track list will be resized together.

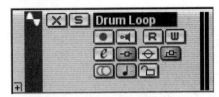

Figure 2.10 An entry in the track list for an audio track

Figure 2.11 The track list settings for a MIDI track.

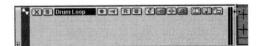

Figure 2.12 Resizing the track information in the track list: Note that the buttons are rearranged automatically to make the best use of available space.

Figure 2.13 The ruler in the Project window

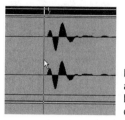

Figure 2.14 An audio track after it has been zoomed by clicking and dragging on the ruler

The Project Window Ruler

The Project window ruler provides a quick and easy way to keep track of your current location in a project and to set the loop and range selection.

Under normal circumstances, the ruler will show time according to the global setting for the project. (To change the time display setting to bars+beats, a video and film frame rate, minutes:seconds, or samples, see "The Transport Bar" earlier in this chapter.) **Figure 2.13** shows the ruler set to bars+beats, the most commonly used time display for music; about two bars from measure 6 to measure 8 are visible.

Also visible on the ruler are the left and right locators, shown as inward-facing arrows connected by a line. The locators are used to set punch points and loop points, which are used to automate some actions with Cubase SX. You'll read more about these in the chapters on recording audio and MIDI. In the example, the locators are set to 1 bar + 1 beat, from the fourth beat of bar 6 to the last beat of bar 8.

Finally, the ruler offers one of the most useful new features in Cubase SX: the ability to move and zoom the Event display with the mouse.

To zoom the Event display:

1. Click the ruler. Anywhere will work, but try to click near where you want to zoom in.

2. *Do one of the following:*
   - ▲ Drag down toward the bottom of the screen. The display will zoom in (**Figure 2.14**).
   - ▲ Drag to the right or left to move forward or backward in time.
   - ▲ Drag up or down to increase of decrease the zoom level.

   Once you get the hang of it, this procedure is by far the easiest way to view events in detail and to find the places to make event edits.

The Project Window Event Display

The Event display (**Figure 2.15**) shows all of the events in a project. Many people think of events as parts or clips or regions, but Cubase SX uses slightly different terminology. In Cubase SX, an event is not necessarily just a piece of audio or MIDI data (though those are the most common kinds of events), but events can be automation data, video data, or MIDI CC information.

You will perform much of your audio and MIDI editing and processing directly in the Event display. In addition, most of the tools selected from the toolbar are used to make changes in events in the Event display. For example, if you select the Mute tool from the toolbar, clicking an event will mute that event (**Figure 2.16**) and dim it in the Event display to indicate that it is muted. You will learn much more about the Event display in the parts of this book that cover audio and MIDI editing.

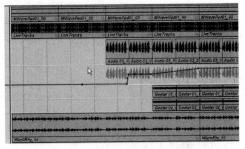

Figure 2.15 The Event display, showing both audio and MIDI tracks

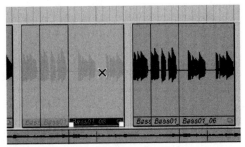

Figure 2.16 This figure shows the same loop twice. The loop on the left has the events dimmed, and will not play back. This is one example of a change made to a project in the Event display, where a great deal of your editing will take place.

The Project Window Info Line

One of the most underused parts of Cubase SX is the Info line. The Info line shows volume, length, and other information about whatever is selected in the Event display. Whenever you select a new event in the Event display, the Info line shows information about it.

A great feature of the Info line is that you can actually change parameters for events directly on it. For example, when an audio event is selected in the Event display (**Figure 2.17**), the Info line shows parameters impor-

tant for an audio event, such as the name, start and end times, length, and so on. Double-clicking one of the parameters (**Figure 2.18**) allows you to edit the setting directly. Cubase SX usually has more than one place to make these sorts of changes, but the Info line is powerful because it collects so much of the information for a particular event in one place.

Of course, the parameters displayed on the Info line will change when a MIDI event is selected (**Figure 2.19**).

Figure 2.17 The Info line showing information for an audio event

Figure 2.18 Making a manual edit on audio event data in the Info display

Figure 2.19 The Info line for a MIDI event

The Project Window Snap Settings

Among the most important things to learn about Cubase SX are the theory and practice of Snap. What Snap does is quite simple: with Snap activated, when you move, resize, change, or otherwise edit an item, the item snaps to the nearest value.

Snap makes it easy to perform actions such as the following:

◆ Drop an audio event at a particular bar location.

◆ Create tempo-synchronized automation information with the Pencil tool.

◆ Snip a long audio file into multiple pieces, each precisely two bars long.

◆ Place a trigger for a sample at a particular frame when editing sound for video.

These are only a few things that Snap can do, but they show how important Snap can be in almost any situation in your work with Cubase SX.

The Snap settings (**Figure 2.20**) are located on the toolbar, on the far right side. Snap can be turned on and off via the Snap button. When Snap is on, the settings to the right of the Snap button determine Snap behavior.

The first drop-down menu for Snap settings (**Figure 2.21**) determines the mode Snap uses when you perform events and edits that can be snapped, as follows:

Grid: When Grid is selected, Cubase SX draws an invisible grid in the project, and Snap uses this grid to guide snapped actions. More settings for the Grid appear on the next two Snap drop-down menus.

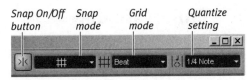

Figure 2.20 Snap is activated and configured here.

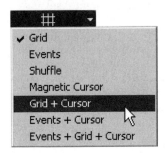

Figure 2.21 The Snap mode menu

Figure 2.22 The Grid mode menu is used to configure the type and granularity of the grid used for snapping.

Events: When Events mode is selected, instead of using a grid, the beginning and end of each event in the Event display is the guide for snapped actions. With Snap in this mode, moving an event will snap to the beginning and end of each other event in the project. This mode can be very useful for editing projects with looser tempo, where a grid is too exact to work with the feel of the music.

Shuffle: When Shuffle is selected, Snap forces events to trade places when they are moved, but maintains a cohesive track.

Magnetic Cursor: The Magnetic Cursor setting turns the cursor (the line that moves from left to right showing the current playback position) into the snap guide. This enables you to snap actions to places that are easy to find manually but may not be on a predictable beat or time line.

Grid + Cursor: This mode combines Grid mode with Magnetic Cursor—the two most convenient Snap settings for music creation, both active at the same time.

Events + Cursor: This mode combines the Events and Magnetic Cursor modes.

Events + Grid + Cursor: This mode combines Events, Grid, and Cursor modes.

The settings for Grid mode determine how the grid interacts with Snap when you make a change in a project that can be snapped. When the project is set to use bars+beats (**Figure 2.22**), the grid can be set so that events snap to each bar or each beat or to the Quantize setting. If a project uses another time format, the grid can be set so that events snap to seconds, milliseconds, frames, or samples.

continues on next page

THE PROJECT WINDOW SNAP SETTINGS

If Use Quantize is selected in the Grid mode menu, the last menu in the Snap settings (**Figure 2.23**) determines the grid. The Quantize setting is explained in detail in this book in Chapter 10: "MIDI Editing." The Use Quantize option here allows you to set the grid so that snapped actions can use very complex rhythmic-based time divisions.

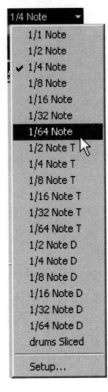

Figure 2.23 Complex tempo and meter divisions are available on the Quantize menu.

The Audio Sample Editor

You can use the Audio Sample editor in Cubase to perform the most exacting audio editing and processing the application offers. Double-click an audio event in the Project window to open the Audio Sample editor (**Figure 2.24**).

Many of the toolbar buttons and pointer tools in the Audio Sample editor are similar to those found in the Project window. The Audio Sample editor is a very powerful component of Cubase SX and is covered in detail in Chapter 9, "Advanced Audio Editing."

Toolbar *Info line* *Thumbnail display* *Waveform display* *Ruler*

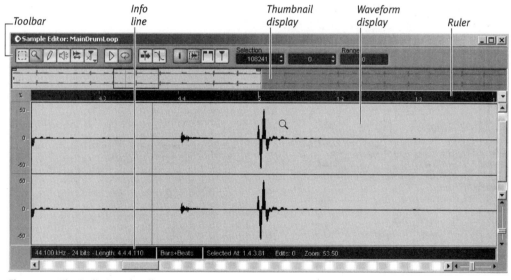

Figure 2.24 The Audio Sample editor

The MIDI Key Editor

Cubase SX includes a full set of specialized MIDI editors. The Key editor has much more flexibility for editing MIDI than the Project window—you can add or delete individual notes for example—but is more intuitive than the List or Logical editors. Chances are you'll do most of your MIDI editing in the MIDI Key editor (**Figure 2.25**). The MIDI Key editor uses a piano roll metaphor to represent data. The piano keyboard at the far left of the window represents a vertical pitch orientation, with low notes towards the bottom of the window, and high notes towards the top. The Note display scrolls from right to left as time passes.

The bottom section of the MIDI Key editor is the Controller display, where you can view and edit MIDI continuous controller (CC) data.

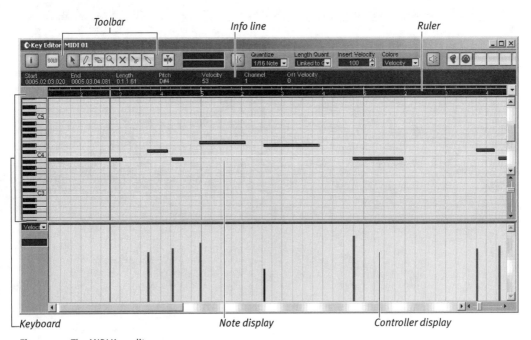

Figure 2.25 The MIDI Key editor

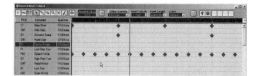

Figure 2.26 The Drum editor, used for programming drum parts

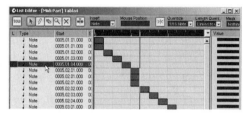

Figure 2.27 The List editor, which provides the deepest control of individual MIDI events

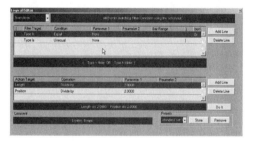

Figure 2.28 The Logical editor: it has been said nobody knows Cubase until he or she knows the Logical editor.

Other MIDI Editors

The Key editor is the most commonly used MIDI editor in Cubase, but there are other, somewhat specialized MIDI editors as well. Sometimes the Drum editor (**Figure 2.26**), List editor (**Figure 2.27**), or Logical editor (**Figure 2.28**) are the best tools for the job.

Drum editor: The Drum editor is a specialized editor for quickly entering percussion parts and creating grooves. The Drum editor was one of the features that made Cubase a hit (way back in the Atari days), and it still offers a great way to program beats.

List editor: The List editor contains a list of every single event in a project. The List editor is not as intuitive or graphical as the Key editor, but the List editor offers complete, exact, super-accurate control over all MIDI data.

Logical editor: The Logical editor lets you modify data in a completely nongraphical way, by building conditional rules and applying them to MIDI data. The Logic editor is probably the least intuitive editor in Cubase SX, but it is extremely powerful if you take the time to learn it.

✔ Tip

■ If you used an earlier version of Cubase, you may be wondering where the Controller editor went. Long a Mac-only feature of Cubase, Windows users finally got the Controller editor when version 5 was released. The Controller editor is gone now, though, replaced by vastly expanded MIDI CC and automation editing capabilities in the Project window and the previously included CC editing tools such as the CC section in the MIDI Key editor.

The Pool

The Pool (**Figure 2.29**) provides a complete listing of all audio and video files contained in a project, as well as a convenient location to add audio and video files to a project without bringing them into the Project window. When Cubase SX starts a project, it insists that a working folder be designated for the audio, MIDI, fade, and other files created during the course of a project. The Pool is a specialized view of the audio and video files in a project.

Using the Pool it's possible to

◆ Add audio files and video files to a project.

◆ Sort files according to time, duration, record date, and many other parameters.

◆ Search for audio and video files by name.

◆ Audition files before adding them to a project.

◆ Create archive and master files for a project, in which all files referenced in a project are collected in one place. This makes moving projects from computer to computer, as well as backing up projects, much easier.

Column headings
Toolbar

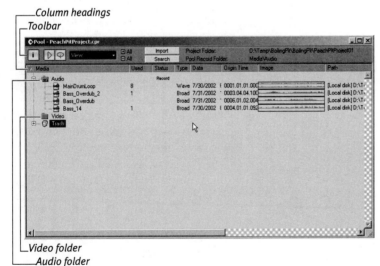

Video folder
Audio folder

Figure 2.29 The Cubase SX Pool

THE POOL

Figure 2.30 Three Mixer channels: two audio channels and one MIDI channel

Audio channels   *Midi channel*

The Cubase SX Mixer

Few parts of the program are more powerful than the Mixer (**Figure 2.30**). In fact, an entire chapter in this book is dedicated to it. Cubase SX has a Mixer that can be customized beyond any hardware interface, and which allows you to take extraordinary control over your mix. You can selectively show and hide elements of the Mixer (**Figure 2.31**), toggle automation on or off, and route audio through a wide range of software effects plug-ins or even to external effects hardware.

The Mixer in Cubase SX includes distinct channels for all MIDI and audio tracks in a project. All channels also have distinct windows that are used to edit all pertinent parameters for a single track (**Figure 2.32**). Unlike in a hardware mixer, in the Cubase SX Mixer, every single parameter, from mix levels to routing to effects, is instantly recalled the next time a project is opened.

Figure 2.31 Three audio channel views: on the left, an audio channel in narrow view; in the middle, an audio channel with the insert effects visible; on the right, an audio channel showing the EQ settings

Channel strip   *Insert effects*   *EQ*   *Send effects*

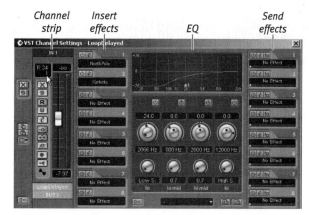

Figure 2.32 The VST channel settings, used to edit all parameters for a single channel

The Cubase SX Effects Racks

Cubase SX builds on the legacy of Cubase VST as a top-quality platform for software-based audio effects. Cubase SX uses VST plug-ins as virtual audio processing effects, some mimicking famous hardware devices, and some doing things to audio that have been heard only in software. In a non-virtual studio, hardware effects units are screwed into 19" racks, and audio is sent to these effects via patch cables from the mixer. In Cubase SX, audio effects are housed in two virtual effects racks: the Send Effects rack (**Figure 2.33**) and the Master Effects rack (**Figure 2.34**).

VST plug-ins (for both Windows and Mac computers) and DirectX plug-ins (for Windows only) are available in the Send and Master effects racks. These effects are used to do the same job as hardware effects in a hardware-based studio. Different effects are used for things like delay, compression, EQ, reverb, and chorus. Cubase SX includes support for automation of effects parameters and the ability to graphically edit that automation after the fact, as well as tools to save and recall preset effects settings. Automation can be used to control the number of repeats on a delay plug-in, or the depth of a flange effect, and can change such parameters over the course of a mix. You will learn much more about using and editing effects later in this book.

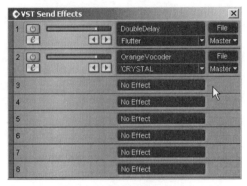

Figure 2.33 The Send Effects rack

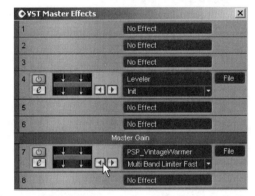

Figure 2.34 The Master Effects rack

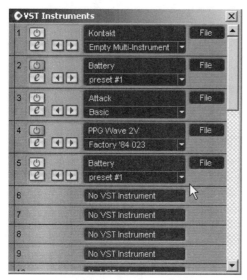

Figure 2.35 The VST Instruments rack, with five VST instruments loaded

VST Instruments

Software-based synthesis and sampling is probably one of the most important capabilities in the history of audio computing. Cubase VST lead the way by creating VST instruments, which are plug-ins that can be played by MIDI. This simple idea has lead to an amazing variety of VST instruments; from dead-on emulations of famous synthesizers, to software samplers that rival the highest-end hardware samplers in complexity and creativity, to previously untried methods of sound creation and transformation.

Cubase SX uses a virtual rack to house VST instruments (**Figure 2.35**). The VST Instruments rack can have up to 32 software synthesizers or samplers running simultaneously. The amount of synthesis power is limited only by the power of the host computer. Cubase SX also includes support for automation of every parameter in a VST instrument and, of course, options to save presets of the sounds you create for use in future projects. A complete chapter of this book is dedicated to VST instruments.

STARTING
A PROJECT

Once you've installed and configured Cubase SX, the next step is to begin working on a Cubase SX project.

A project is the basic file type in Cubase SX, in the same way that a document is the basic file type in Microsoft Word. A Cubase SX project includes the audio, MIDI, automation, and settings for a piece of music. Most people working with Cubase SX create a new project for every song, though not everyone will work this way. Cubase SX allows a great deal of customization; someone working on audio postproduction or audio for video, for example, may set up a very different type of project than a person working on a country song.

In this chapter, you will learn how to start projects, including how to use the templates bundled with Cubase SX and how to create your own templates. You will also learn how Cubase SX manages the various files that are created as a project grows. Many musical projects need tempo information to work properly, so you will learn how to set up a metronome click track. Finally, you will learn how to use the powerful audio-to-tempo matching features in Cubase SX, which allow you to sync the Cubase tempo to an audio snippet or audio drum loop.

Creating a Project

When you start a new project, Cubase automatically asks you where you want to store the files for that project. You can browse an existing folder or create a new one; often it is easiest to create a new folder for each song. As a project grows, Cubase creates new files and folders in this working directory, making it easy for you to manage files and move a project to a new machine if you need to. Be sure to create the working directory on a drive with enough free space to hold your audio files, and give the project and folder identical and logical names. This will allow you to easily find and move the project if you ever need to do so.

In addition to a directory, you'll also be asked to select a template when you start a new project. Cubase offers a standard list to choose from, including 16-track and 24-track templates and MIDI and audio choices. If you don't want to start with a preexisting template, choose Empty. However, whether you're creating music for a soundtrack, a corporate video, a hip-hop tune, a live recording, or any number of other purposes, you'll likely find a template already set up and easily accessible for that particular job. See the sidebar "Templates Included with Cubase SX" for a description of the templates that ship with the Windows and Mac OS versions of Cubase SX. You can customize your own templates as well.

Figure 3.1 Making a selection from the list of installed templates

To start a project:

1. Choose File > New (Windows) or File > New Project (Mac OS).

2. In the New Project dialog box, select a template from the Templates list (**Figure 3.1**).

3. For any new project, you will be asked to find a directory to use for it. Select a directory or create a new one, and click OK.

4. A new project is created; save and name it using File > Save.

Templates Included with Cubase SX

Don't make the use of templates more complicated than it needs to be. Templates in Cubase work just like those in recent versions of many applications such as Microsoft Word. When a new file is created in Word, the application opens a dialog box where you can choose from a group of templates that meet common needs. Word, for instance, offers templates for creating a resume, memo, or Web page, and it also includes a blank, empty document for creating whatever you want from scratch. Cubase SX operates in exactly the same way; out of the box, the program offers a group of templates that you can use to create new projects for common tasks.

Here is a quick rundown of the templates included with the first version of Cubase SX and the most common uses for each one. The templates you have available may differ depending on the version of the program and the platform you use, but this list should give you a good overview.

◆ **Empty** is a completely empty project. You can use it to create a new project or a new template from scratch.

◆ **16 Track MIDI Sequencer** opens with 16 empty MIDI tracks. Use this for MIDI-only projects or to add a few audio tracks as needed.

◆ **16 Track Surround Mix** is for projects that will be mixed in multichannel surround sound rather than stereo. Each of the 16 audio tracks is set up for panning in multiple-channel surround sound, not stereo.

◆ **24 Track Audio Recorder** is the best option if you are going to record only acoustic instruments such as drums, guitars, and vocals. Each of the 24 tracks is ready to record audio and configured for stereo mixing.

◆ **Music for Picture NTSC** opens a project optimized for creation of audio for video using the NTSC video spec common in North America. Cubase SX can play back simple DirectShow video in sync with audio.

◆ **Music for Picture PAL** is identical to Music for Picture NTSC, but it is set to use the frame rate for European PAL video rather than the NTSC frame rate.

◆ **Stereo Mastering Setup** is used for postproduction of stereo mixes, such as those used to create a CD. This type of project is best for tweaking final mixes to make them sound their best before CD burning.

Figure 3.2 You can activate the audio click on the Transport bar.

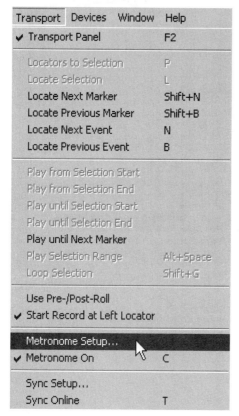

Figure 3.3 Choose Metronome Setup from the Transport menu to configure the metronome.

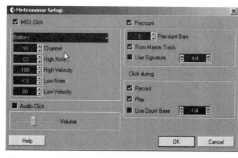

Figure 3.4 In this example, the MIDI metronome note will be sent to the Battery software sampler.

About the Cubase SX Metronome

Some projects, like audio for video or live recordings, do not have a consistent tempo from start to finish. Most musical projects, though, work best when they reference a solid tempo. Assuming that you'll record in a more or less tempo-centric sequencing environment, a solid timing reference is critical for good performances. Cubase SX has a built-in metronome that can be configured to send an audio click over the master output. You can also configure Cubase to send a MIDI note to trigger a sound.

To use an audio click:

◆ On the Transport bar, click the Click button (**Figure 3.2**).

To use a MIDI note as a metronome:

1. From the Transport menu, choose Metronome Setup (**Figure 3.3**).

2. In the Metronome Setup panel, uncheck Audio Click and configure the proper channel and note number for the MIDI device and sound you want to use for the metronome (**Figure 3.4**).

3. Click OK.

✔ Tips

■ The metronome settings are global and are not saved with each project. You may have to change them if you move to a different computer.

■ The slider for the volume of the audio click is at the bottom of the Metronome Setup panel. The click can be *really* loud.

■ A quick way to open the Metronome Setup panel is to Ctrl-click (Windows) or Command-click (Mac OS) the Click button on the Transport bar.

Setting the Project Tempo

Any new Cubase SX project has a particular tempo, which is audible using the metronome, but it might not be the right tempo for the song you want to create. If you're familiar with MIDI sequencers, you will be accustomed to setting tempos before starting to record. If you have recorded exclusively audio, however, this process may be new to you. One of the fundamental differences between MIDI and audio is that MIDI is at its core a tempo-based format. MIDI can't be recorded except in reference to tempo and meter information. If you plan to record only live instruments and will never do any MIDI sequencing or looping, you can pretty much ignore the tempo settings in Cubase SX and just start tracking. Otherwise, you need to set a tempo before you start recording.

To set a tempo in Cubase SX:

1. Click the Transport bar and verify that the Master button is selected (**Figure 3.5**).

2. From the Project menu, choose Tempo Track (**Figure 3.6**).

   The Tempo Track editor opens.

Figure 3.5 When Master is selected, project tempo is controlled by the tempo track, and changes are edited for this track in the Tempo Track editor.

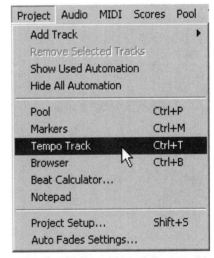

Figure 3.6 Opening the Tempo Track editor

Figure 3.7 Enter the desired tempo in the Tempo box.

3. Do one of the following:
- ▲ Click the Tempo box at the top of the editor and type the desired tempo (**Figure 3.7**)

or

- ▲ Use the up and down buttons next to the Tempo box to set the rate of the desired tempo. If you have a mouse equipped with a scroll wheel, you can use the wheel to increment and decrement many parameters, including the tempo setting in this dialog box.

4. Close the editor when the tempo is set as you want.

✔ Tips

■ Use the Tempo Track editor to make changes in the sequencer tempo. This editor is active only if the Master button on the Transport bar is selected. If you are absolutely sure that you will never want to change tempos in a song, you can unselect the Master button; you can now enter a tempo directly in the Transport window.

■ I strongly recommend that you use the Master button and the Tempo Track editor. They're more flexible than, and a vast improvement over, the tempo editing in VST.

Importing a Loop

Over the past few years, loop-based music production has become increasingly common in all types of music. There are entire audio applications dedicated to nothing but working with audio loops, both on stage and in a recording studio. Cubase SX is not exclusively a looping program, but it includes many tools for creating, importing, editing, and tempo-matching loops. The following section shows you how to use audio loops when recording, as well as how to match a loop to the tempo of a project or to match the project tempo to a particular loop.

Using drum loops

Metronomes and audio clicks are certainly useful, but why record to a click when you can use a drum loop instead? A carefully selected drum loop, from a loop CD or other source, can help you get the feel of a track together right from the start. Setting up a loop across a project, and setting the tempo of a project to match that loop, involves some audio editing tasks that are covered here somewhat out of order. Keep in mind that more advanced audio editing, tempo tricks, and file management are covered later in this book.

To import an audio drum loop:

1. Choose File > Import > Audio File.

2. In the Import Audio dialog box that opens, navigate to the loop you want to import (**Figure 3.8**); then click Open.

   The Import Options dialog box opens (**Figure 3.9**) and asks if the audio file should be copied to the same directory as the current project and also whether the file should be converted if it doesn't match the sample rate or bit depth of the current project. I recommend copying the file to the working directory.

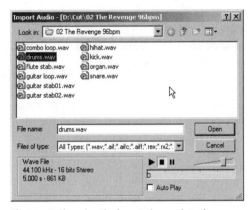

Figure 3.8 Choosing the loop to import into the project; in this example, drums.wav is selected to be imported.

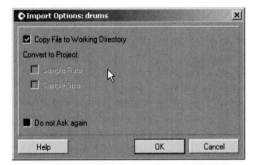

Figure 3.9 Normally, you will want to copy the imported loop to the working directory of the current project.

Figure 3.10 The loop, after it is imported, becomes an event on an audio track in the Project window.

3. Make your selections in the Import Options dialog box and click OK.

The file is imported to an audio track and is added to the Project window (**Figure 3.10**).

✔ Tip

■ The dialog box for importing audio has a small Transport bar on the lower right, which is handy for auditioning audio files before bringing them into a project.

Using Loops and Samples

You need to consider two issues when using drum loops and samples in a program like Cubase SX. One is technical: What file types and formats does the program support? The second is legal: What are you allowed to do with sounds created by someone else?

Cubase SX supports all of the commonly used uncompressed audio file formats and supports the same file types on both platforms.

◆ WAV files are the most common audio files on Windows machines.

◆ AIF files are the standard audio files on Macs.

◆ Sound Designer II files (.sd2) most often come from projects recorded using Digidesign software. Digidesign created .sd2 files as its own proprietary file type; these files are widely found and supported in the audio world.

More often than not, samples you want to import will be in one of these formats. However, Cubase SX will also import compressed MP3 files and will even rip audio directly from an audio CD. In these two situations, the file will be converted to the default file format that the project is using.

The legal questions associated with the use of samples are much more complex. The law regarding sample use is still very much unresolved and can vary from case to case and from country to country. It is certain, though, that if you use an unlicensed sample, no matter how short, you expose yourself to problems if the music is ever released. Because of this, many people purchase sample libraries specifically created for use by musicians and video content creators. These libraries are much more expensive than regular CDs, but they include samples, loops, and sounds that can be used in your music production, and you don't have to pay royalties to the sample CD creator upon release. Whatever you decide to do, always keep track of the samples you use, in case licensing questions arise down the road.

IMPORTING A LOOP

Matching the Tempo to an Audio Loop

On rare occasions, an imported loop will match perfectly with the project tempo, but most of the time there will be at least some discrepancy between the tempo of an imported loop and the project tempo. In years past, fixing this problem in Cubase VST was a circuitous walk through some of the most confusing software panels you could ever have the misfortune to use. Thankfully, Cubase SX makes the whole process *much* easier than before. You have two choices: to match the project tempo to the loop or to match the loop tempo to the project. We will look at both situations.

To match the tempo of a project to an audio loop:

1. Listen to the loop and count its length in beats.

2. Select the loop in the Project window.

3. From the Project menu, choose Beat Calculator (**Figure 3.11**), which opens the Beat Calculator window.

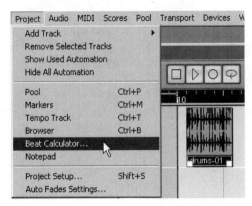

Figure 3.11 Open the Beat Calculator with the loop selected.

Figure 3.12 The Beat Calculator determines the tempo of the loop after you tell it the duration of the loop.

Figure 3.13 The loop in the Project window with the tempo matching exactly

4. In the Beat Calculator window, enter the number of beats in the selected loop. In the example here, the loop is two measures long, or eight beats (**Figure 3.12**).

The Beat Calculator updates in real time to show you the tempo that will result if the selected loop has whatever duration you entered.

5. After you've calculated the tempo, you need to enter it on the tempo track. Usually when starting a project, you should set the tempo at the beginning of the project, so click the At Tempo Track Start button to enter the calculated tempo at the beginning of the project.

6. Close the Beat Calculator and return to the Project window.

7. You can see that the loop now fits into exactly two bars (**Figure 3.13**), but it's always a good idea to check with your ears. Turn on a metronome or audio click, and it will be obvious immediately if the tempo is matched correctly.

MATCHING THE TEMPO TO AN AUDIO LOOP

Matching a Loop to the Project Tempo

The most common situation for matching audio and sequencer tempo is the one just discussed: a loop will be the basis for a track, and the sequencer will need to use that tempo. In certain situations, though, the opposite is true. For example, a song may feel right at one tempo, but a great-sounding loop may not fit it properly. If this is the case, you will need to force the audio loop to match the project tempo.

To match an audio loop to the project tempo:

1. Listen to the loop and determine its length. As you can see in this example, the two-bar loop does not fit the project tempo (**Figure 3.14**).

2. On the Project window toolbar, hold down the mouse on the arrow button. In the pop-up menu, select Sizing Applies Time Stretch (**Figure 3.15**).

3. In the Project window, position the cursor at the end of the audio part that you want to resize. The cursor will change icons to include the word *Stretch* so you know what you are about to do (**Figure 3.16**).

Figure 3.14 This loop is two bars long, but does not match the project tempo.

Figure 3.15 Changing the action of the arrow cursor. In this mode, resizing an audio part will time-stretch the part instead of moving the boundary.

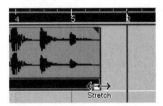

Figure 3.16 The cursor changes to a Stretch icon as the part handle is moved.

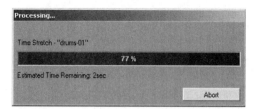

Figure 3.17 Cubase uses an offline process to change the duration of the audio file.

Figure 3.18 The processed audio file fits the project tempo perfectly. Compare this figure to Figure 3.14.

4. Hold down the mouse on the handle on the file and move the handle to where you want the file to end. The Snap value applies here, and in this case, we want the file to be a two-bar loop from the beginning of bar 3 to the beginning of bar 5.

5. Release the mouse when the part is properly resized. Cubase SX displays a status bar as it time-stretches or compresses the file (**Figure 3.17**).

In the Project window, the loop now matches the tempo of the project. In this example, the loop is now two bars long (**Figure 3.18**).

✔ Tip

■ Cubase SX uses probably the best-sounding time-stretch algorithms in the world, the MPEX algorithms from Prosoniq, but there is a sonic penalty for changing the duration of an audio file. The artifacts can vary depending on the source material and amount of time change, but they include things like phase shift in the high end, distortion, slight changes in timing and groove, and general "dirtiness" in the sound. Listen carefully to all such processed audio.

Copying a Loop Throughout a Project

If you use an audio loop as a timing reference when recording, the loop needs to be copied throughout the project. Unlike a metronome, which will click away regardless of the point where the project is playing, a loop has to be copied for as long as you will need it. Once you've mastered looping, you'll be able to record without ever hearing a metronome again.

To copy a loop throughout a song:

1. After the audio loop and project tempo are in sync, click the audio loop in the Project window and drag it to the start of the track (**Figure 3.19**).

2. With the loop selected, click the Edit menu and choose Repeat... (**Figure 3.20**). The Repeat Events dialog box opens.

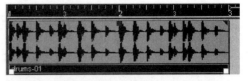

Figure 3.19 The audio loop has been moved to the start of the project.

Figure 3.20 From the Edit menu, choose Repeat ...

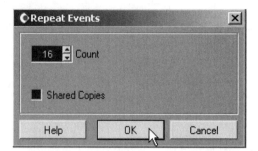

Figure 3.21 This setting will create 16 copies of the selected part.

Figure 3.22 The part copied and repeated in the Project window

3. Select the number of times that you want the loop to be repeated (**Figure 3.21**). A short '60s pop tune will have roughly 80 measures, but most songs written today have significantly more than that. When you have set the number of times you want the loop to repeat, click OK.

In the Project window, the part will be copied the number of time you have specified (**Figure 3.22**).

✔ Tip

■ In the example above, I copied a two-bar loop 16 times, or 32 measures. In addition, I left the original two-bar loop there as a lead-in to get the timing straight, so the loop now repeats for a total of 34 measures. Most rock, pop, hip-hop, electronic, and jazz music is based on phrases or parts that are some multiple of 4 measures long. Jazz standards are four eight-bar phrases or 32 bars long, blues are three four-bar sections for 12 bars, pop songs are almost always based on 8 or 16-bar phrases. As listeners, we've come to expect music to be arranged in those dimensions. While rules are made to be broken, when building a song from loops or phrases, using 4, 8, or 16 bar phrases will sound "right" to most people.

Importing a Cubase Project

You may have upgraded from an earlier version of Cubase VST or Cubasis and may have gigabytes of music created with the older program. Lucky for you, Steinberg built into Cubase SX the ability to import songs and existing projects from previous versions of Cubase VST, Cubasis, and Cubase SL.

To import a song created with an older version of Cubase:

1. Choose File > Import > Cubase Song (**Figure 3.23**).

2. In the Import Cubase Song dialog box that opens, navigate to the file to be imported. Cubase songs previously used the .all file extension. When you have located the file, click Open (**Figure 3.24**).

   Cubase SX needs to create a new folder for the imported song. The same dialog box that opens for a new song is used to find the folder for the imported song.

3. Locate the folder for the new song and click OK.

   Cubase SX converts the old song to an SX project and moves the audio and MIDI files to the directory for the new song. It does not automatically save the song.

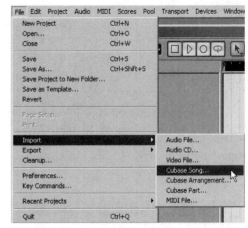

Figure 3.23 Cubase songs can be imported into Cubase SX.

Figure 3.24 The old Cubase song to be imported

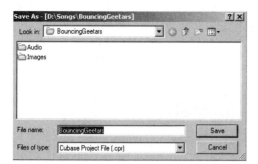

Figure 3.25 Saving the imported song to the new location

4. To complete the import, choose File > Save (**Figure 3.25**).

✔ Tip

■ If you come from the comparatively enlightened world of text or Web publishing, where standards exist to ensure file interoperability between applications, you may be surprised to learn that such standards don't exist in the world of audio software. Projects created in one application are pretty much never usable in another application. Thus, your projects created in Pro Tools, Digital Performer, Logic, or another application can't be directly imported into Cubase SX. If you need to transfer projects from one application to another, you will have to export each MIDI file, audio file, and plug-in preset from the application in which the project was created. Then you'll have to import all of those pieces into Cubase SX and re-create the project as best you can.

IMPORTING A CUBASE PROJECT

Creating a New Template

You can also create new templates that fit your specific needs. A template can include nearly anything that a project can include, meaning that you can set up one or more projects just the way you like and have them available immediately as a template. As you get more experience in Cubase, you'll probably want to create your own templates to save you time.

To create a new Cubase SX template:

1. Set up a project exactly as you want it, including active inputs, routing, tracks, plug-ins, and virtual instruments.

2. Choose File > Save as Template (**Figure 3.26**).

3. In the Save as Template dialog box that opens, give the template a name and click OK (**Figure 3.27**).

4. To use the template, choose File > New and select it from the Templates list (**Figure 3.28**).

✔ Tip

■ Templates save everything in a project, including audio files, MIDI files, and automation data. Sometimes this is precisely what you want; other times, you will want the project to have everything *except* such data. For example, you may want a set of common drum loops at certain tempos for sketching out songs, or you may want routings saved for headphone mixes for musicians. Just be careful to include or exclude the right things.

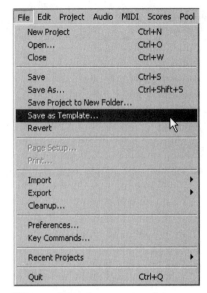

Figure 3.26 Creating a new template

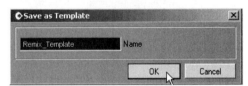

Figure 3.27 Give templates meaningful names.

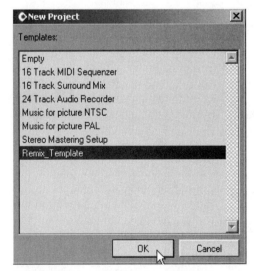

Figure 3.28 The new template is available in the Templates list.

CREATING A NEW TEMPLATE

Creating a Great Template

One of the best things you can do to make your work with Cubase SX efficient and enjoyable is to create a few templates for yourself. Any time you find yourself repeating an action for more than one project—naming inputs or using a certain software synthesizer, for instance—you should think about adding it to a template.

Templates can include the following:

- ◆ Project window settings
- ◆ Effects plug-ins and virtual instruments
- ◆ Audio and MIDI files
- ◆ Markers and navigation tools
- ◆ Anything else you use in a project

What you decide to include in your templates depends, of course, on what you plan to do with Cubase SX, but here are a few examples:

- ◆ If you use virtual instruments extensively with Cubase, in your default template you may want to have a number of them loaded and ready to go (**Figure 3.29**). The plug-ins are not actually running, so they take almost no CPU power, but with one click they are powered on and ready to use.

- ◆ If you use some track names over and over, a template can easily include them (**Figure 3.30**). This also allows recorded audio files to take the name of the track, making keeping track of files easier down the road.

- ◆ You can name hardware inputs so a particular device can easily be wired to them consistently (**Figure 3.31**). It's a lot more intuitive to send a track to "Moog Delay" or to record from "MicroQ" than it is to send a track to "Bus 1L" and to record from "HDSP 3L."

Figure 3.29 Five virtual instruments loaded with empty presets: Note that they are not active, just ready to use.

Figure 3.30 Commonly used track names, such as DrumLoop and Bass DI, can be preset in a template.

Figure 3.31 Hardware inputs and outputs with descriptive names make patching much easier.

Using the Empty Template

When none of the templates fit the needs of a project, you can use the Empty template to start completely from scratch. However, most of the time, you will find starting with a template easier, and if you spend some time making your own templates, you'll rarely find a situation where you have to use the Empty template. If you find yourself using the Empty template often, consider whether you can create a new template for at least some of the situations where you are now starting from a blank slate.

To create a new project with the Empty template:

1. From the File menu, choose New, which opens the New Project dialog box (**Figure 3.32**).

2. Select the Empty project, which creates a blank project with no audio or MIDI tracks; then click OK.

3. In the Select Directory dialog box that opens, navigate to the folder where you want to save a new song or create a new folder (**Figure 3.33**); then click OK.

4. A new, unnamed project opens. Save it right away by choosing File > Save As and naming it (**Figure 3.34**).

✔ Tip

■ Cubase automatically creates folders for audio files, fade files, and other files. Every file created during the life of a project will be stored somewhere in the working directory.

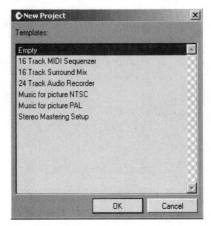

Figure 3.32 The New Project window opens, including the list of available templates; select the Empty template to start a project from scratch.

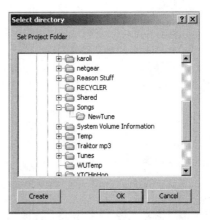

Figure 3.33 Locate a folder for the project or create a new one.

Figure 3.34 Saving the new song in the folder you created

RECORDING AUDIO

Now that we have taken a quick tour of Cubase SX and seen how to set tempos and get a few drum loops percolating, let's move on to the more creative and rewarding tasks of creating some new tracks. If you have spent time recording on any hard-disk recording system, many Cubase SX functions will seem familiar and intuitive. If instead you have worked with tape decks or are new to recording, some functions may take a bit of time to get used to— but soon you will become comfortable with operations that may seem a bit strange and fiddly at first.

You'll start this chapter by recording a single mono track from one of the inputs on a sound card. Then you'll learn how to record multiple tracks and how to record in stereo. You'll also learn how to set up Cubase SX to automatically start and stop recording at selected points in time, and you'll learn how to record more than one take while looping, so you can then select the best takes without interrupting the flow of the recording process.

There is no single preferred way to record; each method is preferable in different situations. Manual recording is easy and quick, particularly if you are operating the computer while other people play. Punch recording is great for fixing mistakes, and it allows hands-free tracking. Cycle recording lets you build up loops and try out ideas without having to fiddle with the machine.

One of the primary goals of the Cubase SX interface is to provide as much power and control as possible in the main Project window, where you'll do most of your work. You'll also learn about particular situations where another window may be easier to use.

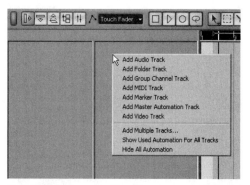

Figure 4.1 You can use this menu to create any kind of track in Cubase.

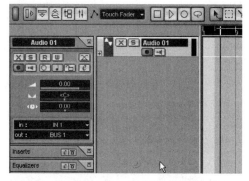

Figure 4.2 A track has been added to the Project window.

Figure 4.3 This setting adds 16 audio tracks to the project at once.

Creating an Audio Track

Before you can record any audio, you need an audio track to which you can record. Cubase SX has many kinds of tracks, including audio tracks, MIDI tracks, and automation tracks. They can be created singly or in groups.

To create a single new audio track:

1. In the Project window, right-click (Windows) or Control-click (Mac OS) the track list.

   A menu opens to let you create a new track (**Figure 4.1**).

2. From the menu, choose Add Audio Track.

   A new audio track is added in the Project window (**Figure 4.2**).

Sometimes, you'll need multiple tracks. For example, you may want to transfer an eight-track live recording for mixing, or you may be setting up to record a full rock band with 16 or more tracks for each take. In these situations, it's much easier and faster to add more than one track at a time.

To create more than one audio track:

1. Right-click (Windows) or Control-click (Mac OS) the track list in the Project window.

2. From the menu that opens, choose Add Multiple Tracks.

3. When the Add Multiple Tracks dialog box opens, specify the number and type of tracks to be added to the project (**Figure 4.3**).

4. Click OK.

   The tracks are added to the project.

✔ Tip

- If you're into menus, you can also add tracks by choosing Project > Add Track > Audio or Project > Add Track > Multiple.

CREATING AN AUDIO TRACK

Setting Audio Recording Preferences

Before you click the Record button to begin recording your audio, you need to be sure that Cubase SX will record the files at the bit depth and sample rate you want.

To set properties for audio recording:

1. From the Project menu, select Project Setup (**Figure 4.4**).

   The Project Setup window opens (**Figure 4.5**). The bottom three options set the sample rate, bit depth (recording format), and type of file to be recorded. The setting for Stereo Pan Law should be left at the default under almost all circumstances.

2. Select your preferred settings. If you don't know where to start, try 44.100 Hz, 24 bit, and Broadcast Wave.

3. Click OK.

✔ Tip

- A Broadcast Wave file is a .wav file that can have extra text added to it, such as the name of the author and the date the file was created. Broadcast Wave files are also time-stamped, meaning that when the file is recorded, the start and end positions of the file within the project are embedded in the file. This makes transfer of files between different projects simple.

Figure 4.4 Select Project Setup from the Project menu, which includes many critical options, including audio record settings.

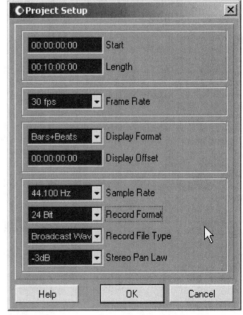

Figure 4.5 You can set the sample rate, bit depth, and file type for your audio recording in the Project Setup window.

File Resolution

The arguments about which sample rate to use may go on forever. On paper, 16-bit, 44.1 kHz audio would seem to cover the entire range of human hearing, leaving no reason ever to use a higher sample rate of 24 or 32 bits. That said, instruments undoubtedly make noises above the range of human hearing. Some people claim that the absence of this information degrades the quality of 44.1 kHz audio.

The most commonly used sample rates are 44.1, 48, 88.2, and 96 kHz. The sample rate for CDs is 44.1 kHz, many DAT decks record at 44.1 or 48 kHz, and DVDs can be either 96 or 88.2 kHz depending on the format and decisions made in production. Though there are still arguments about what is the "best" sample rate to use, there is little argument about one thing; converting sample rates after the fact is generally a very bad idea. The math involved in turning a 48-kHz file into a 44.1-kHz file is very complex and often leaves ugly, harsh artifacts in the resulting file.

What I recommend in the face of these options is to use the sample rate that is used in the intended release format, unless there is a very good reason to do otherwise. This means that if a project is destined for CD release, track it at 44.1 kHz. If you are still worried about not catching enough of your instruments at that sample rate, at least choose 88.2 instead of 96 or 48 kHz. Not surprisingly, the math to turn 88.2 into 44.1 is comparatively simple. Keep in mind, though, that 88.2 kHz doubles the number of samples the system uses, which makes that sample rate precisely twice as demanding on the computer as 44.1.This means half the number of tracks, plug-ins, software synths, and so on at the higher sample rate.

Bit depth for a file is much easier to choose. Nearly every sound card these days can record at 24 bits, and turning a 24-bit file into a 16-bit file for CD release is a benign process. It is strongly recommended that you record 24-bit audio, regardless of the sample rate you choose.

Setting Audio Inputs and Outputs

Before you begin recording, you need to ensure that Cubase recognizes your input device.

1. From the Devices menu, select Device Setup.

2. In the Device Setup dialog box, select the VST Multitrack tab in the left panel (**Figure 4.6**).

3. The right panel shows various settings, including the selected ASIO driver. Click the drop-down menu to select the ASIO driver for the card you want to use (**Figures 4.7** and **4.8**).

4. Click OK in the Device Setup dialog box to save the changes and close the window.

Figure 4.6 Use the VST Multitrack tab of the Device setup panel to select your audio card. It is in the same location on both Windows and Mac OS machines, as shown here.

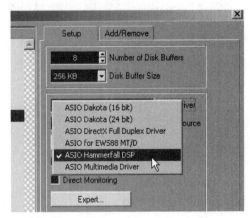

Figure 4.7 This drop-down menu lists all of the sound cards that Cubase SX recognizes as properly installed in Windows and ready to use.

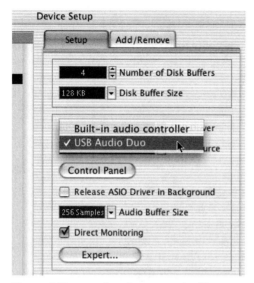

Figure 4.8 The same drop-down menu on a Mac showing all of the available Mac audio cards

✔ Tip

■ If Cubase displays an error message when you select the ASIO driver for your sound card, some other problem exists that needs to be fixed before the program can use the sound card and its audio inputs. Review the configuration sections in Chapter 1, and eventually you will find the problem. No, this isn't the most musically rewarding part of your computer studio experience, but neither is changing a broken guitar string or aligning tape heads on a reel-to-reel deck.

SETTING AUDIO RECORDING PREFERENCES

Recording a Single Track

The simplest way to start recording is to use the Transport bar to start recording exactly the way you would if you were using a tape deck. There are lots of options that we'll cover later; for now, we will simply put a bass loop over a drum loop.

To record a single track with the Transport bar:

1. From the track list, select the track you want to record. Double-click the track name and rename the file. In this example, the file is renamed Bass.

2. Check to be sure that the Record Enable button is red (**Figure 4.9**).

3. In the Track inspector, select the correct input on your sound card. In this example, the bass is patched into input 7 (**Figure 4.10**).

4. Click the ruler so that recording will start some time before the first part of the drum loop.

5. On the Transport bar, be sure that the AQ, Punch-In, Cycle, and Punch-Out buttons are not selected (**Figure 4.11**).

6. Click the Play button on the Transport bar and then immediately click the Record button.

   The selected track turns red to show that it is recording, and you will see that a new audio file is being created (**Figure 4.12**).

7. Click the Stop button on the Transport bar when you are done recording.

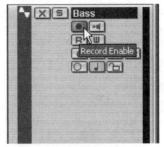

Figure 4.9 The track name is set to Bass, and the Record Enable button is on.

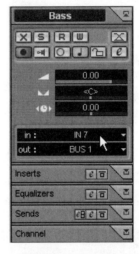

Figure 4.10 Input 7 is selected in the Track inspector.

Figure 4.11 When recording a single track, be sure that the four buttons at the bottom of the Transport bar are not selected.

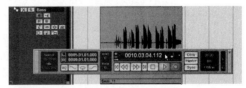

Figure 4.12 Recording in progress: Note the lighted Record and Play buttons and the audio file image in the track.

✔ Tips

- The spacebar on your keyboard starts and stops playback, and the asterisk (*) key on the numeric keypad starts and stops recording, so another quick way to start recording is to press the spacebar and then * on the numeric keypad.

- There are numerous shortcuts for recording, only some of which we will cover here. For example, if you simply click the Record button on the Transport bar, Cubase SX will jump to where the left locator is set and start recording any record-enabled tracks. This shortcut can be very useful for working on a particular section of a tune. The left locator is available from anywhere with a single click. If you find some recording task frustrating, there's a good chance that Cubase SX has a way to make it easier; check the included documentation.

No Signal?

You may still have trouble getting Cubase to recognize your input device. If the meters don't show any input signal when the Record button is selected, or if your audio tracks remain empty when you try to record in them, make sure that your audio input device is selected on the VST Multitrack tab of the Device Setup dialog box under the Device menu. (You may need to quit Cubase and relaunch it after you make your selection.) Make sure that your drivers are installed in the correct locations on your computer, that your ASIO specifications are set up in Cubase, and that the input patch on your sound card matches the input selection number in your Track inspector. For additional help, refer to Chapter 1 for setup instructions.

Remember also that multitrack audio work with a computer inevitably involves a certain number of configuration hassles. You are asking your computer, a highly specialized sound card, equally specialized drivers, and Cubase SX all to deal with each other happily. There will be frustrating moments, but the problems almost always can be fixed. Even the people who get paid good money as consultants to fix these problems have moments of confused and embarrassed head scratching.

Recording Multiple Tracks

There are many situations where more than one track needs to be recorded at the same time: from simple stereo output from a synthesizer to the setup for a full rock band with potentially dozens of microphones. One cannot live on mono alone.

To record multiple audio tracks:

1. For each track to be recorded, select a distinct input in the Track inspector.

   Cubase SX won't enable tracks for recording if they have the same input selected.

2. Select the tracks to be recorded. *Do one of the following:*

   ▲ To select multiple tracks, hold down the Ctrl (Windows) or Option (Mac OS) key and click each individual track to be recorded.

   ▲ To select a group of tracks, click the first track in the group; then hold down the Shift key and click the last track in the group (**Figure 4.13**).

3. Check that all of the tracks have the red Record Enable button selected.

4. Click Play and then Record on the Transport bar.

   The selected tracks will turn red to indicate that they are recording (**Figure 4.14**).

5. When you are done recording, click Stop on the Transport bar or press the spacebar on your keyboard.

Figure 4.13 The track list has been resized to show four tracks selected for recording.

Figure 4.14 All of the selected tracks in the track list are red to indicate that they are recording.

Figure 4.15 Each track with the Record Enable button active will be recorded, even if the track is not selected.

✔ Tips

- Tracks actually don't need to be selected to be recorded. As long as the Record Enable button is selected, a track will start recording when Record is engaged regardless of whether the track is selected (**Figure 4.15**). Assuming that the input is available, selecting a track will enable it for recording, so sometimes it's easier and quicker to select a track, while other times it's easier and quicker to just click the Record Enable button.

- You can monitor the audio while recording by enabling the Monitor button, which is next to the Record Enable button.

Recording Stereo Tracks

The mechanisms for recording stereo tracks are the same as for recording multiple tracks, but there are limitations on the inputs that you can use.

To record stereo tracks:

1. Select the track to be used for stereo recording.

2. In the Track inspector, toggle the Mono/Stereo button (**Figure 4.16**).

3. Set the input selector for the stereo pair that you want to record (**Figure 4.17**). When recording a stereo file, the inputs are "locked" into adjacent pairs on the sound card. The left channel will be recorded from the odd numbered input and the right channel from the even numbered input.

4. Click Play on the Transport bar and then click Record.

   The track will turn red to indicate that it is recording.

5. When you are finished recording, click Stop on the Transport bar.

✔ Tip

■ Cubase SX provides numerous visual indicators to show whether a track is stereo, but one of the easiest to see is in the track list. At the far right of each track is a meter; mono tracks have a single meter, and stereo tracks have two thinner meters (**Figure 4.18**).

Figure 4.16 The Mono/Stereo button is yellow with two interlocking circles for stereo tracks, and it is clear with a single circle for mono tracks.

Figure 4.17 You must select a stereo pair for input on a stereo track.

Figure 4.18 The top track has two meters, telling you that the track is stereo; the bottom track has a single meter, telling you that the track is mono.

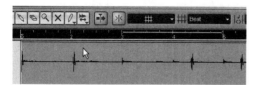

Figure 4.19 The loop selection is indicated by two markers connected by a line. In this case, the loop extends from bar 5, beat 3, to bar 6, beat 1.

Figure 4.20 The left marker (which is the punch-in point) has been dragged to the first beat of bar 5.

Figure 4.21 Punch-in recording activated on the Transport bar

Recording Automatically: Punch Recording

So far, we've been talking about recording manually using the Transport bar or the keys on the computer keyboard. This is an intuitive way to record because you click buttons much like you click tape deck controls, something nearly everyone has used. Cubase SX can go far beyond a tape deck, though, and start and stop recording automatically. Punch recording is a common method for recording automatically and is particularly useful when you have to be engineer, tape operator, and performer all at the same time.

All of the methods in the next few sections use the ruler and the loop markers (**Figure 4.19**). Loop selection governs more than just automatic recording, but for now keep in mind that the left marker indicates the punch-in point (where recording automatically starts), and the right marker indicates the punch-out point (where recording automatically ends).

To start recording audio automatically:

1. Configure one or more stereo or mono tracks to record.

2. On the ruler, click the left loop locator (the triangle with its point toward the right) and move it to the location where recording should start (**Figure 4.20**).

   The cursor will turn into a small hand as the left point is moved.

3. On the Transport bar, click the button to activate punch-in recording (**Figure 4.21**).

   For now, do not click the Cycle or Punch-Out button.

   continues on next page

4. Click the ruler somewhere before the punch-in point.

5. On the Transport bar, click Play.

Playback begins. When Cubase reaches the punch-in point, recording will begin.

6. When you are done recording, click Stop on the Transport bar.

The newly recorded track is highlighted (**Figure 4.22**).

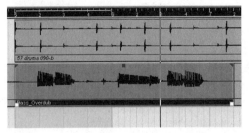

Figure 4.22 The newly recorded track starting at bar 5 is highlighted.

✔ Tip

■ As a shortcut for setting the left and right locators, click the ruler while pressing a key on the computer keyboard. To set the left locator, Ctrl-click (Windows) or Option-click (Mac OS) on the ruler. To set the right locator, Alt-click (Windows) or Command-click (Mac OS) on the ruler.

Punching out while recording audio is accomplished in much the same way as punching in, but uses the right locator to define the punch-out point. By far the most common way to punch out is to set both punch-in and punch-out points. This lets you define very specifically where audio recording will take place. With punch-in and punch-out points set in this way, you can start playback before the punch-in point, and Cubase SX will run the recording operations for you.

Figure 4.23 The ruler with the punch-in point set to bar 5, beat 1, and the punch-out point set to bar 7, beat 1

Figure 4.24 Both punch-in and punch-out settings are activated.

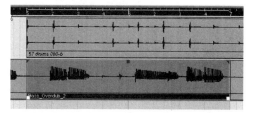

Figure 4.25 A two-bar punch, with the just-recorded part still selected

Setting up good punch-in and punch-out points can provide very convenient, automatic, hands-free tracking.

To start and stop recording automatically:

1. Configure a track or tracks, stereo or mono, to record.

2. Place the left locator where recording should start and the right locator where recording should stop (**Figure 4.23**).

3. Activate both punch-in and punch-out recording on the Transport bar (**Figure 4.24**).

4. Click the ruler at some place before the punch-in point.

5. Click Play on the Transport bar.
   Recording begins at the punch-in point and ends at the punch-out point.

6. To stop playback, click Stop on the Transport bar after the recording has punched out.

✔ Tips

- In these examples, Snap has been turned on and set to either Bar or Beat. With this setup, the locators snap to the nearest snap point when they are moved. Snapping provides a quick and easy way to create a clean two-bar overdub (**Figure 4.25**). However, snapping can be turned off and the punch-in and punch-out points set manually. This allows you to specify surgically precise punches, if that's what you want.

- Double-clicking the L and R settings on the Transport bar allows you to type in the left and right locator positions manually, by entering the bar, beat, or time location using the numbers on the keyboard. This approach can be very handy if you know exactly where you want to punch.

Recording Automatically: Cycle Recording

Cycle recording offers another way to automate audio recording and playback in Cubase SX. Unlike punch recording, cycle recording records in a loop, where each *pass*, or *take*, creates its own part in the editor. Although these takes seem to be unique, stand-alone pieces of audio, Cubase SX creates a single long audio file during cycle recording. That full audio file can be viewed and edited as a group of takes, which makes editing bits and pieces of different passes into a final version much easier.

Exactly what Cubase SX does while cycle recording depends on some Preferences settings. Cubase SX will always record the whole audio file the same way, but the recording can create audio events, audio regions, or both. If you choose to create events, then each pass in the cycle creates a new event, and all events are stacked on top of each other like note cards. This means that each take can be moved individually. When regions are created, the single region in the Project window can quickly point to any of the regions created by cycle recording. For reasons we'll get to later, using regions can make creating composite tracks a bit easier, but you can still do so using events, so don't worry if you have a lot of events created by cycle recording. This setting can be changed by selecting File > Preferences and clicking the Audio tab (**Figure 4.26**).

We'll discuss the differences between audio events and audio regions in detail later in this book. For now, we'll use the default setting, Create Regions. Choose this setting unless you have a reason to choose differently.

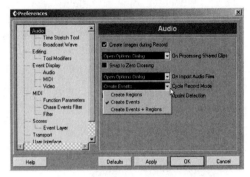

Figure 4.26 Cycle recording settings in the Audio Preferences window

Figure 4.27 Though a bit hard to see in black and white, the Loop button is active on the Transport bar.

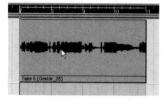

Figure 4.28 All of the individual takes are "behind" this finished part created with cycle recording.

To cycle record audio:

1. Activate the Cycle button on the Transport bar (**Figure 4.27**), as well as the Punch-In and Punch-Out buttons.

2. If you want to hear a click while cycle recording, click the Click button on the Transport bar.

3. Record–enable the track or tracks you want to record.

4. Click the ruler to start playback somewhere before the start of the loop.

5. Click Play on the Transport bar.

   The audio will play back until it reaches the punch-in point at the start of the loop, at which point recording will start.

   The track will keep recording over the loop indefinitely, creating a new region with each loop.

6. When you are finished recording, click the Stop button on the Transport bar. Only the most recent cycle will be shown in the Project window (**Figure 4.28**), but all of the cycles can be played back and edited.

RECORDING AUTOMATICALLY: CYCLE RECORDING

Playing Back Cycle-Recorded Parts

Much of the power of cycle recording audio is in the ability to create master takes of solos or instrumental parts out of bits and pieces of various different takes. The idea is that a perfect solo is a rare thing, so it's handy to be able to replace the occasional clunker note or slack timing with a good part from another take. We'll discuss how to create such a composite take (often called a *comp*) later in the book. For now, we'll explore how to listen to the various takes that were just recorded in cycle mode. After you stop recording, Cubase SX always plays back the last loop recorded, but you can easily hear any of your takes.

To listen to the loops in a cycle-recorded part:

1. Right-click the cycle-recorded part in the Project window.

2. On the menu that opens, select the Set to Region option (**Figure 4.29**).

   The last take is selected because it was just recorded.

3. Select a different take on the Set to Region menu and click it (**Figure 4.30**).

   This other region will appear in the Project window and start playing back (**Figure 4.31**).

✔ Tip

- If you are recording yourself, a good way to start getting tracks is to set the locators so that you can cycle record the whole song. Play or sing the tracks a few times, and often that will give you good material to work with.

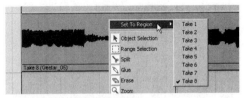

Figure 4.29 This menu determines which cycle-recorded take is played back.

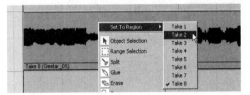

Figure 4.30 Take 2 is selected.

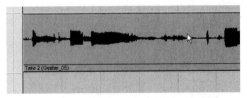

Figure 4.31 Both the waveform in the Project window and the audio playback will switch to the selected take.

RECORDING MIDI

The audio recording and editing capabilities of Cubase SX get so much attention that you may forget that the program also includes world-class tools for recording, editing, and manipulating MIDI data. MIDI tracks live in the Project window next to audio tracks, group tracks, and folder tracks, but they have their own recording and editing tools—along with their own special quirks.

The most common kind of MIDI data is note data. A MIDI controller, such as a keyboard or a wind controller, creates MIDI note-on and note-off events as the instrument is played. A sequencer is used to record and play back these MIDI notes. MIDI offers a great deal of flexibility, allowing you to easily change both the tempo and pitch of MIDI data, and its appeal derives largely from these abilities. You can use MIDI for much more than just recording the note data of a performance on an instrument—you can also use it to control synthesizers, effects, drum machines, and even other software.

In this chapter, you'll learn to record MIDI in Cubase SX, using the MIDI inputs and outputs on your computer. You will also learn how to record in Loop mode, how to punch in parts automatically, and how to record more than one track at a time. Finally, you will learn how to record MIDI continuous controller (CC) data and sysex data.

Naming MIDI Inputs and Outputs

Before you begin to record MIDI in Cubase SX, you should give your MIDI inputs and outputs meaningful names. A complex project can have multiple tracks routed to multiple pieces of MIDI hardware, as well as routing automation and MIDI to software instruments and effects. Having recognizable names is a big advantage as the complexity of a project or your recording setup increases. For example, in my studio, I have a Yamaha Motif synthesizer, and it's a lot easier to figure out where MIDI data is going when I have the option to rout it to "Motif" instead of "Midex8 3." Cubase gives you the option to organize your MIDI devices by names, simplifying the task of keeping track of MIDI comings and goings.

To name MIDI inputs and outputs:

1. From the Devices menu, select Device Setup (**Figure 5.1**).

2. In the Device Setup dialog box, do one of the following:
   ▲ In Windows, from the Devices list, select DirectMusic (**Figure 5.2**).
   ▲ In Mac OS, from the Device Setup dialog box, select MIDI System.

3. The right panel of the Device Setup window will list all installed MIDI inputs and outputs. Click any of the generic names and then type a new name for that MIDI device (**Figure 5.3**).

4. Click OK in the Device Setup window to save the changes and close the window.

Figure 5.1 Opening the Device Setup panel from the Devices menu

Figure 5.2 Select DirectMusic in Windows to see all available MIDI inputs and to rename them.

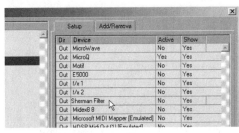

Figure 5.3 Select a generic name, such as Midex8 7, and then simply type a new, more descriptive name, such as the one shown here.

Figure 5.4
Using the track list to add a MIDI track

Creating MIDI Tracks

Cubase SX uses specific track types to record specific types of data. Audio tracks will record audio, automation tracks will record automation, and so on. The default projects that come with Cubase, as well as the projects you create, will often have the correct type of track already available. If not, you can create MIDI tracks in the same way as any other type of track.

To create a MIDI track:

1. Right-click (Windows) or Control-click (Mac OS) the track list.

2. From the context menu that opens, select Add MIDI Track (**Figure 5.4**).

In some situations, you will want to add several MIDI tracks at once. This is very easy with Cubase SX, as you'll see in the exercise on the next page.

What Is MIDI?

MIDI stands for Musical Instrument Digital Interface. Regardless of what you may have heard, it does not stand for Masterfully Incoherent Digital Interface or Mostly Inscrutable Destroyed Inspiration. Honestly. MIDI was created in the early 1980s by a consortium of manufacturers to allow a synthesizer made by one company to communicate with a synthesizer made by a different company. At the time, this was a revolutionary idea. Much-missed American synth legend Sequential Circuits was one of the prime movers behind this open standard that has enabled so much innovation and creativity in the use of synthesizers and sequencers. Almost two decades after its creation, MIDI is still a music production cornerstone, which is a testament to the forward-thinking people who created it. How many other technologies from 1984 still reign at the top of their fields?

To create multiple MIDI tracks:

1. In the Project window's track list, right-click (Windows) or Control-click (Mac OS).

2. From the context menu that opens, select Add Multiple Tracks (**Figure 5.5**).

3. When the Add Multiple Tracks window opens, select MIDI as the type of track to add. Then, in the Count field, enter the number of MIDI tracks you want to create. The example settings in **Figure 5.6** will create eight MIDI tracks.

4. Click OK, and the MIDI tracks will be added to the project.

✔ Tip

■ A great feature of Cubase SX is its extensive use of time-saving context menus. However, if you prefer the regular menus, you can choose Project > Add Track instead of opening the context menu from the track list.

Figure 5.5 Using the track list context menu to create more than one track

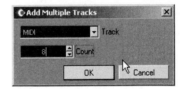

Figure 5.6 The type of track to be created is MIDI; the number of tracks is 8.

Figure 5.7 The Show Inspector button in the Project window

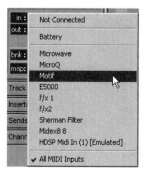

Figure 5.8 Selecting a MIDI input

Configuring a MIDI Track to Record

After adding the appropriate tracks to your project and giving meaningful names to your MIDI inputs and outputs, you need to take one final step before clicking the Record button: you need to select the correct MIDI inputs and outputs. The easiest way to do this is by using the Track inspector.

To select MIDI inputs and outputs:

1. In the track list, select the track you want to record. If the inspector is not already open, click the Show Inspector button at the top left of the Project window (**Figure 5.7**).

2. The top tab of the inspector (the one with the name of the track) is used to display the most common parameters for a track. Click the MIDI input setting to display a drop-down list (**Figure 5.8**).

3. From the MIDI input list, choose your MIDI controller or select All MIDI Inputs.

continues on next page

4. Click the MIDI output setting to open another drop-down list, and in this list, select the MIDI synth, sound module, or VST instrument to which you want the MIDI data sent (**Figure 5.9**).

5. If you want the MIDI data sent to a particular MIDI channel, click the setting marked chn: and select the channel (**Figure 5.10**).

✔ Tip

■ The All MIDI Inputs setting for the MIDI input of a track is a great shortcut. This setting gathers all incoming MIDI data from any active input and uses it as the source for recording. If you are working on your own, this is the easiest setting to use, because you can just grab any MIDI device and record its output on the selected track. More complex MIDI setups with many players or complex routing require you to specify inputs.

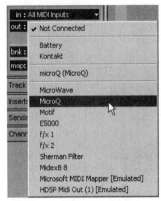

Figure 5.9 Selecting a MIDI output

Figure 5.10 This menu specifies a particular channel for the MIDI output.

Figure 5.11 Record–enabling a MIDI track; note that you can also change the MIDI output settings here, in the track list.

Figure 5.12 Renaming a track; recorded MIDI parts will automatically have this name.

Figure 5.13 The Transport bar while recording

Recording a Single MIDI Track

The track is now ready for recording. A few more clicks and you will be underway.

To record a MIDI track:

1. In the track list or inspector, click the Record Enable button for each track you want to record (**Figure 5.11**).

   Usually it's best to give a track a name before recording. This makes it easier to keep track of MIDI tracks and events as a project progresses.

2. In the track list, double-click the name of the track and then type a new name (**Figure 5.12**).

3. Move the cursor to a location before where you want to start recording.

4. Click the Play button on the Transport bar to start playback.

5. To start recording MIDI data, click the Record button on the Transport bar (**Figure 5.13**).

   The track in the track list will turn red to indicate that it is recording, and MIDI notes will appear as they are recorded in the Event display.

6. When you finish recording, click the Stop button on the Transport bar.

✔ Tip

- Just as when recording audio tracks, you can use the computer keyboard to start and stop playback and recording. By default, the spacebar starts and stops playback, and the * on the numeric keypad toggles recording on and off. You might find typing at the keyboard easier than clicking the Transport bar with the mouse.

No Sound When Playing MIDI?

Most of the examples in this book assume that you are using a MIDI controller and one or more sound modules. Many people will use a single synthesizer with built-in sounds as the sound module, plus the MIDI controller. Some will have a keyboard synthesizer that has its own sounds, which will also be used to trigger sounds from other synthesizers or samplers. Some of you, though, may have nothing but a keyboard, with no built-in sounds, connected via MIDI or USB to your Cubase computer. In this case, you'll be able to view and record MIDI data, but it won't make any noise, which is a less than thrilling experience.

If you are one of those people, probably the best thing for you to do is learn a little bit about VST instruments, which are software-based synthesizers and samplers that run inside of Cubase. Chapter 7 of this book is dedicated to VST instruments and includes descriptions of the VST instruments included with Cubase. Refer to that chapter to learn how to open the rack of virtual VST instruments, and to learn how to load and activate a VST instrument. Once a VST instrument is active, you will be able to select it as an output for a MIDI track, and this will let you trigger software-based sounds with nothing other than a MIDI controller.

Keep in mind also that some VST instruments are multitimbral, and some others are not. Multitimbral synths can generate a different sound on each MIDI channel: a keyboard on channel 1, a synth on channel 2, and so on. Many VST instruments, though, are not multitimbral, which means that the synth can make only one sound. If you want both a bass sound and a synth sound from such a VST instrument, you need to have two instances of it running at the same time. Again, refer to Chapter 7 for a lot more information about VST instruments in Cubase.

Punching In Using the Locators

The left and right locators can make MIDI recording much easier and more convenient, particularly if you are recording alone. The locator basics for MIDI tracks are the same as for audio tracks, so if you can use one set of locators, you can easily use the other. You can use the locators to automatically start, stop, and loop MIDI recording and playback. Using the locators for recording involves both the ruler in the Project window and the Transport bar.

The simplest situation in which you might want to use the locators is when you want to start recording at a certain time. If you set the locator correctly, you can start playback anywhere before the punch-in point, and Cubase SX will automatically start recording at the locator.

To automatically start recording MIDI:

1. Set the left locator to the point where you want to begin recording. You can do this either by clicking the locator in the ruler (**Figure 5.14**) or by double-clicking the setting in the Transport bar and entering the location manually (**Figure 5.15**). Also remember that you can set the left locator by Control-clicking (Windows) or Option-clicking (Mac OS) the ruler. Set the right locator by Alt-clicking (Windows) or Command-clicking (Mac OS) the ruler.

2. On the Transport bar, click the Punch-In button to activate automated recording. Also be sure that the Punch-Out and Loop buttons are not selected (**Figure 5.16**).

3. Record–enable the MIDI tracks you want to record by clicking the Record Enable button for each track.

4. Start playback at a point before the punch-in point defined by the locator.
   When the locator is reached, all record-enabled tracks will begin recording.

5. When you are finished recording, click Stop on the Transport bar or use the computer keyboard to stop playback.

Figure 5.14 Moving the left locator; when the mouse pointer becomes a hand, you can click to grab the locator to move it.

Figure 5.15 You can also move the left locator manually by typing a new location here.

Figure 5.16 Only the Punch-In button is active; Cubase SX will not loop, and you will have to stop recording manually.

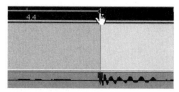

Figure 5.17
Moving the
right locator

Figure 5.18 The Punch-Out button is selected; recording will automatically stop at the right locator.

Figure 5.19 The most common punch setting; Cubase SX will automatically punch in at the left locator and punch out at the right locator.

*Punch In
selected*   *Punch Out
selected*

Punching Out Using the Locators

Naturally, just as you can with audio recording, you can set MIDI recording to automatically punch out at a certain time. You can use the right locator to set a point in the project when all tracks will stop recording.

To automatically stop recording MIDI:

1. Set the right locator by doing one of the following:
   ▲ Drag the ruler (**Figure 5.17**).
   ▲ Double-click the right locator setting on the Transport bar and enter a position manually.

2. On the Transport bar, click the Punch-Out button if it is not already active (**Figure 5.18**).

3. Start recording at a point in the project before the punch-out point.
   When recording reaches the right locator, it will stop.

✔ Tips

■ Remember that the status and setting of the Snap value always determine how the locators move on the ruler.

■ Punching out is most commonly paired with punching in. Set the left and right locators and click both the Punch-In and Punch-Out buttons on the Transport bar (**Figure 5.19**) to define a section of the project where recording automatically starts and stops.

MIDI Recording Mode Options

One way in which working with MIDI is unlike working with audio is that you can add data—both notes and continuous controller data—to a MIDI track after it has been recorded. For example, when you're working with an audio track, you can't add an extra harmony note to an existing file; the harmony note must be recorded on a different audio track and then mixed with the original. Cubase SX has two different ways of recording MIDI: Normal mode and Merge mode. You toggle the mode by clicking at the far left of the Transport bar (**Figure 5.20**).

Normal mode records MIDI like audio. If you are recording and reach a place in the project where MIDI has already been recorded for that track, Cubase SX creates a new MIDI part and leaves the original untouched. The parts can later be edited and spliced, but they remain distinct MIDI events.

Merge mode merges new MIDI data with whatever has been previously recorded for that track. This is the mode to use when you want to build up a part from multiple takes, playing the kick drum on one pass, the snare drum on another pass, and so on. It is also the mode to use when you want to add continuous controller data to a track you have already recorded: for example, if you have a synthesizer part and want to add changes to the volume, pan, filter cutoff, or some other parameter.

It's not too difficult to figure out which recording mode is best for a certain situation, but it's also easy to forget to change the setting before recording starts. Always do a quick mental check before recording MIDI to be sure you are using the right mode for the current task.

Figure 5.20 You toggle the Record mode setting here, at the top left of the Transport bar.

Another Way to Record MIDI

This chapter explains how to record MIDI using an external MIDI device, and in the next chapter, you'll learn how to draw MIDI notes from scratch using the mouse in the Key editor. There is one other option for recording MIDI, though, which is sort of in between the two. If you open the Key editor, you can click on the keyboard on the left side of the editor to trigger MIDI notes. You can start recording in Cubase and it will record those notes, just as if you played them on an external controller, although you might find it more difficult to maintain the tempo while clicking on screen.

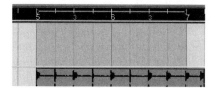

Figure 5.21 The left and right locators set for a two-bar cycle

Figure 5.22 Cycle recording is active, and the left locator is set to punch in recording.

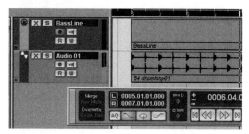

Figure 5.23 The BassLine track is recording in Cycle mode.

■ You don't have to set the starting point for MIDI playback manually. If you just click on the Record button on the Transport bar, a count-off will begin, and recording will start at the left locator. This can be a very convenient shortcut.

Recording MIDI in Cycle Mode

Just like audio, MIDI can be recorded while a specific section of a project is looping. The Cubase SX term for this loop-style recording is cycle recording. Setting up Cubase SX to cycle record MIDI is much like setting up the program to cycle record audio, though there are some extra considerations for MIDI cycle recording, discussed later in this chapter.

To cycle record MIDI:

1. Set the left and right locators to select the section that you want to cycle (**Figure 5.21**).

2. On the Transport bar, click to turn on Cycle mode and also click to make the Punch-In button active (**Figure 5.22**).

3. Move the cursor to a point before where you want the loop to start; then start playback.
   When Cubase SX reaches the point where it will loop, recording will automatically be punched in, and playback/recording will continue indefinitely (**Figure 5.23**).

4. When you are done recording, click Stop on the Transport bar or use the computer keyboard to stop playback.

✔ Tips

■ When cycle recording, you don't want both the Punch-In and Punch-Out buttons selected. That setting will punch out recording after the first pass, though the section will continue to cycle playback.

■ You don't need to use the punch-in capability of Cubase to cycle record. If you are playing along to a section that is in Cycle mode and get a part you like, start recording manually, and you will be cycle recording.

Cycle Recording: Mix vs. Overwrite

Cycle recording audio creates a new audio part for each cycle of the loop. Again, the nature of MIDI allows some choice over how cycle recording works. You can toggle cycle recording between Mix mode and Overwrite mode using the Transport bar.

Mix mode (Figure 5.24) acts much like Merge mode for noncycle recording. Incoming MIDI is added to the already recorded MIDI for that track. This allows a part to be built up over multiple passes, playing the hi hat on one cycle, the kick drum on the next cycle, and so on. When recording is stopped, all MIDI played during all cycles is included in the single MIDI part.

Overwrite mode (Figure 5.25) overwrites any MIDI recorded in previous cycles whenever new MIDI is played. In effect, playing anything during a cycle erases what was played before and creates a new MIDI part. Use this mode when you want to keep playing a part until you get the performance you want, and then stop playback to keep the most recent, good take.

Figure 5.24 The Transport bar set for Mix mode when cycle recording

Figure 5.25 The Transport bar set for Overwrite mode when cycle recording

✔ Tips

- You might prefer a mode in which cycle recording of MIDI acts like cycle recording of audio, creating a new part with each cycle. Cubase SX does not (yet) have such a mode for MIDI recording, so the best approach is to punch in and punch out automatically in Normal recording mode, without using cycle recording.

- If you're cycle recording in Mix mode to build up a drum part or a pad, you should loop a fairly long part. Looping 16- or 32-bar sections will give you numerous shots at a part that will often be a 1-bar loop when recording multiple MIDI tracks.

Figure 5.26
Three tracks record enabled; all will record at the same time.

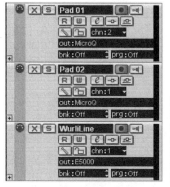

Figure 5.27
Each track that will record is set to its own MIDI output; this is the view in the track list.

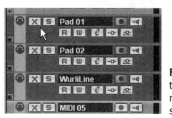

Figure 5.28 All three tracks are recording at the same time.

Recording Multiple MIDI Tracks

Up until now, you have been learning about recording single tracks. That is the most common way MIDI is recorded, but Cubase SX also can record more than one track at a time. There are many situations in which this is a good idea, such as when you want to record more than one musician, to record the same part to more than one destination, or to record MIDI instruments that transmit on more than one channel.

To record multiple MIDI tracks:

1. Record enable all tracks that you want to record (**Figure 5.26**).

2. In the inspector for each track, select the MIDI input you want to use. This may be the same for all tracks, or it may be different, depending on your situation.

3. In the inspector or on the track list, select a MIDI output for each track to be recorded (**Figure 5.27**).

   When you start recording, all record-enabled tracks will record MIDI from their selected MIDI inputs (**Figure 5.28**).

4. When you are finished recording, click Stop on the Transport bar or use the keyboard to stop recording.

✔ Tip

■ All of the features available for recording single MIDI tracks are available for recording multiple tracks. When recording more than one track, you can still cycle, punch in, punch out, and do everything that is possible with single-track recording.

About Multitimbral MIDI Devices

Many synthesizers and samplers are *multi-timbral*, which means that they can play back different sounds triggered by different MIDI channels—that is, MIDI channel 1 will trigger the piano part, MIDI channel 2 will trigger the bass line, MIDI channel 10 will trigger the drum part, and so on.

Some MIDI controllers can also play back on different MIDI channels simultaneously. This can be used to create keyboard splits, where one part of a keyboard triggers a bass sound on MIDI channel 1, and the rest of the keyboard triggers a piano sound on MIDI channel 2. Other parameters can be used to trigger different channels depending on the controller, but the issues remain the same regardless of the particular controller and setup.

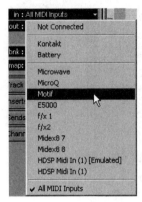

Figure 5.29 When recording multiple tracks and using multitimbral devices, it's usually best not to select All MIDI Inputs.

Multitimbral Recording Considerations

◆ When recording a multitimbral MIDI controller, you don't want All MIDI Inputs selected as the source. Define a unique channel and device for each track that is to be recorded (**Figure 5.29**).

◆ All multitimbral MIDI devices must have the ability to save setups where the whole state of the synthesizer can be recalled. These are often called "multis" or "combis" or something similar. If you will be using multitimbral synths, get familiar with the way that each device manages multitimbral setups. It's easy to get lost in the multitimbral MIDI maze, and knowing how the gear works will keep that from happening.

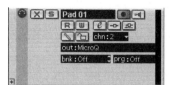

Figure 5.30
A track with previously recorded notes is record–enabled.

Figure 5.31 The CC data is visible in real time as it is recorded.

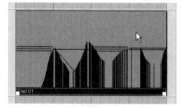

Figure 5.32 The track after recording CC data; the thin horizontal lines are the MIDI notes for the track, and the vertical lines are the recorded CC data.

Recording MIDI Controller Data

MIDI is more than just notes. The MIDI specification also includes continuous controller data, or even sysex data. CC data provides one of the fantastic features of MIDI: it allows you to use the tactile knobs and sliders on a MIDI controller to modify parameters on MIDI devices in real time. Cubase SX can record this data much like it records note data, and if you change a controller during recording (by moving the pitch wheel on your synth, for example), Cubase will record the CC data with the MIDI notes.

CC data is recorded with a performance, but often it can also be used to add dynamic elements to a performance after the fact. For example, the modulation wheel on a MIDI controller can be used to control the way that a filter in a synth behaves.

To record MIDI CC data:

1. Record enable the track to which you want to add the CC data (**Figure 5.30**).

2. Check that recording mode is set to Merge (at the top left of the Transport bar) so the CC data is added to the current MIDI track.

3. Start recording manually, or set a punch-in point and have Cubase start recording automatically.

4. Move the modulation wheel on the controller; the Event display will show the data as it is being recorded (**Figure 5.31**).

5. When you have finished recording, stop playback with the Transport bar or the computer keyboard (**Figure 5.32**).

✔ Tip

- Nearly all MIDI hardware made in the recent past has powerful tools for editing CC sources and destinations. Learning about your MIDI hardware and software will allow you to use the modulation wheel on your MIDI controller to control nearly any parameter on nearly any MIDI device in your studio.

Recording MIDI
Sysex Data

All MIDI devices understand note and CC data in pretty much the same way. The smart people who put together MIDI realized that manufacturers would sometimes need to implement specialized abilities not covered by the basic MIDI specification. This data is called system-exclusive MIDI data, or sysex for short.

Sysex is MIDI data that can be understood only by the particular make and model of MIDI device that created it. For example, all synthesizers should respond to the CC for volume in the same way, but sysex from a Roland synth will do nothing when sent to a Waldorf synth.

Sysex has many uses if you are willing to spend the time to learn about it, but be ready to put your MIDI geek hat on, because sysex is about as technical and computerlike as MIDI gets. There is one use for sysex, however, that nearly everyone should know about: a bulk dump.

Almost all synths, samplers, and other MIDI hardware have the ability to send their complete current state as sysex data. Cubase SX can record this sysex bulk dump, and then it can be played back on the device to return the device to the precise state it was in when the sysex dump was collected.

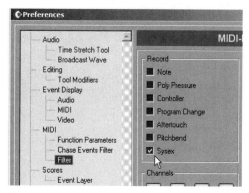

Figure 5.33 With this box checked, sysex is filtered and thus cannot be recorded.

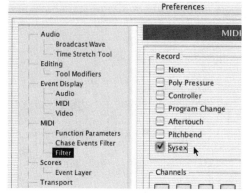

Figure 5.34 The Preferences panel for MIDI filtering when using the Mac OS version of Cubase.

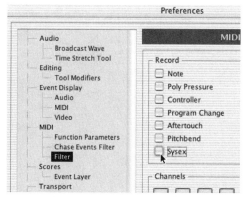

Figure 5.35 Sysex has been unchecked, meaning that it will not be filtered. Now Cubase can record sysex data.

To record MIDI sysex data:

1. By default, Cubase SX filters out sysex data when recording. To enable recording of sysex data, do one of the following:
   - ▲ In Windows, choose File > Preferences and then select MIDI Filter (**Figure 5.33**).
   - ▲ In Mac OS, choose Cubase SX > Preferences and then select MIDI Filter (**Figure 5.34**).

2. Any of the MIDI parameters selected on this panel are being filtered out and not recorded. Uncheck Sysex to allow MIDI sysex data to be recorded (**Figure 5.35**). Click OK to save the changes in the preferences.

3. Record enable a MIDI track and start Cubase MIDI recording.

4. Initiate a sysex dump.

   Each MIDI device has a slightly different method for initiating a sysex bulk dump. Usually, you either push a few buttons simultaneously on the front panel or choose an option in the Global section for the MIDI device. Consult the documentation that came with the MIDI hardware.

   The MIDI In indicator on the Transport bar will light to indicate that MIDI is being received, and Cubase will record the sysex data.

5. When the sysex bulk dump is finished, the MIDI In light will stop flashing. Stop recording with the Transport bar or the computer keyboard.

✔ Tips

- The easiest way to be sure that sysex data was recorded is to play back the part that contains the sysex data and see if the MIDI Out light on the Transport bar lights to show MIDI activity. You can also check in the MIDI List editor, which is covered in Chapter 10, "Editing MIDI."

- Sysex has some voodoo to it, and a lot of data is transferred at the same time. Always check sysex bulk dumps to be sure they work properly. Also, sysex should be recorded and played back at the beginning of a song, since many MIDI devices will not play notes while sysex is being received.

- Dealing with sysex can seem difficult and irritating, but it's still a lot easier than using pencil and paper to write down every parameter of a MIDI device!

ENTERING MIDI MANUALLY

You don't have to use an external device to record MIDI data in Cubase SX. While this is often the best way to get music into Cubase, there are some situations when you simply won't have a controller handy for recording. In addition, some people find creating certain parts, such as bass lines and programmed drum beats, easier to do manually by entering them with the computer keyboard or mouse.

Cubase SX offers many ways to enter MIDI data, but the most commonly used tools are the Key editor and the Drum editor. This chapter will get you going with these editors, showing you how to create MIDI notes and how to edit basic parameters to change the way the notes sound.

You will start by creating an empty MIDI part in the Project window. Then you will learn how to open it in the Key editor and to enter notes with the mouse. You will also learn about the tools Cubase provides to control the duration of notes and how to edit the volume and pan and other properties in the Key editor. In addition, you will learn about the specialized Drum editor, a powerful editor with tools specifically designed for creating programmed beats from scratch.

Creating a MIDI Part

When you record MIDI data onto a MIDI track in Cubase SX, the application automatically creates a MIDI part for the incoming data. However, when you enter MIDI notes using one of Cubase's built-in editors, you need to create a part, or container, for it first. There are two primary ways to create new, empty parts: with the locators and with the Draw tool.

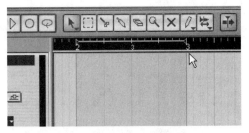

Figure 6.1 The locators set to create a MIDI part

To create a MIDI part using the locators:

1. In the Project window, set the left and right locators where you want the MIDI part to start and end (**Figure 6.1**).

   You can set the locators by moving them on the ruler or by entering their locations on the Transport bar.

2. Select the Object Selection tool (the arrow) and double-click the MIDI track, between the locators, where you want to create the new part.

   A new, empty MIDI part is created and is selected (**Figure 6.2**).

Sometimes, you will want to create a part that does not begin and end precisely at the locators. In this case you can use the Draw tool, as you'll see on the next page.

Figure 6.2 After you double-click with the arrow, a one-bar part is created.

Figure 6.3 You can select any of the tools, including the Draw tool, from this context menu.

Figure 6.4 After you click and drag with the Draw tool, this MIDI part is created.

To create a MIDI part with the Draw tool:

1. In the Project window, right-click (Windows) or Control-click (Mac OS) and select the Draw tool from the context menu (**Figure 6.3**), or choose the Draw tool from the toolbar.

2. With the Draw tool selected, click, but don't release, the location where you want the part to begin. Then hold down the mouse and drag to the location where you want the part to end. Release the mouse.

   A new part is created and selected in the Project window (**Figure 6.4**), with its length determined by the distance you dragged the mouse.

✔ Tip

■ When you use the Draw tool, Snap applies. Turn Snap off to draw a part freehand; keep Snap on to easily create a part of a particular length.

Opening an Editor

The Project window has only minimal tools for editing MIDI data and no tools for creating MIDI data. To put something in an empty MIDI part, you need to open the part in an editor. One method is simply to double-click the MIDI part with the Object Selection tool—the arrow. This opens the MIDI Key editor, which is commonly used for this purpose. However, Cubase also includes Drum, List, and Score editors, which may be more appropriate for your needs. Here's how to open any of these editors.

Figure 6.5 It's hard to see in this illustration, but a red outline surrounding this MIDI part shows that it is selected.

To open a MIDI part in an editor:

1. In the Project window, click the part you want to open to select it (**Figure 6.5**).

2. Right-click (Windows) or Control-click (Mac OS) the part to open the context menu.

3. Choose MIDI and then select the editor you want to open (**Figure 6.6**).
   The MIDI part opens in the editor you select.

Figure 6.6 This context menu includes many options, including options to open a part in any MIDI editor.

✔ Tip

■ By default, Cubase uses the MIDI Key editor when a part is double-clicked. If you prefer to open a part in a different editor when you double click, you can change the default behavior. Choose File > Preferences (Windows) or Cubase SX > Preferences (Mac OS). In the dialog box that opens, under Event Display, select MIDI. In the right panel of this dialog box, open the drop-down Default Edit Action menu and choose a different default MIDI editor (**Figure 6.7**).

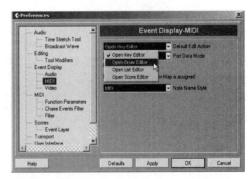

Figure 6.7 The default editor, the one used when you double-click a part in the Project window, can be changed here.

About the Key Editor

The Key editor, described briefly in Chapter 2, lets you enter data through a visual representation of a piano keyboard. (You can also record MIDI data in the Key editor just like you can in the Project window.)

Creating MIDI data in the Key editor involves extensive use of the toolbar and Info line. **Figure 6.8** shows the toolbar with a MIDI note selected, with information about this note displayed on the Info line.

Info Line button: Toggles the Info line on and off.

Solo button: When this button is selected, only the MIDI data in the current editor is audible. All other MIDI data and audio is muted.

Edit tools: The various tools used to create and modify MIDI data. See the next section, "About the Edit Tools," for more information on these tools.

Auto-scroll button: When this button is selected, the window follows along as the project plays back.

Mouse pointer display: Shows the current location of the mouse pointer in both song position and pitch.

Snap button: Toggles Snap on or off for the Key editor.

Quantize menu: Sets both the Snap and Quantize values for MIDI data.

Length Quantize menu: Sets the duration used when a new MIDI note is entered.

Insert Velocity menu: Sets the velocity used when a new MIDI note is entered.

Colors menu: Specifies whether and how MIDI notes are color coded.

Autoplay button: Toggles auditioning on and off. With auditioning on, when a new note is created, it is also played back. When auditioning is off, notes do not play back when they are entered.

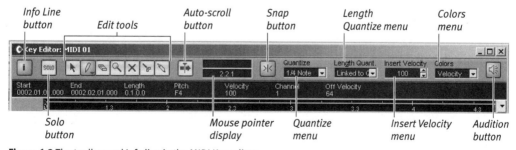

Figure 6.8 The toolbar and Info line in the MIDI Key editor

About the Edit Tools

The edit tools are particularly important when creating MIDI parts. **Figure 6.9** shows the edit tools on the toolbar.

Object Selection tool: Selects one or more notes in the Note or Controller display. This book also refers to this tool as the arrow.

Draw tool: Creates notes and controller data. If you select this tool on the toolbar and then click it again, a menu opens with options for specifying the way the tool creates data.

Eraser tool: Erases notes when they are clicked with this tool.

Zoom tool: Shows more or less information in the editor by enlarging or shrinking the view.

Mute tool: Stops a note from playing back until it's unmuted. Clicking a note with this tool does not erase it permanently (unlike when you use the Eraser tool).

Scissors tool: Splits a MIDI note into two notes.

Glue tool: Combines two MIDI notes into a single note.

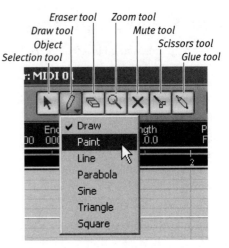

Figure 6.9 The MIDI edit tools on the Key editor toolbar, with the Draw tool options displayed

Figure 6.10 Use this menu to configure the way the Draw tool works. To enter notes with the pencil, select Draw from the list.

Figure 6.11 Clicking will enter a MIDI note. Notice also that the note about to be entered is visible on the keyboard; in this case, the D key is highlighted.

Figure 6.12 After clicking, the D is created in the Note display.

Entering a MIDI Note

The most basic task when creating MIDI data is entering a note. The Draw tool in the Key editor makes this very easy.

To enter a note in the Key editor:

1. Click the Draw tool on the toolbar to select it. Click the tool button again, and when the menu opens, select Draw (**Figure 6.10**).

2. Using the piano-like keyboard on the left side of the Key editor as a guide, place the tool at the pitch and meter position where you want to enter a note (**Figure 6.11**).

3. Click once.
   The note is entered in the Key editor (**Figure 6.12**).

✔ Tips

- The Draw tool defaults to Draw mode, so normally you won't need to set this in the tool's menu. If the tool does not behave the way you expect, go back and check to see if it's in the right mode.

- If you hold down the mouse after clicking, you can drag to the right to make the duration of the note longer.

Hearing MIDI Notes

When entering notes in the Key editor, you can choose whether to hear them or not. When the Autoplay button is selected, Cubase sends each MIDI note as it is created to the device selected for the MIDI part currently in the Key editor. When the Audition button is not selected, notes do not sound when entered.

Each method is best in different situations. If you are looping a drum part in an editor and building the groove by adding notes as the loop plays, you usually won't want the notes to sound; the added note will be heard the next time the loop passes that point in the groove. If you are entering MIDI data for another sound, such as a bass line or a synth bell, and are not also looping the part, you may prefer to hear the pitches as they are entered. It's easy to figure out when to turn Autoplay on or off: essentially, leave it on unless it bothers you. The situations where it's inconvenient to have the notes sounding are usually pretty obvious.

Expanding the Note Display

Most windows in Cubase let you zoom the view on both the vertical and horizontal axes. Because of the way the Key editor works, the vertical axis is particularly important when entering MIDI notes. With too much showing, it's easy to enter the wrong note; with too little showing, it's hard to find the note you want to create. You can set the Key editor so that the keyboard on the left displays as many as seven octaves or as few as one. Viewing more octaves makes it easier to see what is going on with the music, but it's much easier to click the right note when the Note display is zoomed in.

To change the Note display:

1. Click the Zoom slider at the right side of the Key editor (**Figure 6.13**).

2. Drag the slider up to see more notes in the Note display, to get an overview of the whole MIDI part (**Figure 6.14**).

3. Drag the slider down to see fewer notes in the Note display, to see the most detail (**Figure 6.15**).

Figure 6.13 The Zoom slider in the Key editor, here at roughly its default position

Figure 6.14 With the Zoom slider all the way up, many notes can be viewed, but they are quite small on the vertical axis.

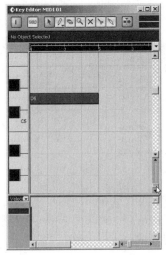

Figure 6.15 The Zoom slider is now all the way down, showing far fewer notes, but the notes are much larger.

Figure 6.16 This is the location and pitch we want: F# at the first tick of beat 2 of measure 2.

Mouse Pointer display

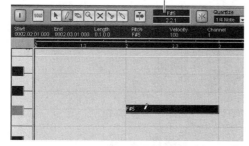

Figure 6.17 Clicking the Note display adds the F# at beat 2 of measure 2, as shown in the Mouse Pointer display.

Using the Mouse Pointer Display

As mentioned previously, one way to see what note you're entering is by looking at the highlight on the Key editor's keyboard. However, the Mouse Pointer display at the top of the Key editor window gives you even more feedback. This display shows the current position of the mouse pointer, with the position constantly updated as you move the mouse around the Note display. It also shows the note that will be entered and the song position where the note will be entered. The song position is shown in *bars.beats.ticks*, so 4.3.1 means bar four, beat three, tick 1. This notation makes it easy to place a note precisely, even without looking at the Note display. For example, assume that you want to enter an F# at the second beat of bar 2. Here's how.

To enter a note using the Mouse Pointer display:

1. Select the Draw tool and move it over the Note display.

2. Watch the Mouse Pointer display as you move the cursor to the location where you want to enter the note (**Figure 6.16**).

3. Click at that location, and the note will be entered at precisely the point you wish (**Figure 6.17**).

Snap and the Key Editor

Like nearly everything else in Cubase, the state and setting of Snap has a great deal to do with what exactly happens when the mouse clicking starts. Having Snap on is convenient when you want to enter notes exactly in time. Snap must be turned off if you want to put notes at places other than at such exact meter divisions.

For example, if you want to enter a part exactly on the eighth notes, the easiest way to do this is with Snap.

To enter notes using Snap:

1. First, you need to set the meter division you want to use. In this example, in the Key editor, the Quantize value is being changed to 1/8 Note (**Figure 6.18**).

2. If Snap is not turned on, click the Snap button to turn it on (**Figure 6.19**).

3. Select the Draw tool.

4. Starting on the left side of the Note display in the Key editor window, click the note you want to enter.

   Clicking where the Draw tool is positioned in **Figure 6.20** will snap the note to the nearest eighth note—in this case, the very beginning of the measure (**Figure 6.21**).

5. Continue to enter notes with Snap on across the whole measure.

   Each note will be placed precisely on an eighth note.

✔ Tip

■ If you turn off Snap when entering the note with the Draw tool positioned exactly as in Figure 6.20, the result is **Figure 6.22**.

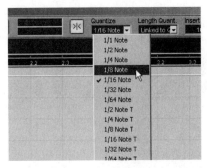

Figure 6.18 Setting the Quantize value (used by Snap in the Key editor) to an eighth note

Figure 6.19 Snap is turned on.

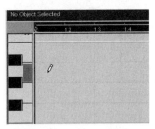

Figure 6.20 The Draw tool is not precisely at the first beat.

Figure 6.21 Clicking at the location shown in Figure 6.20 snaps the note to the exact start of the measure.

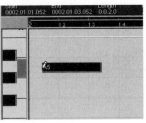

Figure 6.22 With the Draw tool positioned as in Figure 6.20 and Snap turned off, the note will start where the Draw tool is clicked.

SNAP AND THE KEY EDITOR

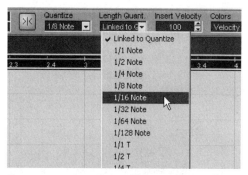

Figure 6.23 This setting will insert sixteenth notes, regardless of the Snap setting, when you use the Draw tool.

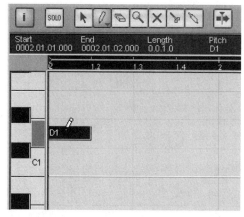

Figure 6.24 This setting enters a sixteenth note at the start of the MIDI part. The figure shows the first beat of measure 2, from 2.1 to 2.2. The duration of the note created is one quarter of this time, or a sixteenth note.

Setting Note Length

In the previous example, you entered eighth notes across a bar using Snap to place the notes precisely. When entering notes in the Key editor, the default note duration will be equal to the Snap value. If Snap is set to eighth notes, then clicking the Note display with the Draw tool will enter an eighth note. In some situations, this is desirable, but not always. For example, you may want to program a techno-style pulsing bass line that is still straight eighth notes, but with each note lasting only the duration of a sixteenth note.

To change the duration of notes created with the Draw tool:

1. Turn Snap on if it not already on, and set the Quantize value to 1/8 note.

2. Select the Draw tool.

3. In the Length Quantize drop-down menu, select 1/16th Note (**Figure 6.23**).

4. With the Draw tool, click the note and meter location where you want the line to start.

   A note of sixteenth note duration will be entered at the nearest eighth note (**Figure 6.24**).

5. Continue clicking across the whole measure, skipping one sixteenth and then adding a note at the next sixteenth The result will look like **Figure 6.25**.

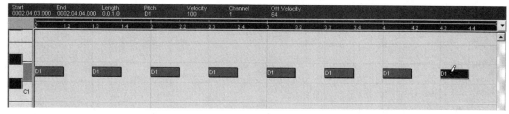

Figure 6.25 A few more clicks, and the Snap and Length Quantize settings create this simple line.

Setting Note Velocity

MIDI involves more parameters than just pitch and duration. One of the more important other parameters is velocity. Velocity relates back to the keyboard and synth origins of MIDI; it is a measure of how hard a key is struck. For non-keyboard sounds, the velocity essentially controls how loudly a note is sounded, though of course not every sound or synth responds in the same way to velocity information.

Like most things MIDI, velocity is recorded using a not terribly intuitive scale that ranges from 1 to 127. By default, the Cubase Key editor uses a velocity of 100 for notes entered by hand with the Draw tool. You'll learn how to change velocity for an individual note later in this chapter, but in some cases you will know ahead of time that you want notes to have a particular velocity. For a techno bass line, for instance, you might want to use maximum velocity, or 127, for each note.

To enter notes with a specific velocity:

1. Select the Draw tool.

2. Click the Insert Velocity field to highlight the setting (**Figure 6.26**).

3. Type a new value; in this example, enter *127* to create notes with the maximum velocity allowed by MIDI (**Figure 6.27**).

4. Use the Draw tool to enter a note in the Note display. When that note is selected, the Info line will show the velocity (**Figure 6.28**).

✔ Tip

- You can also use the small up-and-down arrows beside the Insert Velocity field (**Figure 6.29**) to increase or decrease the velocity by one unit per click. If you have a wheel mouse, you can also click the note and use the wheel to change the velocity.

Figure 6.26 Click the Insert Velocity field and then change it by typing a value on the computer keyboard.

Figure 6.27 This setting will create notes with the maximum velocity for MIDI notes: 127.

Figure 6.28 After you enter and then select a note, check the Info line to see whether the Insert Velocity setting was applied correctly.

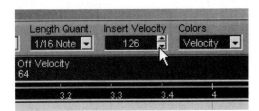

Figure 6.29 You can click the arrows to increase or decrease the velocity of inserted notes.

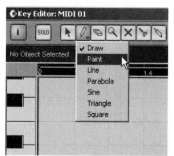

Figure 6.30
Setting the
Draw tool to
Paint mode

Figure 6.31 The Snap, Quantize, and Velocity settings—
the same ones used in the previous example

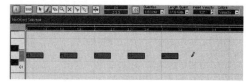

Figure 6.32 Clicking and dragging to paint notes in
the Note display

Entering Multiple Notes by Painting

Cubase makes great efforts to provide short-cuts to let you create music quickly and easily. One of these shortcuts gives you the ability to enter multiple notes in the Key editor with the Draw tool by putting it in Paint mode. When the Draw tool is in Paint mode, dragging will enter notes anywhere and everywhere that the tool is dragged. In fact, you can combine the Snap setting, the Length Quantize setting, and the Insert Velocity setting with the Paint mode shortcut to create in one pass the eighth-note techno bass line we've been working with.

To paint notes:

1. Click the Draw tool on the toolbar to select it. Click it again after it is selected to open a drop-down menu and select Paint (**Figure 6.30**).

2. Turn on Snap by clicking the Snap button.

3. Set the Quantize, Length Quantize, and Insert Velocity values to control the way that notes are entered. For this example, set 1/8 Note for Quantize, 1/16 Note for Length Quantize, and 127 for Insert Velocity (**Figure 6.31**).

4. Click with the Draw tool (which turns into a paint brush) where you want to start entering notes and drag to the right to enter notes for as long as you wish. Release the mouse when you're finished (**Figure 6.32**).

ENTERING MULTIPLE NOTES BY PAINTING

Muting and Deleting Notes

As easy as it is to make mistakes playing a musical instrument, it's probably even easier to make mistakes when entering notes with a mouse. The painting action described in the preceding section is also particularly prone to occasionally creating unwanted notes. Fortunately, you can use the Eraser and Mute tools in Cubase to fix your mistakes by deleting notes or by muting a note or two in a part without actually losing the MIDI data. As their names suggest, the Eraser tool deletes data completely, and the Mute tool prevents the selected note from sounding during playback.

To delete MIDI notes with the Eraser tool:

1. In the Note display, right-click (Windows) or Control-click (Mac OS) and select Erase from the context menu (**Figure 6.33**), or select the Eraser tool from the toolbar.

   The pointer turns into an eraser.

2. Click any note to delete it (**Figure 6.34**).

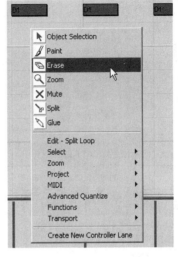

Figure 6.33 Using the context menu to select the Erase tool

Figure 6.34 When you click the note, the note is deleted.

Figure 6.35
Selecting the
Mute tool from
the toolbar

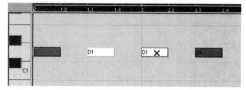

Figure 6.36 The two white notes are muted and will not sound.

To mute notes with the Mute tool:

1. In the Note display, right-click (Windows) or Control-click (Mac OS) and select Mute from the context menu or select the Mute tool from the toolbar (**Figure 6.35**).

2. Using the Mute tool, which looks like an X, click any note that you don't want to hear.

   Muted notes turn white (**Figure 6.36**) and will not be heard at playback.

✔ Tip

- You can use the Mute tool to create interesting effects in existing MIDI tracks, whether the tracks are entered manually or recorded from a MIDI controller. Often in music, less really is more, and setting a project to loop while muting notes a few at a time can lead to much more interesting MIDI lines.

Viewing Continuous Controller Data

Continuous controller (CC) data can be used for an enormous range of tasks with MIDI devices. It can be used to send modulation to synthesizers, change settings on effects devices, and add expression to performances after the fact. There is no room to cover all of that in this chapter—you will learn much more about CC data in Chapter 10—but basic CC skills are useful when creating a MIDI part in Cubase, and that's what we'll focus on here.

There are 127 possible CC messages. Many are just known by number (CC 59), but some are standardized and are generally referred to by name: for example, Velocity, Pan, Modulation, Main Volume, and Pitchbend. Pretty much every MIDI synth made should respond to these standardized controllers, and the Key editor lets you make changes to any CC data you wish. By default, the Key editor shows only one CC at a time, so you need to choose which one to view.

To select a continuous controller to view in the Key editor:

1. Click the pop-up menu at the left of the Controller lane (**Figure 6.37**).

2. In the menu that opens, select the CC you want to view and edit (**Figure 6.38**).

   The controller is visible in the Controller lane (**Figure 6.39**) and is ready for editing.

Figure 6.37 Clicking to the left of the Controller lane opens the pop-up menu to select the CC you want to display.

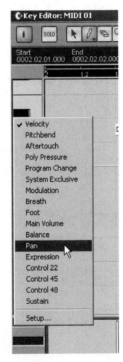

Figure 6.38 Choosing Pan as the CC to be viewed and edited

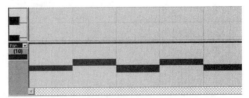

Figure 6.39 CC data for Pan is now visible in the Controller lane.

Figure 6.40 Selecting the Draw tool to create CC data

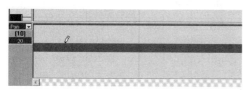

Figure 6.41 Dragging with the Draw tool creates new controller data.

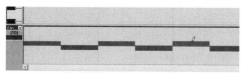

Figure 6.42 With Snap set to eighth notes, you can easily draw a slight pan for each eighth note with the Draw tool.

Entering CC Data with the Draw Tool

Although you can use the various Draw tool modes when creating or modifying MIDI CC data, you'll use the simple Draw mode most often when creating new data. For example, still using that eighth-note pulsing bass line, you can use the Draw tool to pan each note slightly to the left and right by entering CC data.

To enter CC data with the Draw tool:

1. Select the Draw tool. Be sure that it is in Draw mode after it is selected (**Figure 6.40**).

2. Set the Controller lane so it displays the CC you want to edit. In this example, select Pan.

3. Turn on Snap to create data according to meter. In this case, set Quantize to 1/8 Note.

4. With the Draw tool, drag the Controller lane.

   The bar being drawn with the pointer in **Figure 6.41** shows the CC value entered.

5. Repeat step 4 for each eighth note you want to modify.

   Figure 6.42 shows CC data that pans each note alternately slightly to the left and slightly to the right.

✔ Tip

■ MIDI CCs are your friends. They open up possibilities to modulate and modify your synths, samplers, and effects for greatest impact. Learn about CCs in all of your gear, and you will be rewarded.

About the Drum Editor

The Key editor is often the best tool for putting together a MIDI part from scratch. Most of the time, it's the easiest editor to use for building up instrument lines and bass lines and performing similar tasks. One thing it is not terribly good for, though, is creating drum parts. Cubase has a dedicated Drum editor with some unique features and tools specifically for drum parts. The Drum editor was one of the first features that set Cubase apart, way back in the Atari computer days, and it is still a superior tool for building up a good drum loop.

Under normal circumstances, sending MIDI data to a particular device on a particular channel will trigger one sound at different pitches. If you send MIDI data to a synth with a bass patch on that channel, every note will trigger the bass sound, and the notes will control the pitch played back. With drum tracks, each note plays back a different sound: one note will be a kick drum, another note a hi-hat, and so on. The Drum editor is specifically designed for creating and editing such sounds. **Figure 6.43** shows the parts of the Drum editor. With a few exceptions, it is very much like the Key editor.

Toolbar: As in the Key editor, the toolbar has controls for viewing, creating, and editing MIDI data, as well as Snap and Quantize settings.

Note display: Unlike in the Key editor, notes in the Drum editor are represented by diamonds. This makes them easier to see on a grid, a more intuitive arrangement for viewing drum parts.

Drum Sound list: Because each note triggers a different sound, the Drum editor lets you give names to your drum sounds and edit the properties of those sounds. The Drum Sound list is closely related to the drum map.

Controller lane: The Controller lane in the Drum editor is basically identical to the Controller lane in the Key editor.

Drum Map settings: You can use the pop-up menus to select drum maps and display drum map names.

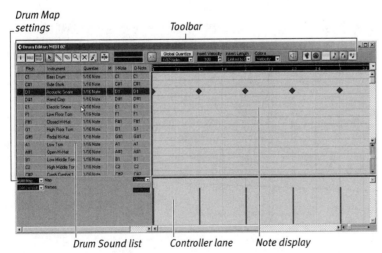

Drum Map settings

Toolbar

Drum Sound list   Controller lane   Note display

Figure 6.43 The Drum editor

Figure 6.44 A MIDI part selected in the Project window

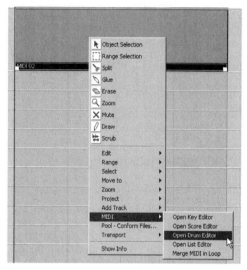

Figure 6.45 Selecting Open Drum Editor from the context menu

Opening the Drum Editor

You access the Drum editor in the same way as all of the other MIDI editors in Cubase. You can open any MIDI part in the Drum editor, regardless of how it was created. Even MIDI parts created in another editor, such as the Key editor, can be opened and edited in the Drum editor if you wish.

To open a MIDI part in the Drum editor:

1. In the Project window, click the MIDI part you want to edit (**Figure 6.44**).

2. Right-click (Windows) or Control-click (Mac OS) to open the context menu for that MIDI part.

3. Select MIDI > Open Drum Editor (**Figure 6.45**).

    The Drum editor opens, displaying any MIDI data already in that part.

Using the Drumstick Tool

The Drumstick tool is the primary means of entering note data in the Drum editor. If you sequence a lot of drums, you'll get to know the Drumstick tool better than some members of your immediate family. Clicking the Note display with the Drumstick will enter a note at that location, while clicking an existing note with the Drumstick will erase it. Put simply, the Drumstick toggles notes on the display grid on and off. To see a very simple example, you can program a kick drum on all four quarter notes of a one-bar loop.

To enter notes with the Drumstick tool:

1. Click the Drumstick tool on the toolbar (**Figure 6.46**), or select it from the context menu.

2. On the toolbar, click the Snap button to turn on Snap, and click the Global Quantize button and set the Quantize value to 1/4 Note.

   These settings are explained in the next few pages. For now, just set them as shown in **Figure 6.47**.

3. Hold the pointer over the Note display until it turns into the Drumstick tool (in other parts of the window, the pointer will be an arrow used for selecting buttons, values, and menus). Move the Drumstick tool to roughly the beginning of the MIDI part and click to enter a note (**Figure 6.48**).

4. Click beats 2, 3, and 4 to create the other notes.

   The result will look like **Figure 6.49**.

Figure 6.46 Clicking this button selects the Drumstick tool; you can also select it by right-clicking (Windows) or Control-clicking (Mac OS) the Note display.

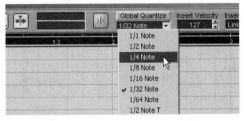

Figure 6.47 Snap is turned on, as is Global Quantize, and 1/4 Note is selected from the Quantize menu.

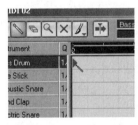

Figure 6.48 Clicking at the first beat enters a note; only half of the diamond is visible, but the note is there.

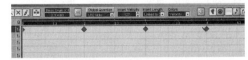

Figure 6.49 The MIDI part after all four quarter notes have been entered

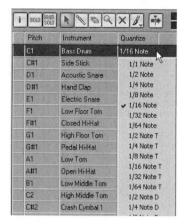

Figure 6.50 The Quantize setting for an individual sound is used by the Drumstick tool if Global Quantize is turned off.

Figure 6.51 With Snap on but Global Quantize off, the Quantize setting for the individual sound will be used.

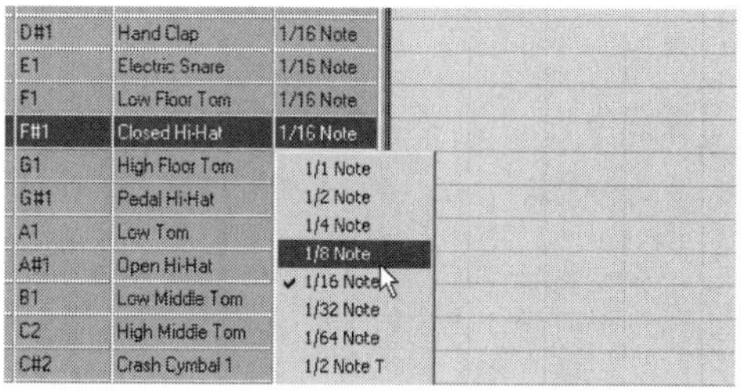

Figure 6.52 This setting will select eighth notes for this sound.

Global Quantize vs. Individual Settings

The Drum editor has more Snap and Quantize options than any other editor in Cubase. For example, the Drumstick tool can use either of two Snap and Quantize settings, depending on what you want to do. The Drum Sound list includes a Quantize setting for each sound, and clicking a setting opens a drop-down menu of meter settings (**Figure 6.50**). You can either assign each drum sound with its own unique Quantize setting, or you can override these settings using Global Quantize.

The Global Quantize button determines how notes are entered with the Drumstick tool regardless of their individual Quantize settings. In the previous example, you turned on Global Quantize and set it to 1/4 Note, so that the Drumstick tool enters notes only on a quarter note in the Note display. If Global Quantize is turned off, the Quantize setting for the particular sound will be used instead of the global setting. In the following example, you'll add an eighth-note pattern to the quarter-note pattern you created on page 124.

To enter notes with the Drumstick tool without Global Quantize:

1. Select the Drumstick tool.

2. Turn off Global Quantize but leave Snap on (**Figure 6.51**).

3. In the Drum Sound list, click the Quantize setting of the sound you want to use. In this case, select 1/8 Note from the menu that opens (**Figure 6.52**).

continues on next page

GLOBAL QUANTIZE VS. INDIVIDUAL SETTINGS

4. Using the Drumstick tool, click at the beginning of the part and drag the tool to the right.

Notes are entered according to the Quantize setting for that sound (**Figure 6.53**).

5. Continue dragging to the right until you have created all of the notes you want.

Figure 6.53 Only eighth notes can be added with these settings. In this situation, the Drumstick tool acts a bit like the Paint tool, creating multiple notes as the tool is dragged.

Drum Maps

Cubase uses drum maps to match names and MIDI notes of drums. Not every synthesizer and sample uses the same note to trigger the same sound, so Cubase allows individuals and synth manufacturers to create their own drum maps to address this issue. With a properly configured drum map, you can use the name of a sound, such as Bass Drum, to enter sounds instead of specifying the note, which could be nearly anything.

Cubase comes with some included drum maps, including the General MIDI (or GM) drum map. General MIDI is a set of parameters for sounds that synth manufacturers have agreed on so that there is a base set of sounds that a GM synth follows. This makes it possible to create a sequence with one GM synth and then play it back with a different GM synth and have it sound roughly the same. Part of the GM setup is a standard drum map, where certain pitches trigger certain sounds. Nearly all newer synths have at least one GM drum kit, as do many software drum machines and software samplers. Also, the manufacturer of your synth may have drum maps available; check the disks that came with it or the manufacturer's Web site.

You can also make your own drum maps if you wish. For more information on loading, saving, creating, and using drum maps, look in Chapter 21, "MIDI Editors," of the electronic documentation that comes with Cubase SX.

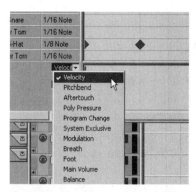

Figure 6.54 Use this menu to select the CC that appears in the Controller lane.

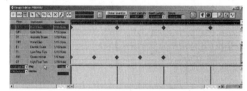

Figure 6.55 With the Bass Drum sound selected, only the velocity of the four quarter notes appears in the Controller lane.

Changing Velocity in the Drum Editor

Creating and editing continuous controller data in the Drum editor is very similar to performing the same tasks in the Key editor. The Controller lane is in the same place and is configured to show CC data in the same way. The main difference is that since each note triggers a different sound, the Controller lane shows data for only that selected sound.

One of the most common parameters for drum and percussion sounds, velocity, needs to be changed fairly often in the Drum editor. Rarely do drum sounds always play back at the same volume. In the preceding examples, all notes were entered with a velocity of 127 (the setting for the Insert Velocity parameter). Using the Controller lane, you can easily change the quarter-note part to a slightly lower velocity, with the eighth-note pattern lower yet.

To change velocity in the Drum editor:

1. Click the Drumstick tool to select it.

2. To the left of the Controller lane, click the drop-down menu and select Velocity if it is not already selected (**Figure 6.54**).

3. In the Drum Sound list, click the sound that you want to edit.

   In **Figure 6.55**, the Bass drum sound is selected, and the Controller lane shows four vertical stalks, which represent the velocity of the four notes entered.

continues on next page

CHANGING VELOCITY IN THE DRUM EDITOR

4. In the Controller lane, click one of the stalks with the Drumstick tool and drag the stalk up or down to the setting you want.

A numerical display to the left of the Controller lane shows the current value of the Drumstick tool, in this example it shows velocity (**Figure 6.56**).

5. Click the next sound in the Drum Sound list whose velocity you want to edit.

The Controller lane now shows the velocity for those notes (**Figure 6.57**).

6. Edit the velocity sticks with the Drumstick tool. Continue selecting sounds in the Drum Sound list and editing with the Drumstick tool until you are finished.

✔ Tip

■ Cubase has lots of tools in addition to the Drumstick tool for editing CC data. Refer to Chapter 10 of this book, "Editing MIDI," and to the electronic documentation that comes with Cubase for more information on CC editing.

Figure 6.56 Editing the velocity with the Drumstick tool: The display with the number 99 shows the current value for the Drumstick tool.

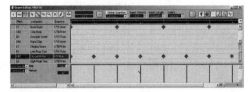

Figure 6.57 Clicking the next sound, the hi-hat, brings the velocity settings for notes on that sound into the Controller lane.

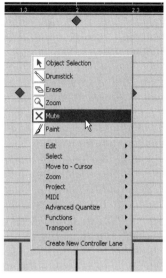

Figure 6.58 Selecting the Mute tool in the context menu

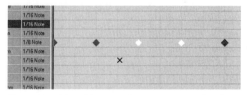

Figure 6.59 The white notes have been muted with the Mute tool. They will unmute and turn back to a color if they are clicked again with the Mute tool.

Deleting and Muting Notes in the Drum Editor

Most of the time, the Drumstick is the easiest tool to use to delete notes in the Drum editor. The whole point of the Drumstick tool is that it lets you toggle notes on and off in a grid, and clicking a note is the easiest way to delete it. One of the best uses of the Drum editor, though, is to set a project to loop over the length of the part currently in the editor and then to build up a part by clicking the Drum editor grid. It can be very helpful in such a situation to selectively mute notes, just to see how the pattern sounds without them, without deleting the notes completely.

To mute notes in the Drum editor:

1. In Note display, open the context menu and select the Mute tool (**Figure 6.58**), or select the tool from the toolbar.

2. Click the note you want to mute.

   Muted notes turn white (**Figure 6.59**) to indicate that they will not sound.

3. To unmute a note, simply click it again with the Mute tool.

✔ Tip

■ In some music styles, programmed drums are crucial to the sound. In particular, if you make electronic music of any kind, you will spend what seems like lifetimes working in the Drum editor. Learn as much about it as you can from the Cubase documentation, your own experimentation, and other Cubase users.

USING VST INSTRUMENTS

7

A VST instrument—usually called a VSTi—is a piece of software that uses the processing power of your computer to generate sounds, turning your audio computer into an actual instrument. Before VSTi, the computer could record, edit, play, and mix audio with effects, but all sound generation had to happen outside of the computer. VSTi changed that and allowed the computer an even greater role in music production.

If you are familiar with VSTi at all, you probably think of VST instruments as famous pieces of hardware re-created as software plug-ins. That is certainly one role they fulfill, but many VST instruments are only slightly related to hardware. There are loop tools, specialized drum samplers, strange otherworldly sound generators, and even applications that let you hand-build your own VST instruments. Don't make the mistake of thinking that VSTi is only for synth geeks without the budget for "real" synthesizers.

In this chapter, you will learn how to open VST instruments, change their settings, and save your own sounds. You will get an overview of each VST instrument that ships with Cubase so you can begin your own exploration of what each instrument can do. You will also learn how to use MIDI to get more out of VST instruments that support MIDI control of their parameters.

What Is a VST Instrument?

A VST instrument is really nothing more than a piece of software that plays back audio when it receives MIDI. This audio can be from any number of sources: some VST instruments are emulations of famous analog synthesizers, some are general-purpose sample players, and others are completely bizarre and unique sound generation tools that are combinations of synthesizers, samplers, and effect devices.

VST instruments come from many sources. Cubase ships with a group of VST instruments—for instance, the a1 (**Figure 7.1**) is an analog-style synthesizer. In addition, many commercial software companies make all sorts of other VST instruments, such as Native Instruments' software emulation of the famous Hammond B3 organ (**Figure 7.2**).

Not all VST instruments are bundled with Cubase or come from traditional software manufacturers. There is a vibrant community of VSTi users and creators, and this community is providing some of the most exciting things in audio software. A great place to learn more about the VSTi options available is www.kvr-vst.com, where you will find information and forums about everything imaginable regarding free, cheap, and expensive virtual instruments.

Figure 7.1 The a1 VSTi is a powerful, complex analog-style synth that runs completely via the CPU of your computer. It's one of the VST instruments that is bundled with Cubase.

Figure 7.2 A very different kind of VSTi is a third-party synth, from Native Instruments, called the B4. It closely mimics the sound and look of a famous console organ.

Why Use VST Instruments?

VST instruments have both an upside and a downside. You may not want to use them for all of your synthesis and sampling, but you may nevertheless find them very useful.

VST instruments have these advantages:

- **Project integration:** Using software for synthesis and sampling means that every setting and change to a device is saved, transparently and automatically, with the project. You never need to use sysex dumps or to write down settings, saving you significant amounts of time.

- **Cost and variety:** The most expensive software instruments cost less than all but the cheapest hardware instruments. You can get very good shareware VST instruments for less than $100, which means they cost about as much as the cables needed to hook up a new sound module or keyboard. VST instruments are also cheaper to make than hardware, meaning that a developer can bring to market as a software instrument a unique idea that would be prohibitively expensive to create as a hardware device.

- **Features that leverage the computer:** Every VSTi gets more power when you upgrade your computer. A faster CPU means more synths, more samplers, and more voices from each.

VSTi instruments have these disadvantages:

◆ **Latency:** Digital synthesizers and samplers have almost no latency (sound delay); the latency of a VSTi is determined by the latency of the sound card and computer being used, which can be a problem when the computer/sound card combination is not state of the art. See Chapter 1 for more information on latency and sound cards.

◆ **Sound quality:** Many VST instruments sound fantastic, some even better than their hardware equivalents, but not all do. Particularly in the realm of emulated analog synthesis, some people find software synths lacking.

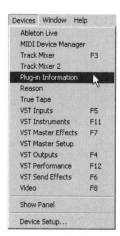

Figure 7.3 Use the Devices menu to open the panel for setting plug-in preferences.

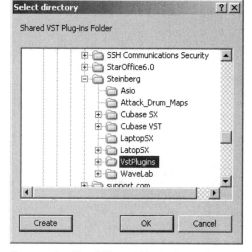

Figure 7.4 Double-clicking a folder in this window sets it as the shared plug-ins folder.

Installing and Managing VST Instruments

Cubase comes with a set of its own VST instruments. These bundled VST instruments are automatically available the first time you run Cubase, and you don't need to worry about where they are installed. Over time, you'll probably add third-party VST instruments made by commercial software companies or shareware developers.

When you install a new VSTi, you'll need to follow the instructions that came with the software. Each installation procedure can have its own requirements. For example, in Windows, Cubase lets you designate a particular folder as the shared plug-in folder. VST instruments are plug-ins, and this folder can provide a convenient way to keep track of your VST applications; VST effect plug-ins and VST instruments in this shared plug-ins folder will be available to any application that supports those protocols.

To assign a shared plug-ins folder (Windows only):

1. Click the Devices menu and select Plug-in Information (**Figure 7.3**).

   The Plug-in Information window opens. The default tab shows all currently installed VST instruments. At the top of the window, there is also a setting for Shared VST Plug-ins Folder.

2. Click the Choose button (next to the Shared VST Plug-ins Folder setting) to open the Select directory dialog box (**Figure 7.4**).

3. On the Select Directory panel, navigate to the folder that you want to designate as the shared VST plug-ins folder and double-click it.

   This folder is now set as your shared plug-ins folder.

✔ Tip

■ As this is written, the Mac version of Cubase does not have a shared VST plug-in folder. This may or may not change in the future.

Opening a VSTi

Many of the features of Cubase covered in
the rest of this book involve virtual racks.
These are software versions of the standard-
sized rack-mount systems used for mount-
ing hardware in recording studios. The VST
instruments mount on a virtual rack.

To open a VSTi:

1. Click the Devices menu and select VST
   Instruments (**Figure 7.5**).

   The VST Instruments panel, or virtual
   rack, opens (**Figure 7.6**). The rack has 32
   slots, though not many computers can
   run 32 simultaneous VST instruments.

2. Click any of the slots labeled No VST
   Instrument.

   A pop-up menu opens, showing all of the
   currently installed VST instruments.

3. Select the instrument you want to use.

   In **Figure 7.7**, the a1 synth is being
   selected from the Synths submenu.

✔ Tip

■ Figure 7.7 shows all of the VST instruments installed on my own version of
  Cubase. Unless you happen to have a
  setup exactly like mine, your menus will
  look somewhat different. Later in this
  chapter, you will read about each of the
  VST instruments included with Cubase.

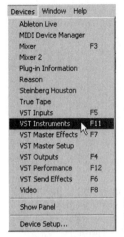

Figure 7.5 Select this
option to open the VST
Instruments rack.

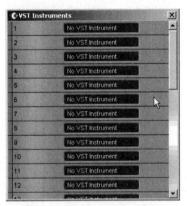

Figure 7.6 All of the slots in the VST rack
are unused in this illustration.

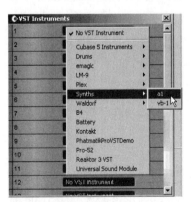

Figure 7.7 All installed VST instruments
are visible in this menu.

Figure 7.8 Click the Edit button to open the edit window for the VSTi in that slot.

Figure 7.9 The VSTi editor for the selected instrument

Figure 7.10 The Track inspector also has an Edit button that you can click to open the editor for a VSTi.

Opening the VSTi Editor

Every VSTi has a window for editing the sound parameters for the instrument. Some instruments are photorealistic renderings of real-world hardware, some are strange, never-before-seen tools for manipulating sounds, and some are just a bunch of sliders and knobs. Regardless of what kind of VSTi you use, you access its parameters in the same way.

To open the editor for a VSTi:

1. Open the VST Instruments panel if is not already open.

2. Find the slot in the virtual rack that contains the VSTi that you want to edit. Click the Edit button—the cursive *e* at the far left of the slot with the instrument name (**Figure 7.8**).

   The editor for that VSTi opens (**Figure 7.9**).

3. When you are done editing the instrument, close the editor.

✔ Tips

- If the output of a MIDI track is routed to a VSTi, the Edit button in the Track inspector (**Figure 7.10**) for that track will also open the editor for that VSTi.

- The F11 button is the keyboard shortcut for opening the VST instrument rack.

Selecting VSTi Presets

Most VST instruments include some number of presets. Listening to the presets for a VSTi is a great way to become familiar with what the VSTi can do. You can listen to the presets by stepping through them one after the other, or you can start by viewing a list of all of the presets for the VSTi.

To step through presets:

1. Open the VST Instruments panel, or the editor for the VSTi.

2. Click the arrow at the right to go up one preset; click the arrow on the left to go down one preset.

   Both the panel and the editor have two arrow buttons. **Figure 7.11** shows these buttons on the panel; **Figure 7.12** shows them in the editor.

To view a list of VSTi presets:

1. Open the VST Instruments panel or the editor for the VSTi.

2. Click the downward-pointing arrow to the right of the preset name field to access a menu (**Figure 7.13**) of all currently available presets for that VSTi.

✔ Tip

■ Keep in mind that more than one MIDI track in the project window can trigger the same sound. If you set a VSTi to a certain preset, you can point more than one track to it in the project window.

Figure 7.11 The two buttons with arrows step through presets for that VSTi

Figure 7.12 You can also use the arrow buttons in the editor for the VSTi to step through the presets.

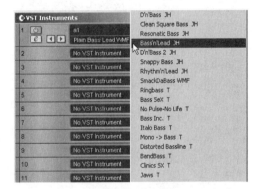

Figure 7.13 You can also use the pop-up menu in the VSTi rack and the editor for a VSTi to select a preset.

Figure 7.14 The most common setting for MIDI input is All MIDI Inputs. It will take MIDI from any available device.

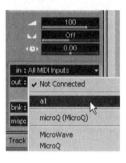

Figure 7.15 If you click the Out setting, any active VST instruments will be listed.

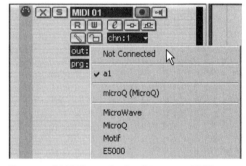

Figure 7.16 A VSTi can also be chosen as a MIDI destination in the track list.

Playing a VSTi

Using a VSTi is not much different than using a hardware synth. The routing and settings are almost identical. VST instruments can be played live if you want; the only potential problem is the latency of your sound card. As this is written, the highest-quality sound cards can achieve latencies below 3 milliseconds, which is as low as most hardware synths and samplers. Not all systems are capable of this quality, though, and you will need to test your system to see if you can comfortably play VST instruments.

To play a VSTi:

1. In the track list, click the track that you want to use for the VSTi.

2. Open the Track inspector. The settings for the selected track will be visible.

3. On the top tab of the Track inspector, check whether the correct setting is chosen for the MIDI In field.

   Figure 7.14 shows All MIDI Inputs selected for the selected MIDI track.

4. Click the MIDI Out setting to open a menu listing available MIDI outputs.

   All active VST instruments are listed, along with any MIDI hardware devices that have been configured (**Figure 7.15**).

5. Select the VSTi you want to play.

6. Play your MIDI controller; it will trigger the VSTi.

✔ Tips

- If you don't want to open the Track inspector, the same options are available in the track list (**Figure 7.16**).

- In Cubase, MIDI is MIDI, regardless of what it triggers. All of the procedures for recording, creating, and editing MIDI data apply in exactly the same way when working with a VSTi.

VSTi Visual Editing Tools

Part of what makes VSTi so great is that the designer can create a software tool that operates according to whatever rules the designer wants. Some VST instruments look and act just like hardware, while others look and act like nothing you have ever seen before. This makes it impossible to say for sure how every VSTi will work, but here are a few examples of the more common interface tools used to change parameters for a VSTi. Always consult the documentation that comes with a software instrument to find out more about how to edit its sound.

Figure 7.17 The sliders on this VSTi work just like mechanical sliders and can be edited simply by dragging them.

◆ **Knobs:** You've encountered them in the real world, and they do just the same jobs in the virtual world. Many (though not all) knobs on software instruments work differently than their hardware counterparts. Often you change the value of a knob by clicking it and dragging up or down, instead of turning it in a circle on the screen. The knobs on the JX16 synth bundled with Cubase work this way.

◆ **Sliders:** Whereas knobs are sometimes tricky to turn on a computer screen, sliders (**Figure 7.17**) are easy to click and drag up and down to set values.

◆ **Buttons:** Like sliders, buttons translate well to the computer screen. Often buttons are backlit and change color when they are selected.

Figure 7.18
This breakpoint editor works differently than any mechanical device.

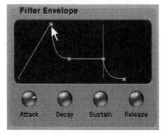

Figure 7.19
If you move one of the breakpoints, the corresponding knob (Attack) moves as well.

◆ **Breakpoint editors:** These are visual, intuitive tools for editing parameters that are normally assigned to knobs. (In the physical world, synth parameters are usually set with knobs.) In **Figure 7.18**, the Attack setting is all the way to the left, at zero. Attack is the parameter used to determine how quickly the envelope reaches its maximum setting. With a computer-based synth, it's easier to click the first breakpoint and drag to the right (**Figure 7.19**). This changes the Attack time, and the setting on the Attack knob reflects this.

Saving and Reusing VSTi Settings

Remember that VST instruments are saved with projects, which is one of the great advantages of using them. You don't need to worry setting the knobs and buttons each time you use the VSTi—they will be set in precisely the same way when you open the project the next time.

In addition, sometimes you may want to save the settings of a VSTi as a preset. For example, you may want to use the same sound in more than one project, or you may want to send the instrument settings to a friend who is using the same VSTi. Cubase refers to these user settings as *instruments*, and Cubase can save these presets as discrete files that you can load into another project or e-mail to another Cubase SX user.

To save a VSTi instrument:

1. Set up the VSTi exactly as you want to save it.

2. In the editor window of every VSTi and on the VST Instruments panel are a set of menus and buttons that control features such as presets; click the File button at the far right to open the File menu.

   A menu opens with options for saving and opening various file types.

3. Choose Save Instrument (**Figure 7.20**).

4. When the Save dialog box opens, name and save the instrument as a file. Type a name for the instrument, navigate to the folder where you want to keep it, and then click Save (**Figure 7.21**).

   You can save an instrument wherever you want.

Figure 7.20 Use the File menu when you want to save your current settings as a distinct file, outside of the current project.

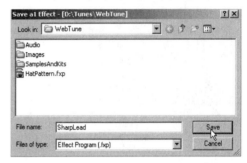

Figure 7.21 Use a standard operating system dialog box to name and save an instrument.

✔ Tips

■ You follow the same procedure to load instruments, but in reverse. Click the File button, select Load Instrument from the menu, and navigate to the file you want to open.

■ A bank is a file that includes multiple instruments. You save and load a bank in exactly the same way as you do single instruments.

Figure 7.22 The Universal Sound Module editor panel—not exactly thrilling

Figure 7.23 Use the prg menu to select a sound in the USM.

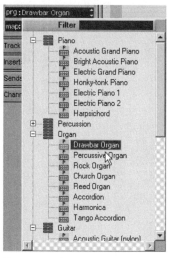

Figure 7.24 The USM offers lots of sounds—which is pretty thrilling.

The Universal Sound Module

The next few pages give you a quick look at each of the VST instruments included with Cubase, starting with the Universal Sound Module, or USM. The USM is a software replacement for a General MIDI sound module. General MIDI (usually referred to as GM) is a superset of MIDI, and its standards were agreed upon by various synth manufacturers to allow some level of predictability when exchanging MIDI files. A synth with a GM bank will have certain sounds at certain preset locations. This means that if a musician creates a song using a GM synth, and if one of the tracks plays an electric piano sound, every other GM synth in the world will also play some kind of electric piano sound when playing back a MIDI file of that song.

The USM is a software version of the General MIDI sound module. The GM bank in a hardware synth is often one the most boring, almost-kitschy sets of sounds on a synth, but the Cubase USM actually sounds pretty good. While some VST instruments have interfaces with flashy graphics and photorealistic renderings of hardware synths, the USM has a very simple settings panel, as you can see in the VSTi editor (**Figure 7.22**).

The USM is multitimbral and polyphonic. The term *polyphonic* means that the USM can play more than one note per sound, so if you play five keys in a piano sound, all five will play. *Multitimbral* means that you can play different sounds simultaneously on each channel; MIDI channel 1 can trigger a sax sound while MIDI channel 2 triggers an organ sound, and so on. To select a sound in the USM, use the Track inspector for a track that is sending MIDI to the USB. Click the prg option (**Figure 7.23**), and a menu opens allowing you to pick any of the sounds in the USM (**Figure 7.24**).

The Neon VSTi

The Neon VSTi (**Figure 7.25**) is quite a different creature than the Universal Sound Module. Neon is a very simple synth that uses retro-style analog/subtractive synthesis to generate its sound. This VSTi is polyphonic, and can play up to 16 voices simultaneously, but it is not multitimbral. This means that if you want two different Neon sounds, you must open two Neon synths, each in its own slot in the VSTi rack. The Neon is found on the Cubase 5 Instruments menu.

All subtractive synths have fundamentally the same architecture. An oscillator generates a signal in response to incoming MIDI. This signal is sent through a filter that can remove some part of the sound spectrum, and then the filtered sound is sent through an output amplifier that controls the rise and fall of the signal volume. Often the filter and amplifier are controlled by *envelopes*. An envelope, when triggered, generates a set of values that can be used to control parameters on a synth automatically.

The Neon lets you pick one of three oscillator shapes (**Figure 7.26**), called waveforms, each with its own sound. The oscillator is sent through a low-pass filter, which is a kind of filter that attenuates (reduces) frequencies above the frequency set with the cutoff knob (**Figure 7.27**), but lets frequencies lower than the cutoff frequency pass through unchanged. In other words, as the cutoff knob is turned counterclockwise, the sound becomes darker, with less treble. One envelope can modulate the cutoff frequency, while the other envelope can modulate the level of the output amplifier. Neon is a very simple synth and is good to use if you want to learn more about the basics of analog-style synthesizers.

Figure 7.25 The Neon VSTi

Figure 7.26 These buttons select the kind of sound that each oscillator produces.

Figure 7.27 This knob controls the all-important cutoff frequency of the filter.

Figure 7.28 The cs40 has more options for each oscillator than the Neon.

Figure 7.29 The cs40 also includes an LFO for adding modulation to some parameters.

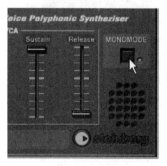

Figure 7.30 When you click the Monomode button to select it, the synth will play back only one voice.

The cs40 VSTi

A synth slightly more complex than Neon is the cs40. Like the Neon, it is polyphonic (although it's restricted to six simultaneous voices) but not multitimbral. You can send MIDI on any channel to the cs40, and the synth will play the same sound.

The first notable difference between the Neon and the cs40 is the Oscillator section (**Figure 7.28**). You can set the two oscillators in the cs40 to use different waveforms, and you can use the Blend slider to mix the two signals together. Each oscillator also has a Tune knob, so that they can be pitched slightly, or dramatically, apart from each other. The cs40 Oscillator section can produce a much wider variety of sounds than the simple oscillator in the Neon.

The cs40 also has a low-frequency oscillator, or LFO, to modulate some of its parameters (**Figure 7.29**). LFOs are staples of analog-style synthesis. As the name suggests, an LFO is an oscillator, but unlike the oscillators used to generate sound in a synthesizer, LFOs operate at such slow rates that they would be inaudible if they were played. Instead, they are used to automatically control another parameter. The speed knob on a chorus or tremolo effect is an example of an LFO that many musicians use. The cs40 LFO has knobs to set the speed of the LFO and the amount that the LFO modulates the selected destinations, which are the filter and amplifier.

The cs40 also has a Monomode button (**Figure 7.30**), which converts the cs40 from a synth that can play six voices at a time (polyphonic) to a synth that can play only one voice. Mono mode is most often used for synth lead sounds or synth sounds that use arpeggios.

The vb-1 VSTi

The vb-1 is a software bass instrument that can produce a wide range of bass sounds. Though its interface strongly mimics a modern electric bass, it can also produce synth bass and even some nonbass sounds when configured to do so.

The vb-1 interface (**Figure 7.31**) has two parameters that at first glance may not seem editable. In fact, you can change the location of both the pick and the pickup simply by dragging them. For instance, **Figure 7.32** shows the vb-1 after the pick and pickup have been moved. You move the pickup by grabbing it under the strings of the bass, as the pointer indicates in Figure 7.32.

The Shape parameter controls the basic type of bass sound used by the plug-in. This is the primary parameter for changing the bass sound from an electric bass to a synth bass. The Damper controls the sustain of each string—the more Damper that is applied, the shorter each note will sound.

The presets (**Figure 7.33**) are a great place to discover what the vb-1 can do.

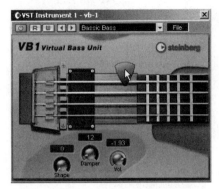

Figure 7.31 The vb-1 VSTi is used mostly for bass sounds.

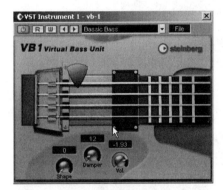

Figure 7.32 You can move the pickup and pick, and the timbre of the bass sound will change as each is moved.

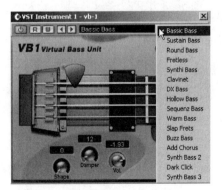

Figure 7.33 The presets menu for the vb-1 has sounds that show its sonic variety.

Figure 7.34 The JX16 VSTi—lots more knobs and sliders.

Figure 7.35 The character of the filter is controlled by the slider marked Mode. HP, the current setting, stands for high pass.

The JX16 VSTi

The JX16 is one level of complexity beyond the cs40 synth (**Figure 7.34**). It's another polyphonic synth with up to 16 simultaneous voices, and it receives MIDI on all channels. Like the cs40 and Neon, the JX16 is one of the instruments originally included with Cubase 5 and appears in the Cubase 5 Instruments menu.

One of the highlights of the JX16 is a multimode filter. The filter is edited in the section of the synth labeled VCF, which is the old-school abbreviation for Voltage Controlled Filter. Pre-MIDI synths used patch cables to send variable voltages to control its parameters, so that terminology has stayed with us into the MIDI and computer age. The filter can act as a low-pass, high-pass, or band-pass filter. Low-pass filters were described earlier. A high-pass filter allows frequencies above the cutoff to pass and attenuates frequencies below the cutoff. A band-pass filter acts something like a high- and low-pass filter combined; the signal at the cutoff frequency is passed unchanged, and frequencies both above and below the cutoff are attenuated. The Mode slider in the filter section (**Figure 7.35**) changes the filter type. A good way to get familiar with the different filter types is to play the same sound with different filters and cutoff frequencies.

Other highlights of the JX16 are the Glide and Chorus sections (**Figure 7.36**). If Glide is turned on, notes will glide from one to the next, instead of each note immediately triggering the new sound. Glide is often used with a synth in mono mode (the JX16 can be a mono synth if the Polyphony knob is set to 1) when the synth is getting a bass line or arpeggio. The Rate knob controls the length of time it takes for the synth to glide from one note to the next; higher settings result in longer glide times. The Chorus section is a simple four-mode effect to thicken and double the sound of the synth.

Check out the JX16—it has many more features for you to learn about if you take the time to investigate.

Figure 7.36 The Glide and Chorus settings

Figure 7.37 The a1 VSTi is the most complex of the analog-style synths that come with Cubase.

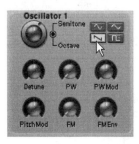

Figure 7.38 Choosing the oscillator shape for Oscillator 1

The a1 VSTi

By far the most complex and powerful VSTi included with Cubase is the a1 (**Figure 7.37**). Like the JX16, the a1 can play up to 16 simultaneous voices and receives MIDI on all channels. This means that you don't have to worry about routing a particular channel to the a1—just select it as the output for a track using the Track inspector.

The a1 is the only of the included synths that allows you to choose a shape for each oscillator. The buttons (**Figure 7.38**) to the right of the controls for the Oscillator 1 and Oscillator 2 select an oscillator waveform, and Oscillator 2 can have a different shape than Oscillator 1. This feature offers a great deal more sonic flexibility when combined with the features of the Mixer section, which can mix any amount of each oscillator together before the signal goes into the filter.

The filter in the a1 is a multimode filter that includes more variety than any of the other included VST instruments. The a1 includes the same three filter types as the JX16 (low pass, high pass, and band pass), but in addition, it features a notch filter. A notch filter is the opposite of a band-pass filter; it attenuates frequencies at the cutoff and allows frequencies above and below to pass through.

The a1 is a complex analog-style synth, with lots of features and great sounds. It offers a huge number of presets for bass, lead, polyphonic, pad, and special-effects sounds. The keyboard at the bottom of the interface is very handy for auditioning the presets: you simply click the keys.

THE A1 VSTI

The lm-7 VSTi

The final VSTi included with Cubase is the lm-7 drum machine (**Figure 7.39**). Each lm-7 preset bank has 12 sounds, each of which can be slightly modified with the sliders and knobs. Clicking any of the virtual drum pads triggers a particular drum sound, and the pads provide a good way to audition the preset drum kits.

Each pad also has a corresponding pair of sliders: one marked Vol, and one marked Tone. The Vol slider determines the relative volume for that pad, and the Tone slider controls the pitch of the drum sound. Cymbal sounds like hi-hats and bass drum sounds are often pitch shifted for effect in dance and electronic music.

When a sound is triggered, the light above the pad turns green to indicate that it is playing; when the sound is done playing, the light turns yellow. You can use the Panorama knob on the right side of the lm-7 interface to modify the drum with the yellow light (**Figure 7.40**). The Panorama knob controls the left-right pan of that pad in the stereo drum mix. You can set each pad to its own pan position.

The lm-7 has three preset kits by default. Compressor uses samples from an acoustic drum kit and is best for rock and pop music, and 909 samples a famous dance music drum machine. The samples in the percussion bank are from famous hand-percussion instruments such as congas and claves. If you use the Load Bank option and navigate to your VST plug-ins folder, you will find a folder called Drums with a bank containing three more drum kits. You can load these into the lm-7 to use Modulation, Fusion, and Drum'n'bass kits.

Figure 7.39 The lm-7 is a dedicated drum VSTi.

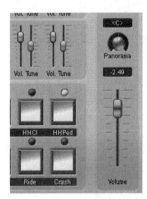

Figure 7.40 You can edit the pan setting of the pad with the yellow light above it. In this black-and-white image, the yellow light is the one that appears lighter than the rest.

THE LM-7 VSTi

Figure 7.41 When the mouse is over the Envelope parameter, the data display shows that CC 18 will modify that parameter.

Controlling VST Instruments with MIDI

By definition, VST instruments respond to MIDI notes. Some, but not all, VST instruments go one step beyond this and also respond to MIDI CC messages. A VSTi that responds to these messages is not only more fun to work with, but is much easier to control with familiar tactile controls like knobs, sliders, and wheels.

Most hardware MIDI controllers such as keyboards allow their knobs and sliders to send CC messages. By matching the CC message being sent by the controller to the parameter that you want to change on the VSTi, you can control any parameter on a VSTi with a physical, tactile controller.

The a1 VSTi has deeper MIDI controls than any of the other VST instruments bundled with Cubase. The following task shows you how to use an external controller to modify a parameter on the a1. The a1 displays controller information in its editor window.

To control a VSTi using MIDI:

1. Select an a1 instrument for a slot in a VSTi rack and open the editor window.

   If you hold the mouse over any knob or button, you will see the CC message for that parameter in the data display. For example, **Figure 7.41** shows the mouse over the Envelope knob, and the data display indicates that CC 18 controls that parameter.

continues on next page

2. Move the mouse over the knob that you want to control and note the controller number. For example, filter resonance, a commonly edited parameter, is CC 71 (**Figure 7.42**).

3. Configure your MIDI controller to send CC 71, or open the Key Editor and manually enter CC data for message 71.

4. Play the MIDI controller, or use the data in the Key Editor.

The VSTi parameter will change to match your setting.

✔ Tip

■ Most VST instruments aren't as easy to set up for CC editing as the a1. Usually, you will have to consult the documentation that came with the VSTi to find out what parameter is mapped to what CC.

Figure 7.42 Resonance is controlled with CC 71 in the a1 VSTi, and you can use a MIDI controller to send that CC data and manually control resonance.

CONTROLLING VST INSTRUMENTS WITH MIDI

BASIC AUDIO EDITING

Figure 8.1 The Project window with three audio tracks: The top track is a looped section, and the bottom two are full takes.

For most of the history of recorded audio, editing involved a razor blade, a cutting block, and some tape. Editing individual tracks was difficult or impossible, and one bad edit with that razor blade could mean redoing the entire song from scratch.

Editing digital audio is a completely different story. Cubase stores audio files on a hard drive, and the visible audio waveforms in the Project window that we call events and parts are actually just pointers to those audio files. This means that any part of any file can play back at any point in a project—there is complete freedom to rearrange and modify the parts of a project. Cubase SX is a world-class audio editing platform.

The techniques that you'll learn in this chapter and in Chapter 9 are accomplished by using advanced editing tools right in the Project window (**Figure 8.1**).

Unlike some other audio applications, Cubase lets you do a huge percentage of the audio editing in the Project window. Its other editors, such as the Audio Part editor and the Sample editor, are available for more advanced uses. You can often accomplish the same thing in many ways.

Context menus are a powerful part of Cubase SX. You open a context menu by right-clicking (Windows) or Control-clicking (Mac OS) the screen (**Figure 8.2**). You'll use context menus extensively while you work.

In this chapter, you will learn how to edit audio events and parts, starting with how to move, copy, and mute them. You will also learn more about Snap and how to use it to move audio precisely in a project. You'll learn the different methods for changing the duration of events and parts. Finally, you'll learn how to fade events in and out, how to crossfade between two audio events, and how to use the Scissors tool.

Figure 8.2 The context menu with the Audio option selected: You'll be using context menus often.

What's the Difference Between an Event and a Part?

The differences between audio events and parts can be confusing even for expert Cubase users. If you record an instrument in Cubase, you've created an audio event in the Project window—the thing with a waveform that you can click, move, edit, and modify. For some projects, you might use nothing but events for your audio. Some events might be as long as the full song, while other events might be loops or single, short snippets of sound.

Parts are used mainly for two purposes. First, you might want to create a part when you have a group of events that you want to use together as a single entity. For instance, if the vocal line in a song is great but the last note is wrong, you can find another place where the singer hit that note right, snip it out, and then align the two events so the good note replaces that bad note in the first event. This leaves you using two events to play back a single line. To make your work easier, you can combine these events into a single part, so you can move and process the events as a single entity. The second main use of parts is in creating comps. Comps are explained later in this chapter, but in general, comping involves using bits of numerous events to achieve a better take.

One reason that parts and events may seem confusing is that different audio programs work with audio in quite different ways. For example, in previous versions of Cubase, all audio events had to be in an audio part. This is no longer true in SX; events can be played, edited, and processed directly in the Project window. If you are learning Cubase SX after using another audio application or an earlier version of Cubase, you might want to take some time to be sure you understand the differences between parts and events.

The final tricky part of distinguishing between parts and events is that in the Project window, audio parts and audio events look very similar. One easy way to see the difference between them is to click something to select it. If you see the blue handles (which are used to change volume and fade), you've clicked an event. If you don't see them, then you have a part on your hands.

Don't fret if the distinction between parts and events seems a bit arcane at first. Parts and events both follow logical rules, and after you've tried a few of the examples in this chapter, you'll understand intuitively which is which and when to use one or the other.

Converting Events to Parts

When editing audio in Cubase SX, it is critical that you understand the difference between events and parts. Both can be used in the Project window, and both can be edited directly in the Project window. Some of what is described in this chapter relates only to audio events, some is useful only with audio parts, and some works with both events and parts.

Audio event: An audio event is a reference to an audio file that has been recorded or imported into Cubase. It is not the audio file itself, but an indication to Cubase to play an audio file (or a part of an audio file) at a particular time in a project.

Audio part: An audio part is a container that can hold one or more audio events. Audio parts are used to manage more easily one or more events in the Project window. If it is convenient to deal with a group of events as a single entity, it's usually best to create a single part that holds all of the events.

To convert audio events to an audio part:

1. Using the Arrow tool, drag over the events you want to convert to a part (**Figure 8.3**).

   This selects the events in the Project window.

2. With the events selected (they will be outlined in red), open the context menu by right-clicking (Windows) or Control-clicking (Mac OS) one of the selected audio parts.

3. From the context menu, select Audio > Events to Part (**Figure 8.4**).

   In the Project window, a new part will be created (**Figure 8.5**) that is large enough to hold all of the events that had been selected.

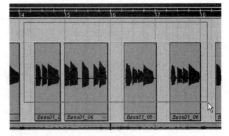

Figure 8.3 Selecting four events on the same audio track

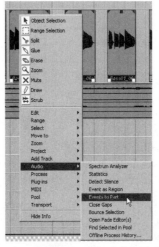

Figure 8.4 This menu command creates a new audio part.

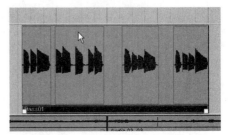

Figure 8.5 The newly created part, with each of the events visible within the part

✔ Tip

■ You also can select multiple events in the Project window by holding down the Shift key and clicking each one.

CONVERTING EVENTS TO PARTS

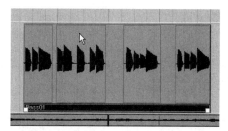

Figure 8.6 Selecting the audio part in the Project window: You can't see this easily here, but the part is outlined in red to show that it is selected.

Figure 8.7 This command dissolves a part into events— the reverse of combining events into a part.

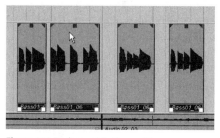

Figure 8.8 Each event in the part is now a discrete element again.

Breaking Parts into Events

Sometimes it's easier to work on smaller events instead of a whole part. If you want to work directly in the Project window on events that are within a part, you can break the part into its constituent events.

To convert an audio part to the audio events it contains:

1. Select the part by clicking it with the Arrow tool (**Figure 8.6**).

2. Open the context menu by right-clicking (Windows) or Control-clicking (Mac OS) the part.

3. In the menu that opens, select Audio > Dissolve Part (**Figure 8.7**).

   The events that were in the part will now be displayed in the Project window (**Figure 8.8**).

Muting Events and Parts

One of the simplest editing operations in the Project window is muting, which simply tells Cubase not to play back the muted event or part during the playback of a project.

Figure 8.9 The Mute tool on the toolbar

To mute parts or events:

1. Select the Mute tool by clicking the Mute button on the toolbar (**Figure 8.9**) or selecting Mute from the context menu in the Project window.

2. Using the pointer (it will turn into an X), click any parts or events that you want to mute.

   They will be dimmed to show their muted status (**Figure 8.10**).

3. To unmute a muted part or event, simply click it again.

   The part or event will now play back normally (**Figure 8.11**).

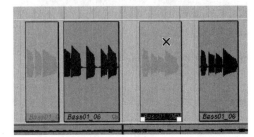

Figure 8.10 The first and third events are muted; the second and third are not.

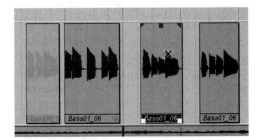

Figure 8.11 The third event is unmuted again.

Figure 8.12 The Use Quantize setting enables more Snap options.

Figure 8.13 With these settings, Snap will constrain movements to quarter notes.

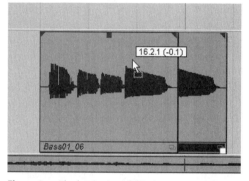

Figure 8.14 The beginning of this event moves along a quarter note grid.

Moving Parts and Events Using Snap

You can move any part or event in Cubase to another place in a project simply by clicking it and dragging it to a new location. If Snap is turned off, parts and events can be moved anywhere, without relation to a beat or grid. When Snap is turned on, parts and events are moved according to the grid created by the Snap settings. In the following task, you will move an event a quarter note at a time to change its place in a beat, but keep in mind that parts are moved exactly the same way.

To move an event using snap:

1. Turn on Snap by clicking the Snap button on the toolbar.

2. From the Snap Settings menu, select Use Quantize (**Figure 8.12**).

3. From the Quantize menu, select 1/4 Note. The snap settings will look like those in **Figure 8.13**.

4. Drag the audio event, which is now constrained to movements of 1/4 note (**Figure 8.14**).

✔ Tips

■ Many people turn Snap on and off constantly. If you are one of those people, you should know that the J key on your computer keyboard is the default shortcut key for Snap; using it will save you a lot of mouse trips to the toolbar and back.

■ Notice the numerical display in Figure 8.14. It shows the current location of the event (16.2.1) and its song position relative to its position before it was moved (–0.1). You can use this information to keep track of the movement of parts and events.

Moving Events and Parts Using the Cursor

Snap provides a convenient method for moving parts and events along a grid. Sometimes, though, it's easier to use the cursor to move a part or event. Using the cursor, you can more easily line up an event or part at the beginning or end of another event or part. The cursor can also help you place events or parts when you are synching dialogue and effects to video material. In this example, you will use the cursor to place an audio part at bar 14, beat 3.

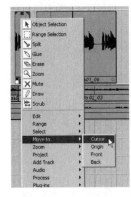

Figure 8.15 The menu option to send the currently selected event or part to the cursor location

To move an audio event using the cursor:

1. Position the cursor where you want to move the audio event by clicking the ruler, or by using the Fast Forward and Rewind buttons, or manually entering the location on the Transport bar.

2. Click the event that you want to move.

3. Right-click (Windows) or Control-click (Mac OS) the event to open the context menu for that event.

4. Choose Move to > Cursor (**Figure 8.15**).

5. The audio part will move to wherever the cursor is located (**Figure 8.16**).

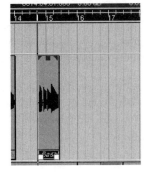

Figure 8.16 The audio event after it is moved to the cursor location

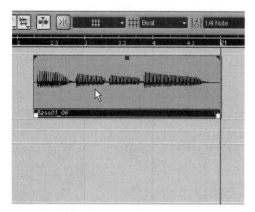

Figure 8.17 This event is selected. It has a red outline around it (not visible in the illustration).

Figure 8.18 When the event is moved to a different track (it's in transit here), it keeps its position in the project.

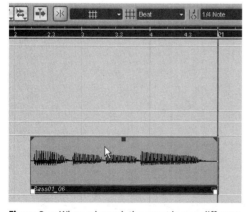

Figure 8.19 When released, the event is on a different track, but at the same point in time.

Constraining Part or Event Movement

Moving an event or a part to a different track is a common operation in Cubase, but in many situations you need the part to play back at the same time in the project as before it was moved. You can constrain the movement of an event or part to a vertical axis when you relocate it. In the following task, you will move an audio event to a new track but won't change its meter position.

To move an event or part while retaining its playback position:

1. Press and hold the Ctrl key (Windows) or the Command key (Mac OS).

2. Click the event or part you want to move (**Figure 8.17**).

3. While still holding the Ctrl or Command key, drag the event or part down or up in the Project window (**Figure 8.18**).

4. When you reach the track to which you want to move the event or part, release the mouse.

   The event or part will move to the new track at the same playback position in the project as before it was moved (**Figure 8.19**).

✔ Tip

- The use of the Ctrl or Command key is one of a small number of operations in Cubase where Snap does *not* matter. In Figures 17 through 19, you can see that Snap is on, with a beat-based grid, but the part does not snap to the nearest beat when moved.

CONSTRAINING PART OR EVENT MOVEMENT

Setting the Snap Point

By default, the snap point for a part or event is the starting point of the part or event. More often than not, this is the most sensible way for Snap to work. In fact, the only way to change the snap point for an audio part is to resize the part itself. The snap point for an audio event, however, does not have to be its starting point.

The snap point for an event determines where Cubase moves the event when Snap is on. Although by default, the snap point is at the beginning of the event, it can be set to any point. Often a different setting is useful for snapping events that do not begin at a musically significant point. An event may have an obvious place where it is rhythmically anchored, and this may be the best place to use as the snap point. In the next task, an event with the downbeat close to its end will be snapped to the beginning of the measure. You will set the snap point with the cursor.

To move an event using the snap point:

1. Turn off Snap while setting the snap point.

2. Determine where in the event the snap point should go.

   It's usually easiest to snap events to quarter notes or, if possible, to the first beat of a measure. In **Figure 8.20**, the last note is the downbeat.

3. Click the Zoom tool on the toolbar to see clearly where the note starts and use the tool to drag over the part of the event where you want to set the snap point (**Figure 8.21**).

4. Move the cursor to the start of the note, where the snap point will be located.

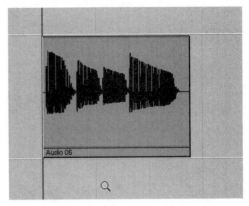

Figure 8.20 In this event, the last note is the first beat of a new measure.

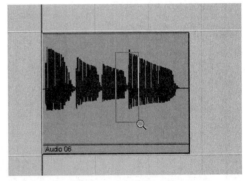

Figure 8.21 Using the Zoom tool to view a small part of the event.

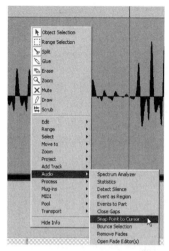

Figure 8.22
This command sets the snap point.

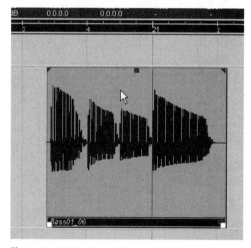

Figure 8.23 Using the newly set snap point, the event can be snapped so that the last note falls at the start of a measure.

5. If the event is not selected, choose the Arrow tool and click the event to select it.

6. Right-click (Windows) or Control-click (Mac OS) to open the context menu for the event. Select Audio > Snap Point to Cursor (**Figure 8.22**).

7. Zoom back out to see the whole event.

The newly created snap point will appear as a thin blue line in the event.

8. Before moving the event, turn Snap back on so Cubase will use the snap point.

9. Click the event and drag it to its new location.

The event now plays from the snap point instead of the beginning. In **Figure 8.23**, the event has been moved so that the downbeat is at measure 21.

Copying Audio Parts or Events

Events and parts are copied in the Project window using the common system-level key commands for click-and-drag copying. Press and hold the Alt key (Windows) or the Option key (Mac OS), click the object to be copied, and move the copy to its new location. Cubase does include, however, a few of its own shortcuts and additions that make copying events and parts easier in some situations.

Shortcuts and Tricks for Copying Events and Parts

◆ If you want to copy an event or part to a new track but keep its position in the project, press Shift+Alt+Ctrl (Windows) or Shift+Option+Command (Mac OS) to create a time-constrained copy (**Figure 8.24**).

◆ Select an event or part, open the context menu, and choose Edit > Duplicate to copy the selected part or event and place the new copy exactly after the original. This is another of the rare operations that ignore Snap. The two events in **Figure 8.25** were created using the Duplicate command with Snap on and set to Beat. The new event did not snap to the nearest beat.

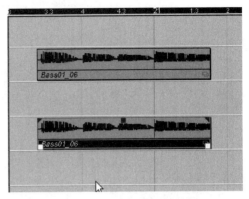

Figure 8.24 An event copied to a new track but constrained vertically

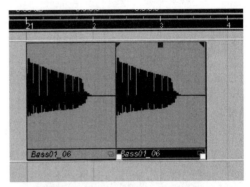

Figure 8.25 Snap was on and set to 1/4 Note, but Duplicate puts the copy directly after the original.

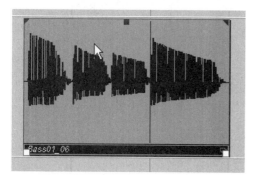

Figure 8.26 This event has been selected; the two triangles and small box at the top of the event will be moved to create a fade-in.

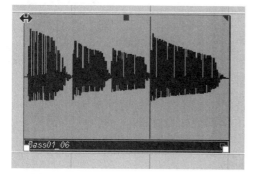

Figure 8.27 The pointer is at the place where the fade-in point can be moved.

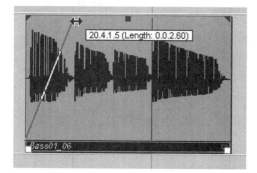

Figure 8.28 Dragging the fade-in point to where the fade-in should end.

Creating a Fade-In

All music and sound production uses effects called fades. A fade-in takes a sound from a lower level and raises it in volume so that it can be heard. A fade-out takes a sound that is playing and decreases its volume until it is not heard. Most people notice fades only when a full mix is faded out at the end of a song on, say, a CD, but parts are faded in and out of mixes constantly.

Cubase has many ways to create fades. One very graphical way to create fades is to use the mouse in the Project window to fade individual events in and out. Only events can be faded in this way. If you need to fade a part, you probably should do that when you are mixing the project.

To fade in an audio event:

1. With the Arrow tool, in the Project window, select the event that you want to fade in.

   The event will have two blue triangles at both top corners and a blue square at the top middle (**Figure 8.26**).

2. Still using the Arrow tool, position the pointer over the top-left blue triangle.

   The pointer will change to a pair of arrows pointing in opposite directions (**Figure 8.27**).

3. Drag to the right to move the blue triangle ahead into the event (**Figure 8.28**).

4. When you reach the point where you want the fade-in to end, release the mouse.

   The triangle shows where the fade-in ends, and the audio waveform will update to show the change in the volume of the part.

Creating a Fade-Out

You use the same procedure that you used to create a fade-in, but you reverse it to create a fade-out.

To fade out an audio event:

1. Click with the Arrow tool to select the event that you want to fade out.

2. Position the pointer over the blue triangle in the upper-right corner of the event.

   The pointer changes to a pair of opposing arrows (**Figure 8.29**).

3. Drag the triangle to the left (**Figure 8.30**).

4. Release the mouse at the point where you want the fade-out to begin.

   The blue triangle shows where the fade-out starts, and the waveform will update to show the change in volume (**Figure 8.31**).

✔ Tip

- The way that the waveform updates when you set a fade is more than just cool looking. The waveform provides excellent visual feedback for setting fade points.

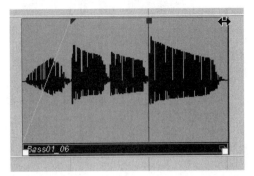

Figure 8.29 The fade-out point is ready to be moved.

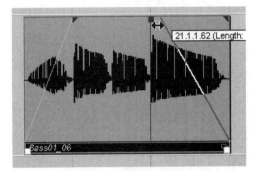

Figure 8.30 Dragging to the left to move the fade-out point

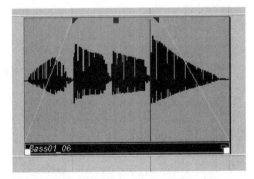

Figure 8.31 The fade-out is set; note that both the fade-in and fade-out are reflected in the change in the waveform.

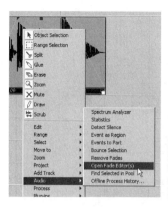

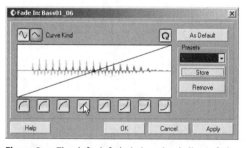

Figure 8.32 This menu item opens the window where fades can be edited.

Figure 8.33 The default fade-in is a simple linear fade.

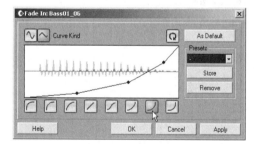

Figure 8.34 One of the fade curves that is available as a preset in Cubase

■ You can also open the fade editors by double-clicking the overlapping section that is to be faded.

Editing Fades

Cubase uses a simple linear fade by default. This default is the rough equivalent of turning a volume knob for the event at precisely the same speed throughout the fade. Although this default fade quite often does the job, Cubase does not restrict fades to this linear shape. Fades can be almost infinitely edited by using the Fade editors.

To edit the curve of a fade:

1. Using the Arrow tool, click an event in which a fade has been created.

2. Right-click (Windows) or Control-click (Mac OS) and select Audio > Open Fade Editor(s) (**Figure 8.32**).

   This opens the Fade In editor, the Fade Out editor, or both. Each editor opens only if the event has the type of fade it can edit.

   The fade editor shows the portion of the event that is faded in or out. **Figure 8.33** shows the Fade In editor with the default linear fade-in.

3. Click the buttons at the bottom of the editor pane to change the shape of the fade (**Figure 8.34**).

4. When the fade has the shape you want, click OK.

   The curve will be applied to the event in the Project window.

✔ Tips

■ If the presets for a fade-in or fade-out are not what you want, you can drag the breakpoints in the fade editor to create your own shape. You can even create new breakpoints by clicking the line of the fade if you wish. Most situations, though, are well covered by the preset fades.

Changing the Volume Level for an Event

You now know how to use the two blue triangles in an event to create fade-ins and fade-outs. You can use the blue square in an event to edit as well to graphically edit the overall volume level for an event when it is played back. This option, in combination with the fade-in and fade-out options, gives you deep control of dynamics for any event in the Project window.

To set the overall volume level for an event:

1. Click an event with the Arrow tool to select it.

2. Position the pointer over the blue square in the middle of the event (**Figure 8.35**).

    The pointer becomes two opposing vertical arrows.

3. Drag up to increase the overall volume level of the event or drag down to decrease the overall volume level (**Figure 8.36**).

4. When the volume level is set where you want it, release the mouse.

    The blue square will show the relative volume level of the event, and the waveform will update to show the result of the change (**Figure 8.37**).

✔ Tip

■ You can also raise the volume level of an event several decibels above its original level using this method.

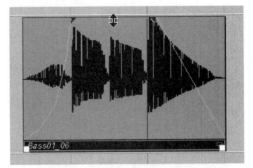

Figure 8.35 The pointer is over the blue box and can now set the overall volume level of the event.

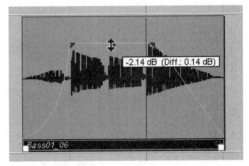

Figure 8.36 Dragging down decreases the volume level.

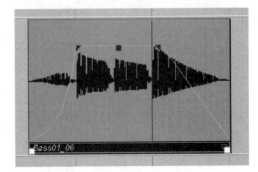

Figure 8.37 After the mouse is released, note that the waveform also changes to reflect the new, lower volume level of the event.

CHANGING THE VOLUME LEVEL FOR AN EVENT

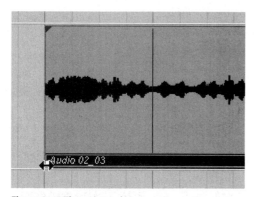

Figure 8.38 The pointer changes to two arrows to show that it is ready to resize an event.

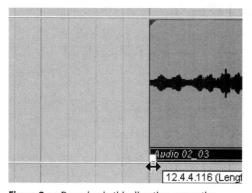

Figure 8.39 Dragging in this direction moves the beginning of the event forward, acting as a mask.

✔ Tips

- If Snap is on, an event will be resized according to the Snap setting.

- To temporarily override Snap without turning it off, hold down Ctrl (Windows) or Command (Mac OS) while resizing the event.

Resizing Events

The edit operations on events and parts that we have discussed so far have allowed you to move or copy an event or part or change its volume, but they have left the event or part itself largely untouched. Another critical aspect of audio editing is changing the duration of events and parts and controlling what exactly an event or part plays.

You can resize events in three ways. The simplest way to resize an event is to change its start or end point. This masks or unmasks the sections of the audio that can be played back by the event, while leaving the content of the event intact. A second way to resize an event is to keep the start or end of the event in the same place, but to move the audio forward or backward in time within the event. A third way is to force the event to change its duration by time stretching, so that it plays back more slowly or quickly than it did originally.

To resize an event by changing its start or end point:

1. Using the Arrow tool, click the event you want to resize to select it.

2. Position the pointer on the bottom corner of the beginning or end of the event (**Figure 8.38**).

   The pointer changes to a pair of opposing horizontal arrows.

3. Drag to the place where you want the event to begin or end (**Figure 8.39**).

4. Release the mouse when the file is resized as you wish.

Moving the Contents of an Event by Resizing

The previous section described one way that you can use resizing to change an event, using the Arrow tool in its default mode. In that mode, resizing an event changes the location in an audio file where the event starts or ends. You can also use the Arrow tool in the Sizing Moves Contents mode. When an event is resized using this mode, moving the start or end point pushes the audio itself back and forth inside the event. This allows the event to start or end at the same place in the project, but moves the audio inside of the event forward or backward in time. In the following task, you will resize a two-measure section using this mode to move the second bar ahead in time by one measure.

To move the contents of an event by resizing:

1. Click the Arrow tool on the toolbar to select it and then click the Arrow tool on the toolbar again to open the context menu. Select the Sizing Moves Contents option (**Figure 8.40**).

2. Turn Snap on or off, depending on your preference. In this example, Snap is on.

3. Move the pointer to the lower-right corner of the event to be changed.

   The arrow changes to two opposing horizontal arrows (**Figure 8.41**).

4. Drag to the left to move the end of the event forward in time.

5. When the event is resized as you wish, release the mouse.

   The audio in the event is moved forward in time, with the end of the event as an anchor (**Figure 8.42**).

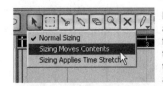

Figure 8.40 Choose a different mode for the Arrow tool to change the way that resizing affects an event.

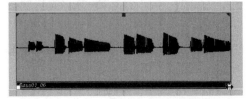

Figure 8.41 Note the different phrase in each bar. The pointer will now resize the event.

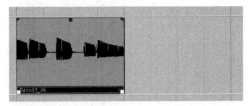

Figure 8.42 The second phrase has now been moved to where the first phrase was originally. The event is also half as long as it was before.

✔ Tips

- Resizing in this way is very useful, but not always easy to understand. Try resizing the same part in the exact same way using each resize mode. The techniques will become clear quickly.

- You can resize an event in this way using either its starting point or ending point.

- Once again, holding down Ctrl (Windows) or Command (Mac) defeats Snap temporarily.

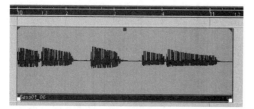

Figure 8.43 This phrase is one bar long, but it does not fit into a bar of the current project.

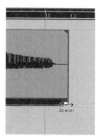

Figure 8.44 The change in the pointer indicates that the event will be time stretched.

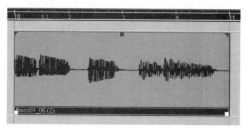

Figure 8.45 The event fits in one bar now; compare to Figure 8.43.

What About Resizing Parts?

Parts are resized in exactly the same way as events, using exactly the same tools. There is really no difference in the way the audio is handled, except when you use Resize Applies Time Stretch. If a part with more than one event is resized in this mode, Cubase has to time stretch each event in the part. Other than this minor difference, the tools for resizing events work in the same way for resizing parts and produce the same results.

Resizing an Event by Time Stretching

The third mode for resizing an event doesn't change the audio that the event plays or the place where the event plays it. Instead, it alters the tempo or duration of the audio to fit the new size of the event. This approach was introduced in Chapter 3 in the context of fitting a drum loop to the tempo of a project. To see how this mode works, you will shorten a one-bar line that does not fit correctly in the project (**Figure 8.43**). You will commonly need to do this when you have samples taken from CDs or vinyl that do not match the tempo of the song in which they will be used.

To resize an event by time stretching:

1. Click the Arrow tool on the toolbar to select it and then click it again to open the context menu. Select Sizing Applies Time Stretch.

2. Turn Snap on or off, as you prefer.

3. Click the event to be resized, to select it.

4. Position the pointer at the bottom corner of the start or end of the event.

   The pointer becomes a pair of opposing arrows with the word *Stretch* beneath them, indicating that the event will be time stretched if it is resized (**Figure 8.44**).

5. Drag the start or end of the event until it is the length you wish.

6. Release the mouse.

   Cubase begins processing the event. A box with a status bar appears showing the progress of the change operation. When the processing is finished, the duration of the event will be changed (**Figure 8.45**).

Creating a Crossfade

A crossfade is a special combination of a fade-in and a fade-out. Crossfades are used in many ways, but their primary use is to create a smooth transition between two different events on the same audio track. For instance, if two takes of a solo part were recorded, and the first half of one take sounds great while the second half of the other take sounds great, the two events can be edited together. In some situations, the transition between the two events will be audible and unpleasant. Crossfading the events together makes the transition nearly inaudible. In this task, you will crossfade two events for just such a transition.

To crossfade two events:

1. Resize both events so the section to be crossfaded is at the very end of the first event and at the very beginning of the second event (**Figure 8.46**).

2. Drag the events over each other so that the sections to be crossfaded overlap.

   The area where the events overlap is indicated by a darkened section (**Figure 8.47**).

3. Select both events by clicking them with the Shift key held down, or use the Arrow tool to draw a box over both events.

4. Right-click (Windows) or Control-click (Mac OS), and in the context menu select Audio > Crossfade. You can also press the X key on the keyboard as a shortcut.

   The overlap of the events is outlined in blue, and the fade curves are displayed in blue (**Figure 8.48**).

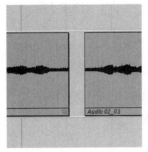

Figure 8.46 These two events need to be joined seamlessly with a crossfade.

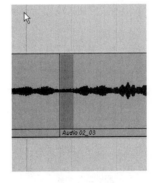

Figure 8.47 Position events so that they overlap in a place in the performance where a fade will not be too obvious.

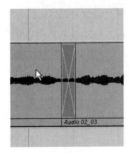

Figure 8.48 After you choose the Crossfade command from the Audio menu, the lines in the crossfade indicate the two fade curves.

✔ Tip

- Creating good crossfades is a craft, if not an art; it takes practice to find the best fade points. The general rule of thumb, however, is to find a place for the crossfade where not much is going on. The less action at the fade point, the more likely it is to be inaudible.

CREATING A CROSSFADE

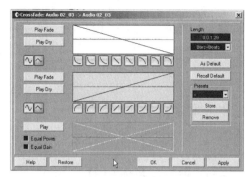

Figure 8.49 The Crossfade panel

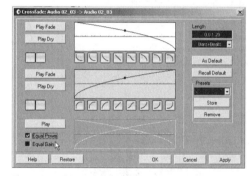

Figure 8.50 The Equal Power box is selected, creating a preset fade curve for both fade-in and fade-out.

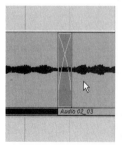

Figure 8.51 The fade curves have changed now that Equal Power is selected in the Crossfade panel.

Changing the Shape of a Crossfade

A crossfade, after all, is nothing but a fade-out of one event and the fade-in of another. Therefore, you can edit a crossfade much like any other fade. Crossfades have a few additional editing options as well.

To edit the shape of a crossfade:

1. After you create a crossfade, select either or both events that are part of the fade.

2. Right-click (Windows) or Control-click (Mac OS), and in the menu that opens, select Audio > Crossfade, or double-click the events where they overlap.

3. When the Crossfade dialog box opens (**Figure 8.49**), select a curve to adjust the fade-in, fade-out, or both; or select either of the check boxes: Equal Power and Equal Gain.

   In **Figure 8.50**, Equal Power has been chosen.

4. Click OK.

   When you return to the Project window, the crossfade will reflect the changes made in the Crossfade panel (**Figure 8.51**).

✔ Tips

■ An Equal Power crossfade maintains the energy, or power, of the sounds throughout the crossfade. An Equal Gain crossfade maintains the gain across the crossfade. A huge percentage of crossfades will sound perfect when using one of these two settings. When in doubt, give them a spin.

■ You can preview each individual fade and the crossfade by clicking the Play buttons to the left of the fade-in, fade-out, and crossfade sections of the Crossfade dialog box.

Splitting Events and Parts

Crossfading and resizing often are applied to snippets of larger takes, used either to grab a loop to be repeated in the song or to create a single version of a line or solo with the best sections from multiple takes. For both looping and editing together multiple takes, the Scissors tool can be invaluable. Using the Scissors tool, you can chop audio parts and events into smaller bits that are easier to work with. In the following task, you will see how to split an event into smaller, two-bar sections.

To split events with the Scissors tool:

1. Click the Scissors tool on the toolbar.

2. Turn on Snap and select Bar. Snap matters when using the Scissors tool, so it needs to be turned on or off depending on the job. In this case, two-bar loops are the goal, so you need snap to align them (**Figure 8.52**).

3. Position the pointer over the event to be snipped.

   A thin line shows where a cut will be made if the mouse is clicked at the current location (**Figure 8.53**).

4. Move the pointer until the line is on the location where you want to snip the audio event; then click.

   The event is split into two pieces (**Figure 8.54**).

✔ Tips

- Parts can be snipped just like events. The only real difference is that when a part is split with the Scissors tool, the corresponding events are also split to create a new part.

Figure 8.52 Setup to use the Scissors tool: The tool is selected on the toolbar, and Snap is turned on and set to Bar.

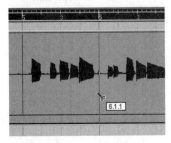

Figure 8.53 The thin, light line at measure 6 indicates the place where the Scissors tool will cut the event if the mouse is clicked.

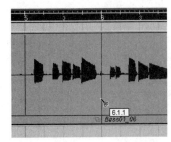

Figure 8.54 The darker line in this illustration shows where the event was cut. The line is actually blue in Cubase.

- Remember that after a part is snipped with the Scissors tool, all of the audio from the original event is still there and can be viewed/heard by resizing the event.

SPLITTING EVENTS AND PARTS

Figure 8.55 The Audio Part editor with two events shown.

The Audio Part Editor

Audio parts are useful for a number of reasons; in particular, after a group of events has been edited together into a part, you can move, copy, process, and otherwise treat them as a single entity. You use the Audio Part editor (**Figure 8.55**), as you might guess, to edit audio parts.

The Audio Part editor creates composite takes, or *comps*. A comp is a single musical phrase, line, or groove that is composed of pieces from more than one performance. Sometimes a comp is created to cover a mistake, such a single flat note by a singer in an otherwise solid performance. Comps can also be heavily edited masterpieces of audio artifice. The following pages walk you through the basics of creating a comp in the Audio Part editor.

Keep in mind that an audio part is just a container in which audio events are kept, so much of what you do in the Audio Part editor you could also do in the Project window. Comping, though, is done only in the Part editor.

Preparing Events for a Comp

A comp can be created from many sources. For example, a single long take can be cut into pieces for comping. Events or regions created with cycle recording are also very common sources. Comps can also be created out of completely unrelated and distinct pieces of audio, although this is not a common practice. In the task here, a longer event was snipped into two-bar loops and will be comped from these pieces. You will get the events ready for comping.

To arrange events for comping in the Audio Part editor:

1. Set the start and end points for the loop so they correspond to the length of the section to be comped. In this case, set a two-bar loop (**Figure 8.56**).

2. On the Transport bar, click the Loop button to turn on looping.

3. Drag all of the events that will be used into the range of the loop (**Figure 8.57**). This puts together all of the constituent events that will be used to create the comp.

✔ Tip

■ When comping, and particularly when arranging elements for a comp, you may find it useful to set the lanes in the Audio Part editor so that they are quite narrow, so the editor can show more events. To adjust the height of the lanes, you use the vertical slider at the lower-right corner of the Audio Part editor (**Figure 8.58**).

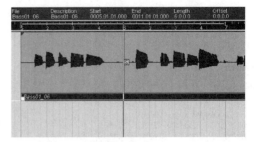

Figure 8.56 A two-bar loop, from measures 5 to 7, is set in the Audio Part editor.

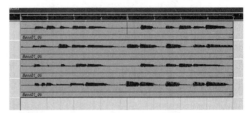

Figure 8.57 Each of these events has been created from a longer take by using the Scissors tool.

Figure 8.58 Use the vertical slider to adjust the lanes when you are managing a lot of events in the Audio Part editor.

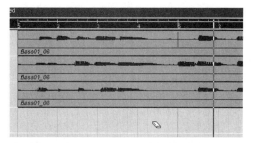

Figure 8.59 The Eraser tool just deleted the bottom event; the event newly on the bottom will now play.

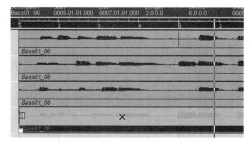

Figure 8.60 Muting an event has the same effect as deleting it, except that a muted event can be unmuted easily.

Figure 8.61 The resized event will not play until the cursor moves to the point where it is the bottom event in the editor.

Hearing the Events in a Comp

When you are creating a comp, you can hear each of the events in the Audio Part editor. The Audio Part editor plays back only one event at a time, and—if you have events stacked vertically—the event at the bottom of the Audio Part editor is the one that will play back. In Figure 8.57, for example, the bottommost part will play back throughout the loop. However, there are multiple ways to hear events that are not on the bottom:

◆ Use the Eraser tool to delete the event that's closest to the bottom (**Figure 8.59**).

◆ Apply the Mute tool to the bottom event to leave it in its current location but hear the event directly above it (**Figure 8.60**)

◆ Resize the bottom event so that a section of the event above it will be heard (**Figure 8.61**).

In Figures 8.59 through 8.61, at least a section of the third event from the top will play instead of the bottom event. Of course, muting, deleting or resizing any of the events can change which one gets priority in playback.

Finishing a Comp

In Cubase, probably the best way to create a comp is to start the loop playing and listen to each part play by alternately muting each of the other parts. The good parts will usually be pretty obvious, and the bad parts can be resized or muted out of the comp. **Figure 8.62** shows one possible comp that was created from the lines in Figures 8.59 through 8.61. The top event plays for the first measure, then the second event plays until the bottom part plays one note, and then the second and top events play, finishing the line.

When the Audio Part editor is closed, the comped part looks like **Figure 8.63**. Some sections of the part are dimmed because of the muted event in the Audio Part editor. If the muted event is deleted, the part in the Project window looks like **Figure 8.64**.

✔ Tip

■ Comping is another editing operation that is part art, part science, and part craft. The Audio Part editor in Cubase is one of the better software comping tools currently available. Comping practice will pay off mightily over time.

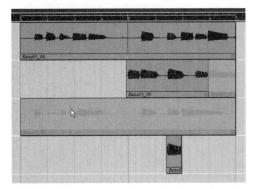

Figure 8.62 This is one of a nearly infinite number of possible comps.

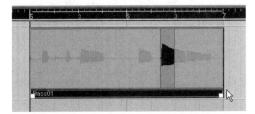

Figure 8.63 In the Project window, the comp looks like this. It plays back just as shown in Figure 8.62.

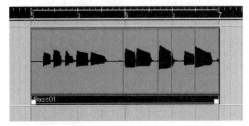

Figure 8.64 After you remove the muted events, you can more easily see that this part is comped from more than one event.

ADVANCED
AUDIO EDITING

Audio applications are generally divided into two main categories: multitrack recording applications and sample editors. Sample-editing applications give users lots of control over a single stereo or mono audio file; multitrack applications substitute nicely for multitrack tape decks but have limited options for editing and processing the tracks.

Cubase, however, breaks free of these categories, allowing you to perform both sample editing and multitrack recording in the same window. What's more, Cubase provides tons of processing options, and you can perform a lot of processing with almost no strain on your CPU. In addition, because all editing in Cubase is nondestructive, you can save a history of the effects you've applied so that, if necessary, you can undo them afterward.

In this chapter, you will delve deeper into the audio-editing abilities of Cubase, learning how to process and change the audio you have recorded. You will learn about some of the audio processing options that come bundled with Cubase and how to apply them to events and parts in a project. You will also learn about third-party VST plug-ins and their uses, and how to manage and modify all of the changes made to an event, even after the fact. Finally, you will learn about the high-resolution Sample Editor and some of its regions-based editing options.

Types of Audio Editing

You can perform two main types or styles of
audio editing in Cubase. The first type, discussed in Chapter 8, "Basic Audio Editing,"
involves changes to parts and events, including changes in duration, location, and basic
sonic parameters such as fade and level. The
second type of audio editing makes changes
to the audio itself so that it doesn't sound
the same after it has been edited. This second kind of audio editing involves such
modifications as changes to the gain struc-
ture of a sample, addition of reverb, time
correction, and pitch shifting.

Once again, you will be spending a lot of time
with the context menus that open when you
right-click (Windows) or Control-click (Mac
OS) an event or part. Most of the actions in
this chapter use the Process menu (**Figure
9.1**) or the Plug-ins menu (**Figure 9.2**).

Even though the work you do in this chapter
will involve mucking around with the way
your audio sounds, as mentioned earlier all
editing in Cubase is nondestructive. When
Cubase processes a piece of audio, it always
keeps the original, and you can return to
this original sound if you decide you want it
back. Later in this chapter, you'll learn how
to restore your original files using the Offline
Process History feature of Cubase.

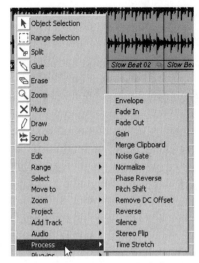

Figure 9.1 The Process menu includes
many of the utility processing tools that
are bundled with Cubase.

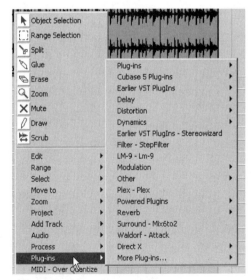

Figure 9.2 The Plug-ins menu lists all installed
VST/DirectX plug-ins—both those bundled with
Cubase and those from third parties.

Figure 9.3 Selecting the Zoom tool on the toolbar

Figure 9.4 Drag over a section of an event to zoom in and display it in closeup view in the Project window.

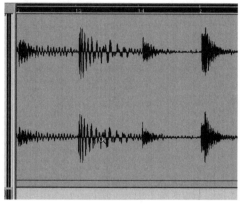

Figure 9.5 The Events display after zooming

Using the Zoom Tool

Until now, the actions described in this book have been on a comparatively large scale. More advanced audio editing, however, often necessitates a much closer look at the event or part being edited. For this purpose, the Zoom tool is invaluable. You can select the Zoom tool from either the toolbar (**Figure 9.3**) or the context menu opened by right-clicking (Windows) or Control-clicking (Mac OS). You can use the Zoom tool to zoom in on a particular section of the Project window.

To zoom a section of the Project window:

1. Select the Zoom tool by clicking the Zoom button on the toolbar or choosing Zoom from the context menu.

   The pointer turns into a magnifying glass.

2. Using the magnifying glass, drag over the section of the Project window that you want to see more closely (**Figure 9.4**).

   The section appears zoomed and centered in the Events display (**Figure 9.5**).

✔ Tip

- Holding down the Shift key while clicking anywhere with the Zoom tool will zoom the project significantly.

Extracting Events from Parts

You can use the Range Selection tool for more controlled editing in the Project window or the Audio Part editor, for example, to select a specific section of an audio event or part. After you select the range, it functions as if it were its own event. This gives you incredible flexibility when working with events and parts. In the task here, you will see how to copy a single drum hit from an event using the Range Selection tool. The event will not be resized at all.

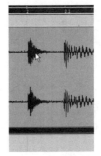

Figure 9.6 The solid, dark drum hit will be selected.

To extract a section of an event with the Range Selection tool:

1. Zoom in closely on the section you want to select.

   This example uses the drum hit on beat 2, under the pointer in **Figure 9.6**.

2. Turn off Snap.

   Snap matters with the Range Selection tool—you can turn it on or off as you wish, but in this example, it should be off.

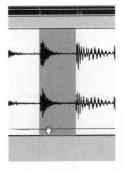

Figure 9.7 Only this one note in the larger event is selected. In Cubase, the selection will be blue.

3. Click the Range Selection button 🔲 on the toolbar or select the tool with the context menu.

   The pointer turns into a crossbar.

4. Using the crossbar pointer, drag over the section of the event you want to select (**Figure 9.7**).

   The pointer becomes a small hand.

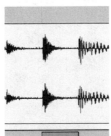

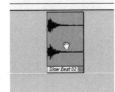

Figure 9.8 The single sample has been copied to a new track, with no need to resize or modify the event.

5. Hold down Alt (Windows) or Option (Mac OS) and drag the selected range to an adjacent track.

6. Release the mouse.

   A new event is created from the selected material (**Figure 9.8**).

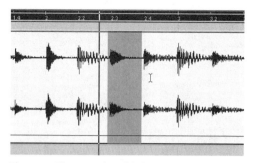

Figure 9.9 The same drum hit that you saw in Figure 9.6: The start of the selection will be fine-tuned.

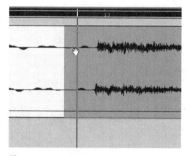

Figure 9.10 Using the cursor to zoom in close to the start of the selection

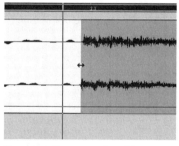

Figure 9.11 The start point of the selection has been modified.

Adjusting a Range Selection

The range stays selected only when the Range Selection tool is active. Once you click the Zoom tool, the range selection is gone. If you make a range selection and decide that it is not what you want, you have to start over again. In addition, you may need a very exact range that is also fairly long, making it nearly impossible to select without the use of different zoom levels. The only way to make an exacting change in a selected range is to zoom using the ruler and cursor. The following task shows you a couple of navigational shortcuts you can use to select with precision the single drum beat that's next to the cursor in **Figure 9.9**.

To zoom in and adjust a range selection:

1. Unselect Snap if it is on.

   When you make exacting edits, Snap almost always needs to be off.

2. Click the ruler near where you want to zoom in. Drag to the bottom of the screen to increase the zoom, and drag horizontally to either edge to move left or right. Release the mouse when you've zoomed in close enough in to see your selection (**Figure 9.10**).

3. Position the Range Selection tool at the border of the selection. It will turn into a pair of opposing horizontal arrows. Use this pointer to drag the selection border to where you want the range to begin (**Figure 9.11**).

4. Zoom out by clicking the ruler and dragging up; then zoom back in at the end of the selected range and repeat until you get the exact range that you want.

Navigating with the Locators

Cubase includes a huge range of options for navigation within projects. Anyone doing detailed audio editing should learn some of the key combinations and shortcuts for moving around in events, parts, and selections. These will save you a great deal of time in zooming in and out to find places to edit. For example, you could accomplish the sample extraction described in the previous section with much less zooming by moving the locators and using them as guides for viewing the selection, as you'll learn here.

To use the locators to view a selection:

1. In the Sample Editor's main window, zoom in and set the selection starting point as in Figure 9.11.

   Now you need to set the end point.

2. Right-click (Windows) or Control-click (Mac OS) and in the context menu that opens, select Transport > Locators to Selection (**Figure 9.12**).

   This sets the left locator to the start of the current selected range, and the right locator to the end of the selected range. You can also simply press the P key on your keyboard, and this shortcut will set both the right and left locators, as well.

✔ Tip

- You can use the numeric keypad to navigate through a project. The numeric 1 key always moves the cursor to the left locator, and the numeric 2 key always moves it to the right locator. **Figure 9.13** shows how, after pressing the 2 key on the numeric keypad, the cursor jumps to the end of the selection range, which makes it easier for you to move it to a new location.

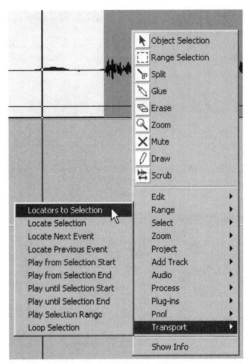

Figure 9.12 This menu choice sets the locators as bookends around the current selection.

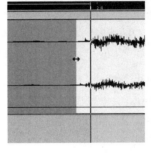

Figure 9.13 It's easy to get the selection ending right when you can jump to it with the keypad.

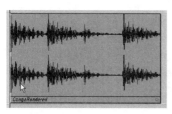

Figure 9.14
The event
before it is
reversed

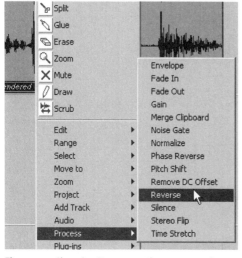

Figure 9.15 Choosing Reverse as the process to be performed on the event

Figure 9.16 Cubase prompts you to be sure that the processing changes only the events you want it to change.

Processing an Event or Part

Cubase supports two primary ways of processing audio. You can use such processes included within Cubase as noise gating, time stretching, and envelope modification, or you can apply third-party VST (Windows and Mac OS) and DirectX (Windows only) audio plug-ins to a selection, event, or part.

There isn't room here to cover all of the Cubase processes and options (much less all of the VST and DX plug-ins). We'll explore a few examples of the more important processes, but you should take some time to experiment with the audio processes bundled with Cubase.

In this task, you will learn how to reverse the audio in an event.

To reverse the audio in an event:

1. Use the arrow tool to select the event to be reversed.

   Figure 9.14 shows the event before it is processed.

2. Right-click (Windows) or Control-click (Mac OS) the event and select Process > Reverse (**Figure 9.15**).

   If the event you're processing is used more than once, a dialog box opens and asks whether you want the processing to apply to each event that uses that audio, or whether Cubase should create a new event with the processing applied (**Figure 9.16**).

   continues on next page

3. Click Continue or New Version in the message box, depending on your needs.

A status bar shows the progress of the audio processing. When the processing is complete, the new processed event—with the audio waveforms in reverse order—will appear in the Project window (**Figure 9.17**).

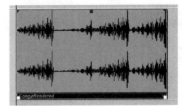

Figure 9.17 The event in the Project window after it has been reversed

✔ Tip

■ For more information about the options for processing audio, and about the processes themselves, read "Audio Processing Functions," in the electronic documentation that comes with Cubase.

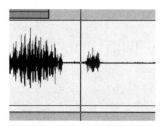

Figure 9.18 The blip next to the cursor will be decreased in volume.

Figure 9.19 Use this panel to set the increase or decrease in gain.

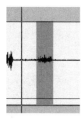

Figure 9.20 The Project window shows the change that results from the processing.

Adjusting Gain in an Event

Often you may want to selectively boost or cut the volume of a section of audio. For example, one note may stick out in a performance, or the sound of the singer taking a breath before singing may be too prominent. There are multiple ways to tackle such a problem, but one of the easier approaches is to process the audio by changing the gain at the level of the event.

To change the gain of a selection in an event:

1. Zoom in until you can easily see the section you want to change.

   In this example, the note just to the right of the cursor is too loud (**Figure 9.18**).

2. Turn off Snap.

3. Use the Range Selection tool to select only the section that needs to be changed.

4. Right-click (Windows) or Control-click (Mac OS) and select Process > Gain.

   The Gain panel opens (**Figure 9.19**).

5. Select an amount of gain reduction by using the slider or the arrow buttons. Click the Preview button to hear the effect.

6. When the selection sounds right, click the Process button.

   When the audio has been processed, you will be returned to the Project Window, where you can see the change in the event (**Figure 9.20**).

Pitch Shifting an Event

Anyone who has ever used samples or loops has encountered a situation where a piece of audio sounds great, except that it's not quite in tune. Cubase includes a full-featured pitch-shifting process that can be applied to events, parts, or selections of an event or part. Using pitch shifting, you can change the global pitch of an event or surgically alter a note or two that does not sound right. In the following task, you will see how to pitch shift an entire event to match the key of the project.

To change the pitch of an event:

1. Using the Arrow tool, select the event that needs to have its pitch altered.

2. Right-click (Windows) or Control-click (Mac OS) and select Process > Pitch Shift.

   The Pitch Shift dialog box opens (**Figure 9.21**). This dialog box contains many parameters, but we will discuss only some of them here.

   You can set the amount of pitch shift by entering a number of semitones in the Pitch Shift Settings section, as you will do here, or by using the keyboard.

3. In the Pitch Shift Settings area, click the up arrow on the Transpose box twice to specify two semitones (**Figure 9.22**).

   Cubase plays back a root tone and then a second tone that shows how far the event will be pitch shifted. Pitch shifting cannot be previewed.

4. Click the Process button.

   A status bar shows the progress of the processing (**Figure 9.23**). When processing is complete, you will be returned to the Project window.

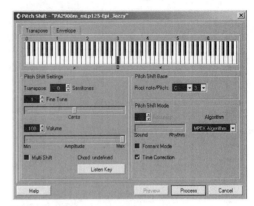

Figure 9.21 The Pitch Shift dialog box

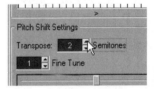

Figure 9.22 This setting will pitch shift the event by two semitones.

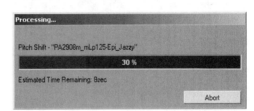

Figure 9.23 You can monitor processing by watching this status bar.

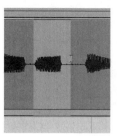

Figure 9.24 Selecting the note that needs to be pitch corrected

Figure 9.25 Use the Fine Tune arrows (where the pointer is) or with the Cents slider to adjust the pitch.

Correcting a Mistake Using Pitch Shift

Pitch shifting is often used to correct small tuning mistakes in a live musician's performance. Most often, it is used with vocals, but any performance with a small pitch mistake on a monophonic instrument can be corrected in this way. This pitch-correction process is usually called tuning and can be done in many ways. In the "Dark Ages" before about 1998, people used hardware samplers as the preferred tool for correcting pitch mistakes, with the retuned words or syllables fired back to tape or disk via MIDI. One of the most famous VST plug-ins, Autotune, automated the pitch-correction process, forever relieving vocalists of the requirement of singing the correct pitch. All of these tools still work, but using only your ears and Cubase you can single out a note and tune a performance.

To correct pitch mistakes in a performance:

1. Turn off Snap, unless your performer made mistakes for precisely one bar or beat.

2. Listen to the event in question to determine which note is incorrect. Then use the Range Selection tool to select just the note you want to change (**Figure 9.24**).

3. Right-click (Windows) or Control-click (Mac OS) and select Process > Pitch Shift to open the Pitch Shift window.

   Now comes the tricky part. When tuning a performance, usually the pitch changes are very minor.

4. Use the Cents slider or Fine Tune arrows to pitch shift the selection slightly sharp or flat, as needed (**Figure 9.25**).

continues on next page

CORRECTING A MISTAKE USING PITCH SHIFT

5. When the pitch-shifted audio sounds right (often it's a good idea to use a correctly tuned piano or guitar as a reference), click the Process button to apply the changes.

You may be asked it you want to create a new event with the processed audio (**Figure 9.26**). Under most circumstances, you will.

Figure 9.26 The dialog box asks if you want to create a new event with the pitch-shifted audio. Usually, you will want to select New Version.

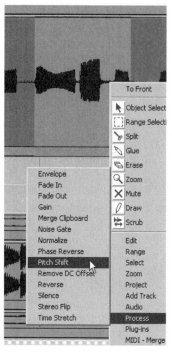

Figure 9.27 Choosing Pitch Shift after the correct range has been selected

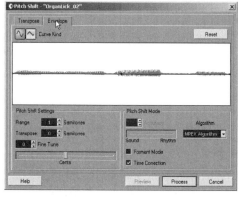

Figure 9.28 The Envelope panel allows you to apply pitch shifting according to user-specified curves.

Pitch Shifting with an Envelope

Cubase has a large number of options available for pitch shifting; we will cover only a few of them here. One pitch shifting option worth considering is the envelope, which you can use as a guide.

Envelopes are commonly used in synthesizers to create curves to control parameters automatically, and if you understand a synth envelope, you'll have no trouble using the Cubase pitch-shifting envelope. If you are not familiar with synthesizers, just remember that the envelopes for pitch shifting let you create a smooth curve that changes the amount of pitch shifting over time.

When are envelopes useful? Often live musicians will begin off-pitch and slowly drift back to pitch as their ears lead them back into tune. A singer may start out flat and swoop up to the right pitch, or a saxophone player may be too aggressive and play sharp for a few notes before drifting back down into tune. In situations like this, the envelope can be a very effective tool for tuning the performance.

To pitch shift using an envelope:

1. Turn off Snap.

2. Listen to the event and find the section that needs to be tuned.

3. Using the Range Selection tool, select the range of the performance that needs to be pitch shifted.

4. Open the context menu and select Process > Pitch Shift (**Figure 9.27**).

5. In the Pitch Shift panel, select the Envelope tab (**Figure 9.28**).

continues on next page

6. Drag a point to edit the curve; double-click to create any new points needed on the curve.

You can edit envelopes here just like you can edit fades in the Fade-in and Fade-out editors.

The Range setting determines the overall pitch shifting capability of the editor. The value of this parameter is set in semitones, or half steps on a piano keyboard. **Figure 9.29** shows a fairly wide range of pitch shifting (up to three semitones) with a curve set to pitch up the first two notes but leave the last note mostly unchanged.

7. When you have the curve set as you wish, click the Process button to apply the changes to the audio.

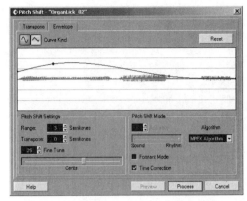

Figure 9.29 A curve has been created with three breakpoints; each horizontal line in the waveform display represents a semitone of possible pitch shifting. In this illustration, the range is set to three semitones, so there are three lines above and below the waveform, allowing the audio to be pitched up or down a maximum of three semitones.

A Stylistic Warning

I have carefully avoided telling you how your music should sound, or what is musically "right" or "wrong." However, in this case, I have a cautionary tale.

On March 18 and 19, 1963, jazz saxophone virtuoso Stan Getz was in New York City with Brazilian legends Joao Gilberto and Antonio Carlos Jobim recording an album that eventually received the understated name of *Getz/Gilberto*. One of the Jobim's songs, written in Portuguese, was called "The Girl from Ipanema." The first version was in Portuguese, but the decision was made to include a version with the lyrics translated into English. That created a problem: Brazilian singer Joao Gilberto was not comfortable singing English. Over the objections of nearly everyone, Getz had Gilberto's wife Astrud (who could sing English) brought to the studio to give the song a try. Astrud was not a professional musician and had little previous performance experience. Instead of the train wreck some expected, the exquisite "The Girl from Ipanema" we know was the result. For 5 minutes and 22 seconds, the music of three continents sang in rare harmony.

However, it also sang flat. Astrud gave a staggering performance, but it was certainly not on pitch. But it was precisely that flatness that gave the vocals the languorous, tropical feel of the beaches of Rio. Brazilian vocalists to this day reference that wonderfully flat vocal in their own singing, and it's become a stylistic signature. Even so, I'm sure if that performance were recorded today, someone at some point would demand that the vocals be tuned and run through five limiters and slathered with reverb, thus depriving the world of one of the sublime moments in recording history.

The moral of this story? If every vocal were tuned, and if every take were made perfect, much of what we consider the best recorded music would not exist. Don't automatically airbrush every sound in a project, unless you're making beer commercials.

Processing Audio with VST Effects

VST stands for virtual studio technology. In a virtual studio, the entire processing, recording, and mixing process occurs inside a computer. Among the key components that make a virtual studio possible are effects such as delays, flangers, reverbs, and compressors. Cubase ships with a nice complement of built-in VST plug-ins, but Steinberg also opened its plug-in specification so that third parties could make plug-ins that would work in Cubase.

VST plug-ins can be used in many different ways. Most often, they are used in the VST mixer. You will learn more about them in Chapter 11, "The Cubase Mixer," and Chapter 12, "Audio Effect Plug-ins." In the following task, you will see how to apply a Phaser plug-in, included with Cubase, to an audio event (a drum loop).

To process an event with a VST effect:

1. Use the Arrow tool to select the event to be processed.

2. Right-click (Windows) or Control-click (Mac OS) and select Plug-ins > Modulation > Phaser from the context menu (**Figure 9.30**). The VST plug-in window opens (**Figure 9.31**).

3. Click the Preview button to hear the event with the effect.

4. Adjust the parameters until the effect sounds the way you want.

5. When you are satisfied with the effect, click the Process button.

   The audio will be processed with the effect, and you will be returned to the Project window.

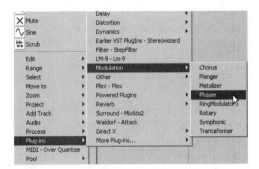

Figure 9.30 Opening the Phaser plug-in that comes with Cubase

Figure 9.31 The editor panel for the phase-shifter plug-in

✔ Tip

■ If you are unfamiliar with the way that a phase shifter works, consult Chapter 8, "Audio Effects," in the Cubase manual.

Figure 9.32 Extra buttons lurk beneath the main VST plug-in processing window.

Figure 9.33 The Wet Mix and Dry Mix controls move in opposition to each other.

Additional Settings for Processing Audio

Many of the VST plug-ins and the built-in Cubase audio processes have additional parameters that may be useful depending on the kind of effect you are using and what you doing with it. Many of the panels used to set up processing have a button on the bottom marked More that when clicked, opens another set of options that control the use of the plug-in. In many cases, you will not need to use these parameters, but you still should know about them so you can use them to make changes when necessary.

Click the More button on the plug-in's panel to display additional parameters for audio processing (**Figure 9.32**). In this case, we'll look at the Mod Delay panel.

◆ **Wet Mix** or **Dry Mix**: These settings control the percentage of the output that is modified by the effect. At 100 percent wet, the entire signal is changed by the effect; at 100 percent dry, none of the signal is modified by the effect. The sliders are ganged, meaning that when you move one, the other moves automatically, so the total of the two is always 100 percent (**Figure 9.33**).

◆ **Tail**: Some effects (notably delays and reverbs) create additional audio that needs to be tacked on to the end of the processed selection or event. If you select the Tail check box, Cubase will make the event longer to allow the effect to die away as it is designed. The slider controls the amount of audio added to the processed event or selection, in milliseconds.

continues on next page

♦ **Pre-CrossFade**: Selecting this option mixes the effect-altered signal with the dry signal. The slider determines how long the crossfade lasts.

♦ **Post-CrossFade**: If you select this option, the plug-in will be faded out before the end of the selection or event. The slider sets the duration of the crossfade.

✔ Tip

■ Keep in mind that on a Windows machine, DirectX plug-in effects are used in exactly the same way as VST effects.

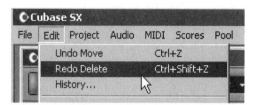

Figure 9.34 Undo and Redo options on the Edit menu of Cubase; the program keeps all edits since the last time the project was opened.

Removing Audio Processing

Sometimes you will want to remove an effect after processing your audio. Cubase has a powerful set of tools for undoing changes made to a project or file. Some undo features are global, but Cubase also includes some more specialized tools for managing changes made in audio processing. Of course, the most recent action can always be undone by pressing Control-Z (Windows) or Command-Z (Macintosh). However, Cubase also keeps a list of every edit made to a project, and you can continue to undo actions all the way to the state of the project when it was opened. You can also choose from the Edit menu to undo and redo changes to a project (**Figure 9.34**).

Although many audio applications have this level of undo and redo at the project level, Cubase's specialized tools for modifying and undoing audio processes are pretty amazing. It's possible to remove, reorder, and modify all processing done to an audio event or part. For example, you can remove only one process after a series of modifications have been made to an event. You can decide later in a project that you would rather have a slower chorus sound, or less delay, or stronger compression. These changes, amazingly, can be made at any time, even after a project has been saved. You have complete control over the history of processed audio in Cubase.

To remove audio processing from an event:

1. Use the Arrow tool to select the event.

2. Right-click (Windows) or Command-click (Mac OS) and select Audio > Offline Process History from the context menu.

3. The Offline Process History dialog box lists every process that has been applied to a file (**Figure 9.35**).

   In this example, the first process, Fade In, is selected.

4. Select the process you want to delete and click the Remove button.

   A dialog box opens asking for confirmation to remove the process (**Figure 9.36**).

5. Click Remove to delete the process.

   The event will be processed again and placed in the Project window with the new version.

Figure 9.35 This history list shows all processes that have been performed on an event.

Figure 9.36 Cubase prompts you before making changes.

Figure 9.37 The Phaser will be edited, so it is selected in the list.

Figure 9.38 When you choose to make changes to a process, the original editor will open.

Modifying Effects on Processed Audio

Just as you can undo effects that you've applied to your audio, you can modify a process that you've applied to an event or range. For example, you might notice—after processing—that a Phaser effect is too pronounced. You can edit this effect, even at this point, by using Offline Process History.

To change the processing settings for an event or range:

1. Use the Arrow tool to select the event that you want to change.

2. Right-click (Windows) or Control-click (Mac OS) and select Audio > Offline Process History from the context menu.

3. When the Offline Process History dialog box opens, select the process that you want to edit (**Figure 9.37**). Then click the Modify button.

   The editor for that process opens, displaying the same settings used when the audio was processed (**Figure 9.38**).

4. Change the parameters as you like and then click the Process button.

   Cubase reprocesses the audio with the new settings (status bars will show the progress) and replaces the event in the Project window.

5. Click the Close button to dismiss the Offline Process History window.

Replacing One Process with Another

Cubase offers so much flexibility in its audio processing that you can even replace one process with another. For example, you might process a file using a simple delay plug-in, but later you decide that a more complex delay would be better. Making this swap is not only possible, but quite easy, using the Offline Process History window.

To replace processing already performed on an event:

1. Use the Arrow tool to select the event that you want to change.

2. Right-click (Windows) or Control-click (Mac OS) and select Audio > Offline Process History from the context menu.

3. In the Offline Process History dialog box, select the process you want to replace (**Figure 9.39**).

4. Click the pull-down menu in the right panel to select a new process or plug-in to replace the original process. For example, as shown here, choose Plug-ins > Delay > ModDelay (**Figure 9.40**).

   A dialog box opens to confirm that you really want to replace the processing.

5. Click Replace. The editor for the new process or plug-in opens in a new window (**Figure 9.41**).

6. Change the parameters for that plug-in as you wish.

7. Click the Process button.

   The event is reprocessed, as indicated by the activity in the status bars. When processing is complete, you are returned to the Offline Process History window.

8. Click Close to dismiss this window and return to the Project window.

REPLACING ONE PROCESS WITH ANOTHER

Figure 9.39 The Double Delay effect will be replaced with a Mod Delay effect.

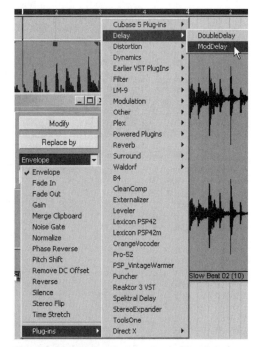

Figure 9.40 Selecting the new plug-in (Mod Delay) to use in place of the original delay

Figure 9.41 The editor for the replacement plug-in

The Sample Editor

It has been said more than once in this book that Cubase lets you do as much as possible from the Project window. Most of your audio editing and processing can be done in the Project window. This window offers the widest view of audio, MIDI, and automation in a project, and this comprehensive view is preferred for many operations.

However, Cubase has always included a Sample editor (**Figure 9.42**), and there are still compelling reasons to use it. The Sample editor provides a large-scale, high-resolution view of a single audio file, which makes sample-level editing easy—for example, you can easily create regions in the Sample editor. Also, the Sample editor is the only place where you can use the Draw tool to manually change the actual audio data.

By default, the Sample editor opens to the full size of the Cubase screen. It's designed to give the most complete, high-resolution look possible for a single piece of mono or stereo audio. For the illustrations that follow, I resized the editor smaller to show more in the illustrations. You should *not* do the same, however; leave the Sample editor windows big and proud.

Figure 9.42 The Sample editor

Zooming in the Sample Editor

The Sample editor has a Zoom tool that works just like the Zoom tool in the Project window. You can also click the ruler and drag vertically to zoom in or out and then navigate in your sample with more precision by using the thumbnail display at the top of the Sample editor's window.

To select a view in the waveform display:

1. Position the pointer over the top half of the thumbnail display at the top of the Sample editor.

    Regardless of the tool that you've selected, the pointer will be an arrow (**Figure 9.43**).

2. Drag over the section of the audio that you want to see in detail in the waveform display (**Figure 9.44**).

    After you release the mouse, just that section will be visible in the waveform display (**Figure 9.45**).

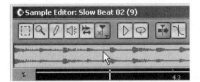

Figure 9.43 When positioned over the top half of the thumbnail display, the pointer will be an arrow.

Figure 9.44 Drag over the part of the event that you want to see in the Waveform display.

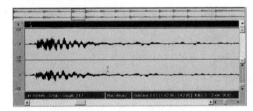

Figure 9.45 The waveform display now shows only the section selected in the thumbnail display.

Figure 9.46 The pointer turns into a double-headed arrow when it is over the bottom half of the thumbnail display.

Figure 9.47 Resizing the selection in the thumbnail display by dragging the border

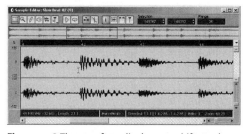

Figure 9.48 The waveform display now shifts to show the newly selected area.

To resize your view in the waveform display:

1. To resize the selected region, position the Pointer over the bottom half of the thumbnail display.

   Regardless of what tool is selected, the Pointer will turn into a pair of opposing arrows (**Figure 9.46**).

2. Drag anywhere on the thumbnail display to resize the selected area (**Figure 9.47**).

   The newly selected area will appear in the waveform display (**Figure 9.48**).

✔ Tip

- The Sample editor is particularly easy to navigate because it shows a great deal of detail for a single piece of audio. However, other windows also have thumbnail displays, including the Project window.

Using Scrub in the Sample Editor

Scrubbing is a term that comes from the era when editing was done with analog tape. To find the correct place for an edit, tape was manually shuttled back and forth—or scrubbed—over the tape head. Scrubbing is a very intuitive way to find exact locations for edit actions, and Cubase has an excellent digital scrub system built into the Sample editor.

To navigate audio by scrubbing:

1. In the Sample editor, click the Scrub tool on the toolbar (**Figure 9.49**).

2. Click the waveform display near the section you want to hear (**Figure 9.50**) and drag to the left or right.

   The cursor will catch up to the pointer, playing the audio as it moves (**Figure 9.51**).

   Moving the pointer to the left and right and more quickly or more slowly plays the audio forward, backward, and at varying pitches. This is precisely the way real scrubbing works.

✔ Tip

- If you really dig the Scrub tool, there is also one in the Project window. You can use it in the same way if you wish.

Figure 9.49 Clicking the Scrub tool to select it

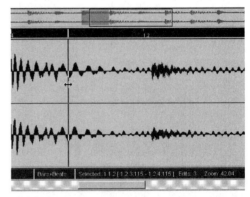

Figure 9.50 Moving the pointer over the area that is to be played

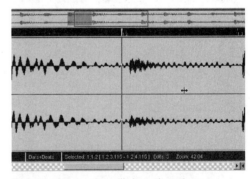

Figure 9.51 The cursor will chase the pointer, scrubbing the audio at different speeds.

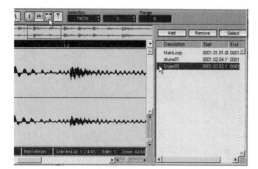

Figure 9.52 Click the Show Regions button (under the pointer) to display a list of regions on the right.

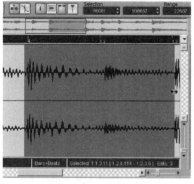

Figure 9.53 A selection in the waveform display, which will be converted to a region

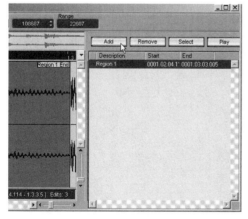

Figure 9.54 Click the Add button to create a new region from the selection.

Creating Regions with the Sample Editor

One of the primary uses of the Sample editor is in creating, editing, and otherwise working with regions. A region is simply a section of an audio clip. Regions were discussed in Chapter 4 as they related to cycle recording of audio. One way to cycle record is to record a single clip but have each pass of the loop create a new region. Regions can be converted to events and also exported as discrete audio files if you wish.

To create a region:

1. On the toolbar in the Sample editor, click the Show Regions button (**Figure 9.52**).

2. Use the Range Selection tool to select part of the clip in the waveform display (**Figure 9.53**).

3. In the Regions display, click the Add button.

   This converts your selection to a new region (**Figure 9.54**).

✔ Tip

■ If you do much intense editing with regions, the list of regions can grow fast and become confusing. If you name your regions, they'll be much easier to locate and manage. Click a region in the list in the Description column and then give it a useful name.

Creating an Event from a Region

You can easily drop regions into the Project window to create new events. This is a very simple way to grab the right take from within a larger clip that was cycle recorded, or to place single sounds, samples, or hits somewhere in a project. Any region in the Regions list can be moved into the project window as an event.

To convert a region to an event:

1. Move the pointer to the Regions list.

   Regardless of the tool being used in the Sample editor, if you move the pointer to the Regions list, it will turn into an arrow.

2. Click to the left of the region name (**Figure 9.55**) and drag over the Events display in the Project window.

   In the Project window, a blue outline shows where the event will be created if the region is dropped at the current mouse position (**Figure 9.56**).

3. Release the mouse to create the event in that location.

   The new event appears in the Project window (**Figure 9.57**).

✔ Tip

- The Snap value is important when you drop a region in the Project window. You may need to adjust your Snap value to get your newly converted event into the right location.

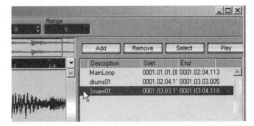

Figure 9.55 You must click to the far left of the region name for this process to work.

Figure 9.56 Dragging over the Project window; the outline and numeric display show where the region will be dropped.

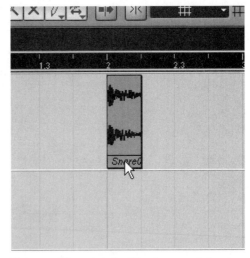

Figure 9.57 The event after it has been created and placed in the Project window

Additional Processing Functions

Envelope: Functions similar to a fade-in or fade-out, but changing the envelope of an event allows you to draw in a volume curve for the entire event, not just the beginning or end. Use an envelope for breakpoint editing when a fade-in or fade-out is not precise enough.

Fade-In: Identical in sound and function to the fade described in Chapter 8. The difference is that the fade will be applied to the event offline, and not as a real-time playback parameter.

Fade-Out: The flip side of a fade-in.

Gain: Processes an event to change the overall level of the entire event.

Merge Clipboard: Mixes audio that was copied to the clipboard (usually from the Sample editor) with the selected event and creates a new event using both parts.

Noise Gate: Allows you to set a level below which Cubase will mute the part. Often used as a noise-reduction tool.

Normalize: Raises the level of the audio in an event to the highest level possible with no clipping.

Phase Reverse: Swaps the phase of the audio, so that where the waveform goes up, it will instead go down. Sometimes when an instrument is recorded with more than one microphone, one part may cancel out another, and reversing the phase of one of the tracks sometimes helps fix this problem.

Pitch Shift: Changes the pitch of audio and is edited in the same panel as the Time Stretch process.

continues on next page

ADDITIONAL PROCESSING FUNCTIONS

Remove DC Offset: In some circumstances, audio will be recorded incorrectly with too large a DC current. If this happens, the waveform will not look centered, and clicks and pops will often occur when events are snipped. Using this process fixes these problems.

Reverse: Changes the audio so that it plays backward.

Silence: Reduces the output of the selected event or selection in an event to zero. It has the same result as muting the audio, but it works as a process.

Stereo Flip: Swaps the left and right channels in an audio file.

Time Stretch: Changes the duration of an audio file using the same tools as for pitch shifting.

ADDITIONAL PROCESSING FUNCTIONS

10

EDITING MIDI

MIDI is more than just notes—it's a powerful tool that's fantastic for experimentation, because MIDI data is almost infinitely editable. After you record or enter MIDI, you can instantly change the pitch, timing, key, duration, and nearly any other parameter, with no loss in quality. And you can also use MIDI to control effects processors, synthesizers, samplers, and, in some instances, mixers or even lights.

Cubase includes very advanced tools for editing and transforming MIDI once it has been recorded. In this chapter, you will learn some of the differences between editing audio and editing MIDI. You will learn much more about the Key editor, including how to modify MIDI notes and how to view and modify MIDI continuous controller (CC) data. You will learn about quantizing, which you can use to make detailed and exacting edits to the timing of a MIDI part. At the end of this chapter, you will learn to use the List editor, which offers an extremely detailed look at all MIDI data in a project and enables precision editing of MIDI.

Audio Editing Versus MIDI Editing

Because audio and MIDI are different, you edit them in different ways. When you work with audio, you can edit at the level of a single sample. You can modify the timbre of a sound—its equalization, for example—through processing. In contrast, when you edit MIDI, you must use the sampler or synth triggered by the MIDI track to make changes to the EQ of a sound.

One of the major differences between editing MIDI and editing audio in Cubase is that you can do much less MIDI editing in the Project window. When you edit audio, you can see and edit both events and parts directly in the Project window. With MIDI, the events are the notes and data, and these cannot be edited in the Project window. For example, you cannot use the Draw tool to add a MIDI note to a part in the Project window—the tool is supposed to be used in the MIDI editors. If you drag with the Draw tool in the Project window, you'll simply create a new part (**Figure 10.1**). So while you'll learn some MIDI editing tasks that you can do in the Project window, most of this chapter concentrates on the MIDI editors.

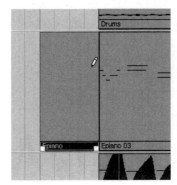

Figure 10.1 You cannot use the Draw tool in the Project window to create or change MIDI notes. You can use it only to create new MIDI parts.

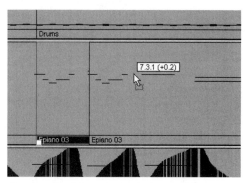

Figure 10.2 A MIDI part as it is being moved: The (+0.2) indicates that the part has been moved two beats forward.

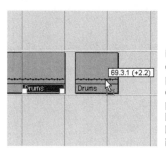

Figure 10.3 A different MIDI part is being copied. At this point it is two bars and two beats forward in time.

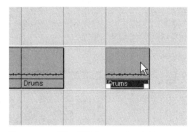

Figure 10.4 The MIDI part after it has been copied

✔ Tip

- You can also move or copy multiple parts simply by holding down the Shift key and selecting more than one part before making the edit.

Moving and Copying MIDI Parts

You can perform a few large-scale editing operations in the Project window, such as moving and copying MIDI parts. You perform these operations essentially the same way as you perform them for audio parts.

To move a MIDI part:

1. Select the Arrow tool.

2. Click the part that you want to move and drag it.

   As you drag, the current location of the part will be displayed next to the pointer, along with the distance that the part has been moved (**Figure 10.2**). This information tells you exactly where a part will wind up as it is moved.

3. When the part is where you want it, release the mouse.

✔ Tip

- Snap matters when moving parts; if it's on, parts will move only in the increments set in the Snap menu. In this example, Snap is on and set to Beat.

To copy a MIDI part:

1. Select the Arrow tool.

2. Turn Snap on or off.

   Snap also matters when copying parts.

3. While holding down Alt (Windows) or Option (Mac), click the part you want to copy and drag to the place where you want the part pasted (**Figure 10.3**).

4. Release the mouse.

   The copy will be at its new location in the Project window (**Figure 10.4**).

Muting and Splitting MIDI Parts

The actions used to mute and split MIDI parts are similar to those used for working with audio parts.

To mute a MIDI part:

1. Select the Mute tool from the toolbar or the context menu (Right-click Windows, Control-click Mac OS).

   The pointer will change into an X to indicate that the tool has been selected.

2. Click the part or parts you want to mute. The muted parts will become dimmed (**Figure 10.5**).

3. To unmute a part, click it again.

To split a MIDI part:

1. Select the Split tool from the context menu.

2. Turn Snap on to make a tempo–restricted split or turn it off to split anywhere in the part.

3. Position the Split (scissors) tool at the location where you want to make the split.

   You'll see a thin line across the part and a numerical display that shows where the split will be made (**Figure 10.6**).

4. Click the mouse to split the MIDI part into two new parts (**Figure 10.7**).

✔ Tip

■ If a MIDI note spans a part that is split in two, only the section of the note in the first part will play. In other words, the note will not be triggered again in the second part. Figure 10.7 shows how the two lines in the part almost disappear when the part is split in half.

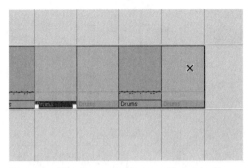

Figure 10.5 The dimmed parts are muted and will not play.

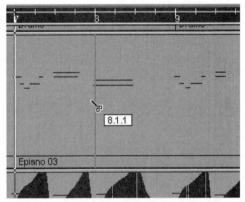

Figure 10.6 The thin vertical line on the MIDI part is a guide to where the part will be snipped.

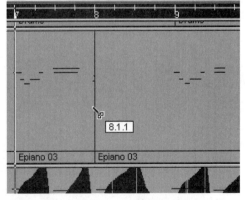

Figure 10.7 After the mouse is clicked, two piano parts are created from the original part. The notes that span the split, however, will not be triggered in the second part.

Figure 10.8 Use this button to show and hide the Track inspector.

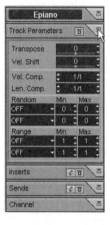

Figure 10.9 The Track Parameters tab has been selected for a MIDI track.

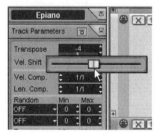

Figure 10.10 This slider controls transposition for the entire track. All notes on the track will be transposed by the amount set here in the Track inspector.

Transposing a MIDI Track with the Inspector

The MIDI Track inspector was introduced in Chapter 5, "Recording MIDI." The Track inspector can be used for more than just selecting MIDI inputs and outputs, however, because it offers control over a number of parameters, such as volume, pan, and timing offset. The inspector for a MIDI track also offers an option to transpose all notes on the track by a specified amount. This can be very useful when a song written in one key later needs to be changed to another key to make it easier for a performer to work with. Transposing can also come in handy to match a pitched audio sample that isn't in the key of the song.

To transpose a MIDI track using the Track inspector:

1. If the Track inspector is not visible, open it by clicking the Show Inspector button on the Project window toolbar (**Figure 10.8**).

2. Click a MIDI track. The Inspector for a MIDI track has five tabs that show different information about the track. Click the Track Parameters tab to display it (**Figure 10.9**).

3. On the Track Parameters tab, select Transpose. Then do one of the following:
   - ▲ Click the up and down arrows to transpose up or down in increments of one semitone.
   - ▲ Click the numeric value in the Transpose field and enter a new value directly.
   - ▲ Click below the number to open a slider (**Figure 10.10**) to change the amount of transposition.

✔ Tips

- Remember that, unlike with audio notes, you can change the pitch and tempo of MIDI notes with no loss of quality.

- The Track inspector will change the pitch of all notes and parts on the entire track. If you want to transpose only one part, you should use a MIDI editor.

Dissolving One Part into Multiple Parts

You can also use the Project window to break a MIDI part into multiple parts. This capability comes in handy in two situations. First, some MIDI files that play back more than one instrument sound have each instrument assigned to its own channel: channel 1 will play a piano sound, channel 2 will play a bass sound, and so on. In this case, it is easier to place a part for each instrument on its own track so you can assign sounds to each track individually and so the MIDI file will play back correctly. Second, when you're working with drum parts, it is often convenient to have each drum on its own track. Even if the tracks trigger the same instrument, it's great to have individual control over the volume and pan of the kick, snare, hi-hat, and other drums.

The following example shows how to dissolve a drumbeat (**Figure 10.11**) into multiple parts: one for each drum sound and with each part on its own track.

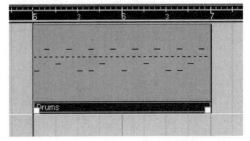

Figure 10.11 This drum part uses only four notes: one for each drum sound that is triggered.

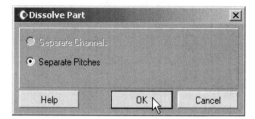

Figure 10.12 In the Dissolve Part dialog box, specify how the part should be dissolved. Here, the part will be dissolved by note.

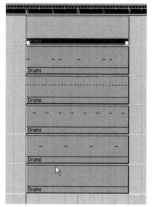

Figure 10.13 After the part is broken into multiple parts, each is visible in the Project window, and the original is muted.

To dissolve a MIDI part:

1. Right-click (Windows) or Control-click (Mac OS) the part you want to dissolve; in the context menu, select MIDI > Dissolve Part.

2. When the Dissolve Part dialog box opens, choose whether to dissolve each channel into a part or dissolve each pitch into a part. Multitimbral MIDI files will usually be dissolved with the channel options; dissolving a drum part to individual drum hits will normally use the pitch option. Then click OK.

   In **Figure 10.12**, only the Pitch option is available because the MIDI part has only one channel. Cubase will extract all of the notes of each pitch and create a new MIDI part for each one. It will also mute the MIDI part that was dissolved (**Figure 10.13**).

Editing Multiple Parts in the Key Editor

The Key editor (**Figure 10.14**) is the default editor that opens when you double-click a MIDI file in the Project window. You can also access any of the editors by selecting MIDI from the context menu that opens from a MIDI part.

Often it is useful to see more than one part at a time in the Key editor. For example, having both a keyboard and a drum part open in the same editor makes it easy to see when notes might be getting in the way of each other. The following task shows how to open three MIDI parts in the Key editor.

To view multiple parts in the Key editor:

1. In the Project window, hold down the Shift key and click all parts that you want opened in the Key editor.

   Holding the Shift key allows you to select multiple, noncontiguous parts.

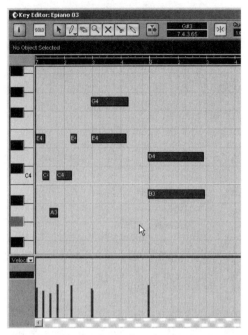

Figure 10.14 The MIDI Key editor

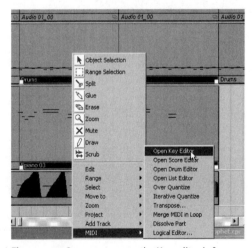

Figure 10.15 One way to open the Key editor is from the context menu.

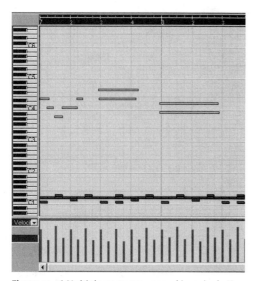

Figure 10.16 Multiple parts are opened in a single Key editor. The active part is highlighted (the darker notes near the bottom of this illustration).

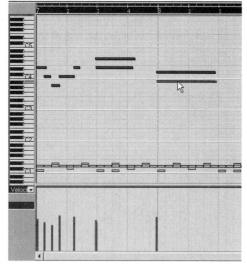

Figure 10.17 Clicking a MIDI note from another part makes it active, and the velocity stalks in the Controller lane make this obvious.

2. Double-click one of the selected parts, or right-click (Windows) or Control-click (Mac OS) and select MIDI > Open Key Editor (**Figure 10.15**, previous page).

The MIDI Key editor opens, but only some of the notes will be highlighted (**Figure 10.16**). That's because although you can view MIDI from more than one part in the editor, you can edit MIDI from only one part at a time. In Figure 10.16, the solid notes are the ones that can be edited. If you click one of the notes in a different part, then those notes become active and can be edited (**Figure 10.17**).

More About the Key Editor

You will often use the Key editor to edit MIDI notes and continuous controller data because it offers many more editing options than does the Project window, and it is much more intuitive and musical than the List editor. However, if you're working with drum parts, you're likely to prefer the Drum editor.

However, because this section is about what you can do in the Key editor, you might want to quickly review Chapter 6, "Entering MIDI Manually," to refresh your memory of such elements as the Note display, the Controller lane, and the tools on the Key editor toolbar.

Copying Notes in the Key Editor

You can use the Key editor to copy a MIDI note or a group of notes. The following task shows you how to copy all notes in one measure to the next measure and then use Snap to drop the copied notes precisely at the start of the next measure.

To copy MIDI notes:

1. Turn on Snap and set the Quantize value to a 1/4 note or so, to make the move easier.

2. Select the Arrow tool if it is not already selected and drag over the notes that you want copied (**Figure 10.18**).

3. With the notes selected, hold down Alt (Windows) or Option (Mac OS) and click one of the selected notes.

4. Drag the mouse to where you want to copy the notes.

   A numeric display will show how far you have moved the copy from the original (**Figure 10.19**).

5. When the copied notes are where you want them, release the mouse and then the Alt or Option key.

✔ Tips

- If you want to copy notes, but restrict movement to the vertical or horizontal axis, hold down Ctrl-Shift-Alt (Windows) or Command-Shift-Option (Mac OS). This allows you to copy the notes to a new song position but forces the pitch to remain the same. If you copy notes on the vertical axis using this technique, the notes will stay at the same song position but change pitch.

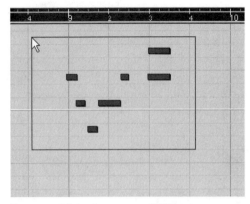

Figure 10.18 Selecting a group of MIDI notes

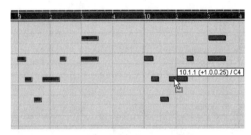

Figure 10.19 Copying the notes: The original notes are outlined, and the copied notes are solid bars. Note that Snap is on while the notes are copied.

- If you accidentally release the Alt or Option key before releasing the mouse, you will move the notes instead of copying them. Just undo the change and try again.

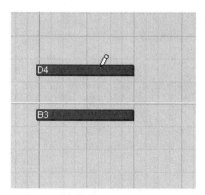

Figure 10.20 The D4 note is about to be changed with the Draw tool.

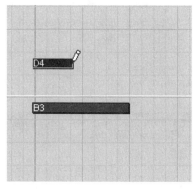

Figure 10.21 Clicking the note with the Draw allows it to be resized.

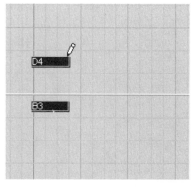

Figure 10.22 If both notes are selected, resizing actions resize both notes simultaneously.

Changing the Duration of MIDI Notes

A very common MIDI operation is changing the duration of a note. Notes can be easily lengthened or shortened by using the Draw tool in the Key editor.

To change the duration of a MIDI note:

1. Turn off Snap and select the Draw tool. The pointer will change to a pencil.

2. Move the pointer over the note that you want to change (**Figure 10.20**) and drag until the note is the duration that you want (**Figure 10.21**).

✔ Tips

- Multiple notes can also be changed using the Draw tool. In the illustration, one of two notes was changed, but if both notes were selected in this example, both notes would have their duration modified. The result would look like **Figure 10.22**.

- You can also change the starting point of a note using the Draw tool. Hold down Ctrl (Windows) or Command (Mac OS), and the Draw tool will change the starting point of the note instead of the ending point of the note without changing the note's duration.

Editing Notes with Identical Pitch

In many situations, you'll need to edit all notes of a particular pitch. If a phrase was difficult to play, the resulting part may contain multiple incorrect notes with the same pitch. A part may also contain a good performance, but you might decide that a particular chord sounds better without one of the notes.

If you are creating drum parts, each pitch plays a different sound; a C note might play a snare drum, and a C# note might play a snare drum with a hi-hat. Editing all notes on one pitch is very handy in this situation, because when you change the note, you will change the drum sound that is triggered. The following task shows you how to do precisely that: move the notes triggering one drum sound so that they trigger another drum sound.

To change all notes of the same pitch:

1. In the Key editor, select the Arrow tool and double-click a drum part to open it.

2. Hold down Ctrl (Windows) or Command (Mac OS) and click the note that you want to select on the keyboard at the left of the editor window (**Figure 10.23**).

   This selects all of the notes with that pitch in the Key editor window.

3. Keeping the notes selected, press the Up Arrow key on the keyboard twice.

   This transposes the selected notes up two semitones and constrains them to only vertical movement (**Figure 10.24**).

✔ Tips

■ While multiple notes are selected, you can also edit other parameters, such as note length. **Figure 10.25** shows the same MIDI part after changing length with multiple notes selected.

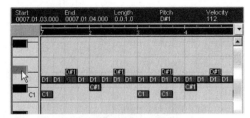

Figure 10.23 Clicking the keyboard with Ctrl or Command held down will select all notes in the editor with that pitch.

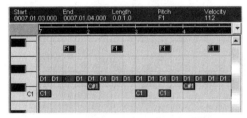

Figure 10.24 Simply pressing the up arrow key twice moves these notes to new pitches.

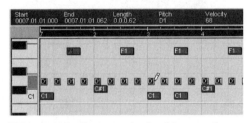

Figure 10.25 Another example of resizing more than one note at a time: All of the D1 notes were selected and then resized together.

■ You can also use the mouse to drag the selected notes. Just remember that Snap matters when you make a change in this way, and that holding down the Ctrl or Command key allows you to move the notes vertically (pitch) without changing their horizontal (song position) location.

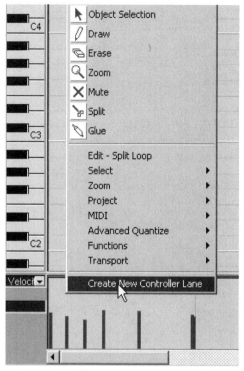

Figure 10.26 This context menu option opens a new Controller lane.

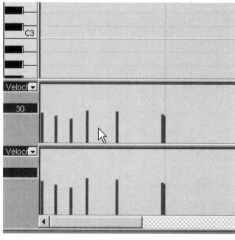

Figure 10.27 The new Controller lane, in this case showing the same parameter a second time

Viewing Continuous Controller Lanes

Some basic continuous controller (CC) concepts were introduced in Chapter 6, "Entering MIDI Manually." We'll cover some of the more advanced options and tools for CC editing in the next few pages, but there is more to CC editing than can be covered here. For more information about continuous controller data and how to edit it, see the section about the Key editor in Chapter 21, "The MIDI Editors," in the electronic documentation that came with Cubase.

One of the first things you should know about editing CC data is that you can view more than one Controller lane in the Key editor at the same time. Two of the MIDI values most commonly edited in the Key editor are Velocity and Pan. Here is how to see them both simultaneously.

To see multiple Controller lanes in the Key editor:

1. Right-click (Windows) or Control-click (Mac OS) and select Create New Controller Lane (**Figure 10.26**).

   A new Controller lane is created, and the Key editor will look something like **Figure 10.27**. The precise sizes and parameters of the two lanes may be different.

   continues on next page

2. Click the pop-up menu at the left of the Controller lane.

You use this menu to select the CC displayed in that particular lane. Most likely, your Controller lane displays the default parameter, which is Velocity.

3. From the pop-up menu, select Pan as the visible parameter in the new lane (**Figure 10.28**).

Each Controller lane now displays a distinct parameter that you can edit and modify.

✔ Tip

■ Controller lanes can be resized by moving the borders between lanes up and down, just as tracks can be resized in the track list.

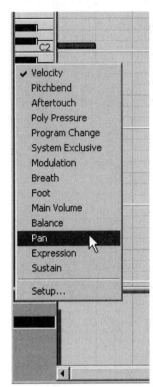

Figure 10.28
Selecting a different parameter to be viewed in the new Controller lane—in this case, Pan

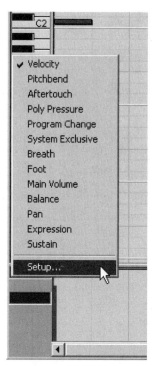

Figure 10.29
Choose Setup to open the dialog box and customize the list of CCs that can be viewed in Controller lanes.

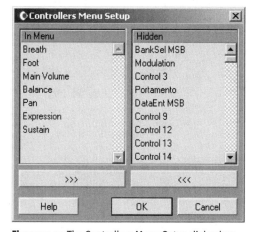

Figure 10.30 The Controllers Menu Setup dialog box

Viewing Any CC Message

The menu in Figure 10.28 shows only some of the more common CC messages that you can create and edit in Cubase. In fact, there are 128 CC messages, and there are situations in which you might want to use any one of them.

One of the most commonly used parameters is Modulation. Nearly every keyboard synth made, and most other MIDI controllers, have two wheel controllers on them somewhere. One is called the pitchbend wheel and is used to bend the pitch of the notes being produced. The other, called the modulation wheel—or mod wheel—sends CC data that is usually connected to one or more parameters on the presets in the keyboard. The mod wheel is invaluable for controlling both hardware synths and VST instruments because almost every keyboard has this tactile controller. The following example demonstrates how to show modulation data in a Controller lane in the Key editor.

To view additional CC messages:

1. Click the pop-up menu at the left of the Controller lane and select Setup (**Figure 10.29**).

   The Controllers Menu Setup dialog box opens (**Figure 10.30**). The CCs on the left side of the pane, in the In Menu list, are available in the pop-up menu for the Controller lanes in the Key editor. The CCs in the right half of the dialog box, in the Hidden list, are not on that menu.

2. Click one of the CCs in the Hidden list. Choose Modulation if it's there.

continues on next page

3. Below the Hidden list is a button marked <<<. With a CC selected, click that button to move the CC to the In Menu list (**Figure 10.31**).

4. In the Controllers Menu Setup panel, click OK to save the change and close the panel.

Now when you click the pop-up menu for a Controller lane, Modulation will be available for viewing in the Controller lane (**Figure 10.32**).

✔ Tip

■ If you want to get an idea of just how many parameters MIDI can control, take a look at all of the available options in the Controllers Menu Setup panel. You can use all of these normally hidden parameters, and there are many general CC messages that you can use for nearly anything (**Figure 10.33**). Your MIDI devices and MIDI-aware effects should come with lists indicating what CC message controls what parameter, and Cubase gives you graphic control over those parameters.

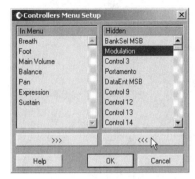

Figure 10.31 Clicking the button at the bottom of the Hidden list will add the Modulation CC to those available in the Controller lanes.

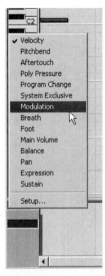

Figure 10.32 Selecting the newly added Modulation parameter for a Controller lane

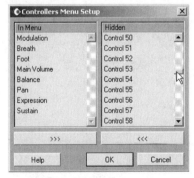

Figure 10.33 A few of the generic CCs: Any CC can be viewed in a Controller lane.

Creating Tempo-Based CC Data

One of the really fun musical things that you can do with CC data in Cubase is creating tempo-based effects with MIDI instruments and MIDI-addressable effects processors. Nearly all MIDI instruments have most of their internal parameters mapped to one CC or another, and you can do a lot of creative things by changing these parameters with CC messages synced to the current tempo of the project. The Cubase Draw tool has multiple modes that make creating such tempo-based data very simple.

It's up to you which parameter you want to affect, but some common ones are the cut-off frequency on a synth filter, the amount of feedback on a delay unit, and the amount of reverb applied from an effects processor. To find out which CC message changes what parameter, you need to consult the documentation that came with your MIDI device.

In the following task, you create tempo-based CC data using the Cubase Snap settings and drawing tools. Nearly all MIDI devices, and many VST instruments, map something important to the Modulation CC message, so this next task is a good place to start.

To create tempo-based CC data:

1. On the toolbar, click the Draw tool. In the tool-selection menu that opens, select Triangle (**Figure 10.34**).

2. Turn on Snap, set Quantize to 1/4 or 1/2 note, and set Length Quantize to 1/64 note.

3. Set the Controller lane to Modulation and position the mouse pointer in or near the Controller lane.

   The pointer will change shape to show that it is in Triangle mode (**Figure 10.35**).

4. Drag to the right and slightly down or up.

   A line with a triangle shape shows the values that will be created for the CC message (**Figure 10.36**).

5. Release the mouse button when you have a curve that looks right. You can also play back the MIDI part to hear the change the CC data creates in the MIDI device and adjust the curve audibly and in real time.

   The new CC data is perfectly synced to the tempo, and it's visible in the Controller lane (**Figure 10.37**).

Figure 10.34 The Draw tool has more than one mode. The Triangle mode allows you to draw triangle-shaped curves in the Controller lanes.

Figure 10.35 In Triangle mode, the pointer changes to this shape in a Controller lane.

Figure 10.36 Drawing a curve in Triangle mode

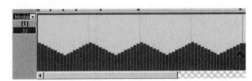

Figure 10.37 After you draw the curve, Cubase enters these values automatically.

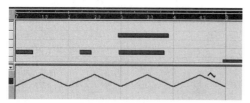

Figure 10.38 With Quantize set to 1/4, one measure will have four triangles drawn in it.

Figure 10.39 This triangle was drawn with Quantize set to 1/1 and Length Quantize set to 1/16.

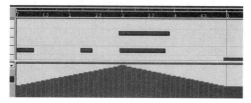

Figure 10.40 With Length Quantize set to 1/128, a much smoother curve is drawn.

✔ Tip

- If you are a bit of a synth geek, you may notice that these edits mimic a triangle-wave low-frequency oscillator (LFO). Indeed; using these drawing tools to create CC messages is very much like using an LFO on a synth.

About Snap and CC Editing

You don't have to turn on Snap to create every type of CC data, but you must turn it on if you want to create CC data using the project tempo as a reference. Once Snap is on, each quantize setting—which snaps data to a particular beat or subdivision of a beat—changes the way CC data is created and visually displayed by the curves in the Controller lanes. Smaller Snap settings will create more finely grained curves, which will usually sound smoother when sent to a MIDI device, though they will also create a lot more MIDI data.

Quantize controls the length of the curve. If you are drawing a triangle wave, the Quantize setting determines the number of triangle shapes that are drawn in each measure. **Figure 10.38** shows one measure being drawn with the triangle set to 1/4-note quantize. One triangle is created for each quarter note.

Length Quantize controls the density of the CC events that are created. Shorter note values create more finely grained CC data. For example, consider **Figure 10.39** and **Figure 10.40**, which use the Triangle tool again. To make things clear, the Quantize setting is 1/1, or a whole note, so only one triangle is drawn for the whole measure. In Figure 10.39, Length Quantize is set to 1/16, and in Figure 10.40, Length Quantize is set to 1/128. The higher Length Quantize value in Figure 10.40 creates 128 steps of MIDI data, while in Figure 10.39 the same overall change in MIDI value is accomplished with only 16 steps. It's not hard to see that the CC data in Figure 10.40 has a much smoother curve, and under most circumstances the change will be audibly smoother.

Other Curves for CC Messages

The Draw tool has more than one option for creating MIDI CC messages. Here is a short explanation of the other Draw tool modes and their use for creating tempo-based CC data.

Draw (pencil): Use this tool to create freehand curves; you can create pretty much any shape you want with the tool in Draw mode. With Snap off, you can create very fine curves (**Figure 10.41**).

Paint: When working with CC messages, Paint is identical to Draw.

Line: Use this tool to create CC data as if it were drawn with a ruler (**Figure 10.42**). Just like the Draw tool, with Snap off, the Line tool creates a lot of finely grained MIDI data.

Parabola: Use this tool to create smooth curves of MIDI data as in **Figure 10.43**. If Snap is on, the CC data curve ends on a particular beat.

Sine: Sine creates a smooth, curved wave that can be used easily for tempo-based effects.

Triangle: This tool creates the triangle or sawtooth waveform shown in Figure 10.37.

Square: Use this tool to create jagged values (**Figure 10.44**) with no curve as they rise and fall. The Snap and Quantize settings determine the number of teeth created per measure.

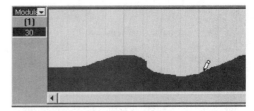

Figure 10.41 The freehand Pencil tool

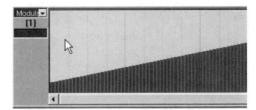

Figure 10.42 The result of using the Line tool

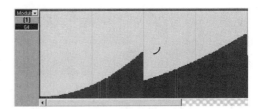

Figure 10.43 You can use the Parabola tool to draw curves.

Figure 10.44 Controller data drawn by the Square tool

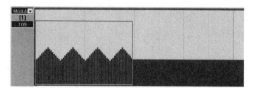

Figure 10.45 Selecting CC data to be copied

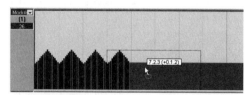

Figure 10.46 The thin outline shows that the copy is taking place.

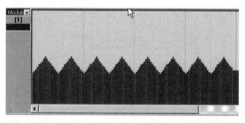

Figure 10.47 After the copy operation is completed

Deleting, Moving, and Copying CC Messages

You can move CC data freely within a project or within a part. You can delete CC events with the Eraser tool, select them with the Arrow tool, and move them with the standard Cut, Copy, and Paste commands. The following task describes how to perform one of the more complex operations: copying a triangle curve to a new location.

To copy CC data in a Controller lane:

1. Using the Arrow tool, draw a box around the CC messages that you want to copy (**Figure 10.45**).

2. Turn on Snap.

   Snap can be on or off, but turning Snap on makes it easier to copy CC data to a new measure or beat.

3. Hold down Alt (Windows) or Option (Mac OS) and click the selected CC data.

4. Drag the CC data to the new location.

   An outline shows you where the data is being moved (**Figure 10.46**).

5. Release the mouse when the copy is where you want it.

   The CC data is copied to the new location in the Controller lane, and the original CC data remains in its original location (**Figure 10.47**).

DELETING, MOVING, AND COPYING CC MESSAGES

Quantizing

In previous sections of this book, the term *quantize* referred to the Quantize setting or Length Quantize setting of Snap. These settings determine the influence of Snap on the precise movement or copying of MIDI data.

However, MIDI data can also be quantized—that is, by quantizing MIDI data, you change its timing. The changes can be subtle or dramatic, but whenever a MIDI part or note is quantized, the rhythm changes. The simplest kind of quantizing in Cubase is used to clean up notes so that each note begins at a specific meter division. In other words, each note is moved so that it begins on the nearest eighth, sixteenth, or other user-defined note.

To quantize MIDI notes:

1. Use the Arrow tool to select the notes to be quantized.

2. Set Quantize to the tempo value that you want Cubase to use for placing the MIDI notes.

   In this example, a setting of 1/8 note is used (**Figure 10.48**).

3. Right-click (Windows) or Control-click (Mac OS) and select MIDI > Over Quantize (**Figure 10.49**).

   Cubase moves all selected notes according to the Quantize setting. In this case, all notes will begin on an eighth-note (**Figure 10.50**).

✔ Tip

■ All quantizing can apply either to particular notes selected in a MIDI editor or to an entire MIDI part or parts. Anything selected when the quantize action is applied will be quantized.

Figure 10.48 Selecting the MIDI notes to be quantized

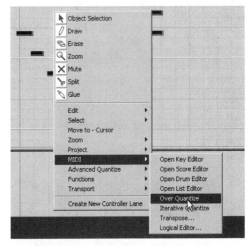

Figure 10.49 This command will quantize the selected notes.

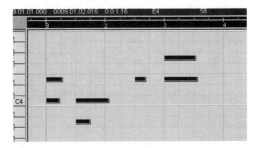

Figure 10.50 After quantizing is applied, each MIDI note starts on an eighth-note.

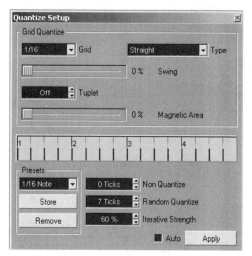

Figure 10.51 The Quantize Setup dialog box

Adjusting the Quantize Grid

Many musicians think that anything quantized is automatically "bad." It is true that quantized MIDI can sound very machinelike and robotic, and depending on the kind of music, that can be very bad. Like most MIDI applications, Cubase has many options for quantizing MIDI that are designed to make the result sound natural and not quantized. In Cubase, most of these options are on the Quantize Setup panel (**Figure 10.51**).

One of the most important options on the Quantize Setup panel is the option to create user-defined grids to use for quantizing. For example, instead of quantizing to straight robotic eighth-notes as in the previous example, you might want robotic sixteenth notes, or you might want to quantize using a sixteenth-note grid but with a swing feel. The following tasks introduce you to the quantizing options available on the Quantize Setup panel.

To customize the quantize grid:

1. Select the notes you want to quantize.

2. From the main Project window menus, select MIDI > Quantize Setup (**Figure 10.52**).

3. In the Quantize Setup dialog box, select 1/8 for the grid setting and Triplet for the Type setting to create an eighth-note triplet grid.

   As the settings are changed for the grid and type, the grid display changes to reflect the current quantize settings (**Figure 10.53**). Compare this grid display to the one in Figure 10.51.

4. To use the setting, click the Apply button; the selected MIDI notes will be quantized using the current grid. To leave the Quantize Setup in its current state without quantizing the selected notes, click the close box in the upper corner of the panel to close the window.

Figure 10.52 The Quantize Setup dialog box is available only from the MIDI menu.

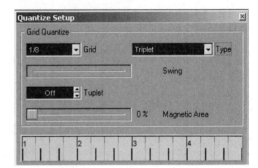

Figure 10.53 The quantize grid has been changed from Figure 10.51 to a triplet grid.

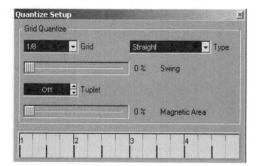

Figure 10.54 The Quantize Setup dialog box starts with a plain eighth-note grid.

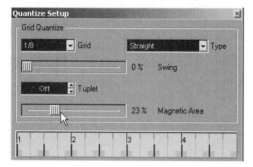

Figure 10.55 The Magnetic Area slider adjusts the range in which notes will be quantized, indicated by the lightly colored area next to the grid markers. Notes outside the gray range will be ignored.

Controlling Which Notes Are Quantized

Cubase provides a useful way to exclude and include only some of the notes in the quantize setup. Quantizing all the notes in a part often produces a more sweeping effect than you need. You might want to tighten up only the timing of notes that fall near a beat grid if some of the other notes were played quite intentionally away from the beat. Normally all notes will be moved when a part is quantized, unless you specify otherwise. In this next task, you'll quantize notes close to the grid and at the same time leave other notes alone.

To quantize only some MIDI notes:

1. Select the notes, part, or parts to be quantized.

2. Open the Quantize Setup dialog box by clicking the MIDI menu and selecting Quantize Setup.

3. Set the grid as you want it.

   In this example (again, so it is a bit easier to see), the panel has a straight eighth-note grid (**Figure 10.54**).

4. Use the Magnetic Area slider to set limits on what is quantized.

   As the slider is moved, an area on either side of each point in the grid is highlighted (**Figure 10.55**). Only notes within this range will be affected by quantizing.

5. Click Apply to quantize according to the current setting, or click the close box to close the panel without quantizing.

Making Quantized MIDI Sound More Natural

A method for making quantized MIDI parts sound less robotic and more similar to "live" sound is to use what Cubase calls iterative quantize. The dictionary definition of iterative is "characterized by repetition or repetitiousness." In fact, iterative quantize is actually used to avoid quantizing MIDI to overly exact, robotic, repetitious timing values. Instead of moving MIDI notes to the nearest, most exact grid location, iterative quantize moves MIDI notes by a percentage of the distance to the nearest grid location. This approach is often the best way to quantize a MIDI part to make it sound realistic—the timing is tighter than the original performance but retains enough slop to sound like it was played by a person.

To apply iterative quantize to MIDI notes:

1. Select the MIDI notes or parts to be quantized.

   To give you a good view of what iterative quantize does, **Figure 10.56** shows a few MIDI notes zoomed in quite close.

2. Open the Quantize Setup dialog box by clicking the MIDI menu and selecting Quantize Setup.

3. Near the bottom of this panel, enter the iterative strength. Start with a setting of 50% (**Figure 10.57**).

   The higher the value, the more the MIDI is quantized by iterative quantizing. At 0%, iterative quantize does nothing; at 100%, it acts just like Over Quantize.

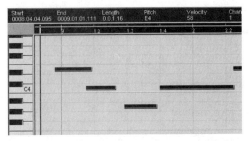

Figure 10.56 The MIDI notes before being quantized

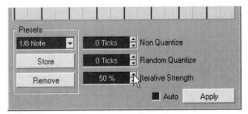

Figure 10.57 This setting determines how strong or weak the iterative quantize effect is.

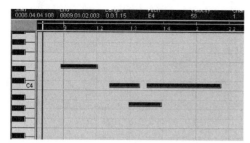

Figure 10.58 The notes after iterative quantize is applied: Compare them to the other quantize results described in this chapter.

4. Close this window without clicking Apply.

5. With the notes still selected, right-click (Windows) or Control-click (Mac OS) and select MIDI > Iterative Quantize.

    The notes are moved with 50 percent of the quantize strength of Over Quantizing. **Figure 10.58** shows the result. Compare this figure to Figure 10.50, in which all notes started precisely on an eighth-note. You may want to experiment by moving the value up and down to understand how these changes affect the rhythmic feel of the section.

✔ **Tip**

■ The discussion here only scratches the surface of what can be done with quantizing in Cubase. If you edit a lot of MIDI parts, dig deep into the Cubase documentation to find out more.

The List Editor

Up to now, all of the MIDI editors you've used were comparatively musical. The Key editor uses a keyboard to represent pitch and a grid to represent time. The Drum editor is similar but has some tools specifically for making drum beats. The List editor (**Figure 10.59**), however, offers a very computerish way of working with MIDI. Although it's not the most intuitive editor in Cubase, it offers precise MIDI editing and allows precision placement in the creation of MIDI data. You'll want to use the List editor when you know exactly what you want to change in a MIDI part. It's not something to use for sketching out tunes or figuring out new ways to play a chord. It's for actions like precisely inserting a MIDI command to make a synth change sound at a certain point in a song.

The List editor provides these interface elements:

Toolbar: The List editor toolbar includes familiar tools such as Draw, Mute, and Zoom, as well as List editor-specific tools such as the Insert menu.

Insert menu: You use this menu to select the type of event that you create with the Draw tool.

Filter button: Huge amounts of MIDI data can be displayed in the List editor, and sometimes it can be nearly impossible to find the data you want. The Filter button lets you filter out unwanted information so you can concentrate on the material you need.

Filter settings: When the Filter button is active, the filter settings check boxes allow you to determine what data is visible and what is not.

List: This pane lists all MIDI events in the part being displayed in the editor.

Event display: This pane provides a visual representation of all of the data in the event list.

Value display: This pane provides a visual representation of the value of each event in the event list.

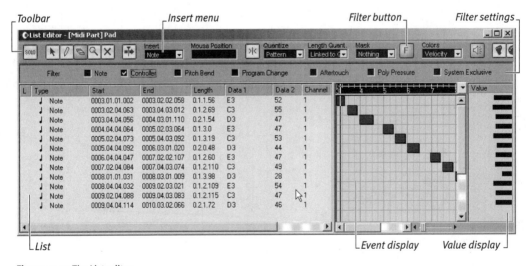

Figure 10.59 The List editor

Figure 10.60 Use these check boxes to show and hide different types of MIDI data.

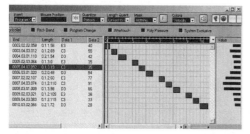

Figure 10.61 With only note data visible, you can more easily see what is going on.

Filtering Data in the List Editor

One of the most important tools in the List editor lets you specify not what the editor shows, but what it does not show. The List editor can contain thousands of pieces of MIDI data, and finding the information you want can be next to impossible unless some of the data is filtered out of the view. To do this, Cubase uses a clever set of check boxes available via the Filter button. In the following task, you will see how to filter controller information to get a better view of note data. This particular part has a ton of CC messages, but dozens of screens would be needed if all the data were displayed.

To filter MIDI data in the List editor:

1. From the main menu bar, choose MIDI > Open List Editor. On the toolbar, click the Filter button.

A row of settings for indicating what MIDI data should be filtered opens.

2. Click the types of controller data you do not wish to see (**Figure 10.60**).

In this example, selecting the Controller button will mask out controller data in the editor. With controller data filtered, all of the notes in the MIDI part can be seen easily (**Figure 10.61**).

✔ Tip

■ Of course, all kinds of data can be viewed or hidden, depending on what you check in the boxes for the Filter settings. Just remember that filtering is a negative system. You can't choose to see some data: you can only choose *not* to see some data.

Changing Values in the Event List

The List editor isn't the easiest editor to use, but it offers powerful control for editing MIDI data values. Other editors may be a bit more musical, but nothing can beat the List editor for control. Any of the parameters shown in the event list can be edited. In the following task, you will see how to change the pitch of a note.

To modify MIDI data in the event list:

1. Open the List editor. In the event list, click the MIDI event you want to edit.

   The event will be highlighted (**Figure 10.62**). Note that you can widen this list view by grabbing and moving the line between the event and note windows.

2. To edit a value, simply click it and enter a new value.

   For example, clicking E3 (the pitch of the selected note) will select it for editing (**Figure 10.63**).

   You can enter values manually, or you can use the Up and Down Arrow keys on the keyboard to change values.

3. Press the Down Arrow a few times to set the new note value to C3 (**Figure 10.64**).

✔ Tip

■ Different kinds of MIDI data have different values that can be edited in the List editor. For MIDI notes, for instance, you can edit the start, end, duration, pitch, and velocity parameters. For a CC message, though, you can edit only the time it starts and the message and the value that is being sent.

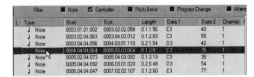

Figure 10.62 Clicking the note allows it to be edited.

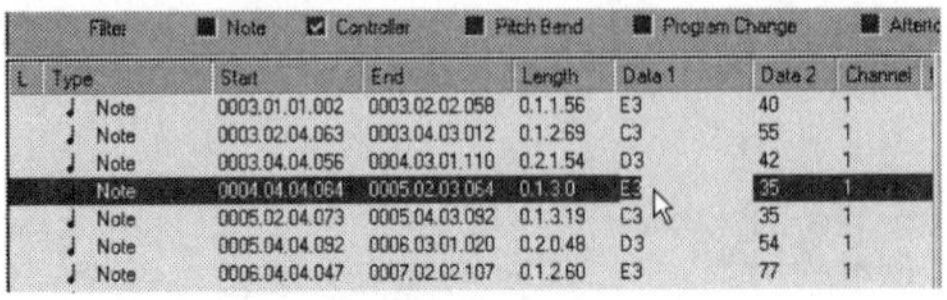

Figure 10.63 Clicking E3 allows the note to be edited for this MIDI event.

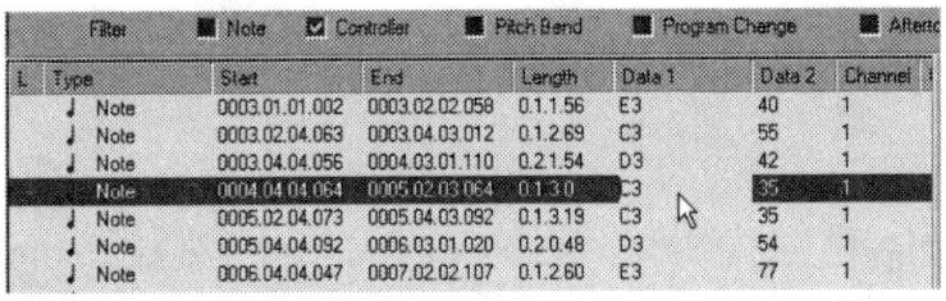

Figure 10.64 After the value is changed, the note will play C3 instead of E3.

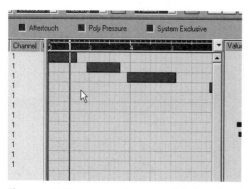

Figure 10.65 The program change needs to be entered before the second note shown here.

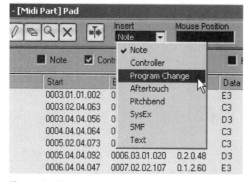

Figure 10.66 Selecting Program Change as the type of data to be inserted

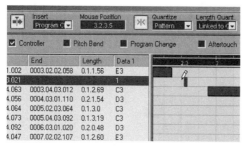

Figure 10.67 Creating the program change with the Draw tool

Creating a New Event in the Event List

If you need to do a lot of exacting MIDI editing, the List editor is a great tool to know about. A common use for the List editor is to enter a program change at a particular location in a song. Many synthesizers and hardware effects processors can't switch instantly to a new sound or new effects program; they will produce a short glitch, which can sound really awful. This next task shows how to insert a program change message with the List editor so that a synth can change smoothly in time.

Entering a program change in the List editor:

1. In the Event display, find the place where the program change needs to be entered.

   In **Figure 10.65**, the program change should go before the second note in the Event display.

2. Using the Zoom tool, zoom in close to the location where you want to enter the program change.

3. Select the Draw (or pencil) tool, click the Insert menu, and select Program Change (**Figure 10.66**).

   The Insert menu determines what kind of Event is created with the pencil tool.

4. Click the Event display with the Draw tool wherever you want to create a program change.

   This creates a new event, which will be added to the list as well (**Figure 10.67**).

THE CUBASE MIXER

You've recorded, edited, and tweaked each individual sound that makes up a song—now you need to turn the whole track into a cohesive statement. In audio circles, this is called *mixing*, and it is as much an art as playing an instrument. A good number of audio professionals make a lot of money doing nothing but mixing tracks or remixing tracks already produced by someone else. They rarely, if ever, track an instrument or work with live musicians.

The Cubase mixer is extremely flexible and powerful. As with all digital mixers, all of its settings are saved with the project, meaning that you never have to worry about getting back to where you were the last time you worked on a particular mix. In Cubase, MIDI is mixed right along with audio, and the Cubase mixer gives you a wealth of options for routing and modifying both audio and MIDI data.

In this chapter, you will learn about the different channels you can use in a Cubase mixer project and how to route audio and MIDI to them and to hardware outputs on your sound card. Cubase also includes some special MIDI effects, as you will see. If you are interested, you can check out a sample mix with commentary, available at my Web site (www.thadbrown.com/cubase), that demonstrates many of the ideas in this chapter.

Why Stereo Mixes?

Hearing is a spatial, as well as an aural, sense. Our ears perceive not only changes in the volume and timbre of a sound, but also the direction from which a sound originated. They can even give us a fairly reliable idea of how far away we are from a sound generator. Presumably, these capabilities evolved as survival tools: We need to know to run when our eyes tell us that a lion is set to pounce, but we also need to be able to read the meaning of sounds so we can react quickly when we hear a few sticks break right behind us.

Although innovations in playback systems continue to appear, a stereo mix with one left speaker and one right speaker can go a very long way toward convincing our ears of a three-dimensional acoustic space. Consider these three basic parameters for creating a stereo mix:

◆ **Level** is the relative loudness of a sound. Humans tend to notice loud sounds more than soft ones and also to use level to help calculate the distance of a sound source. We know that a full drum kit is louder than an acoustic guitar, so if an acoustic guitar is louder than a drum kit, our ears will guess that the drum kit is far away and the guitar is close.

◆ **Pan** is the placement of a sound in the left-right field. We perceive a sound played in only the right channel of a stereo mix to be located at our extreme right. We perceive sounds played equally through both speakers to be at the center of the stereo field.

◆ **Timbre** is the frequency makeup of a sound. The character of the sound generator is the primary factor in determining the timbre of a sound, but a sound's distance and location and the space in which the sound is created also change the timbre of a sound. For example, a hand clap 20 feet away in a gymnasium sounds very different than the same hand clap 2 feet away in a closet.

All of the techniques discussed in this chapter and the next fundamentally involve changing these three parameters to paint a sonic picture for your listener.

Channels in the Cubase Mixer

Figure 11.1 shows a mixer for a typical Cubase project. As you can see, this one screen contains a great deal of information. Each of the mixer's components will be covered in detail later in this chapter. For now, simply note the variety of channels available in the Cubase mixer and the variety of views available for each track.

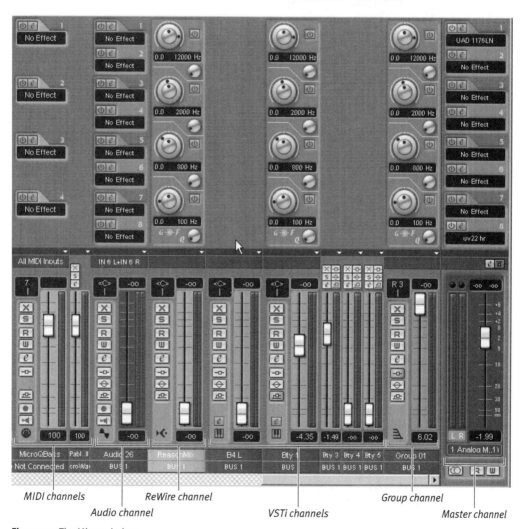

MIDI channels   *ReWire channel*   *Group channel*

　　　Audio channel   *VSTi channels*   *Master channel*

Figure 11.1 The Mixer window

MIDI channels: Each MIDI track in a project has a MIDI channel in the mixer. Cubase uses a lot of audio-style tools for mixing MIDI.

Audio channel: Just like MIDI tracks, each audio track in a project has a channel in the mixer. The mixer channel can also be used for processing, applying EQ settings, adding effects, and routing audio for that track.

ReWire channel: ReWire is a protocol for transferring audio, MIDI, and synchronization information between applications running on the same computer. In Cubase, ReWire is most often used to route audio from another application (such as Reason or Live) to the Cubase mixer.

VSTi channels: Each VSTi in use also has at least one channel in the Cubase mixer. Some VST instruments may use more than one channel, depending on their configuration. Both the ReWire and VSTi channels have the same controls as audio channels.

Group channel: A group channel is an audio channel that is not wired directly to any particular audio track. Group channels are used to route audio to a specific source, such as a set of headphones, or to apply effects to multiple tracks or to apply multiple effects in a series.

Master channel: The master channel holds the final, stereo output of the full mix created by combining all other channels in the Cubase mixer. It contains one fader to control the overall volume of the mix and has its own unique effects settings and even its own stereo/mono button. You should view the master level of your mix to avoid overload distortion and to see how changes you are making in individual mixer channels change the general level of a song. You can turn your view of the master channel off and on with a click of the button on the Common panel, on the left side of the mixer.

Figure 11.2 Each button shows or hides all of one kind of channel.

Figure 11.3 With all buttons unselected, the Cubase mixer is empty. Clicking any button displays all channels of that type.

Managing Your Mixer On-Screen

The mixer includes knobs, sliders, and buttons for every track in your composition and can quickly overwhelm the screen of your computer. A single project can easily contain dozens, or even hundreds, of tracks. Most users won't break that century mark, but even a project with 24 audio tracks, a few VST instruments, and some group channels for effects can get hard to manage in a reasonable amount of screen space.

Luckily, Cubase provides a number of ways for you to adjust your view—one channel at a time; or by the panel, for an individual effect; or for the full mix—so that you can fine-tune your work. One of the simplest ways to manipulate your screen space is to use the buttons at the lower left of the Cubase mixer (**Figure 11.2**). These buttons show or hide entire groups of tracks. A button (or track) is green when selected and gray when it isn't selected. Unselecting all of these buttons yields an empty mixer (**Figure 11.3**). The buttons in Figure 11.3 show or hide, from top to bottom, audio, group, VSTi, ReWire, and MIDI tracks.

In addition to selecting the tracks that you want visible, you'll often toggle back and forth between the normal and extended (or expanded) views to display their effects. In normal view (**Figure 11.4**), you'll see controls that you've worked with before—such as faders and buttons for solo/mute and pan—for each individual track.

continues on next page

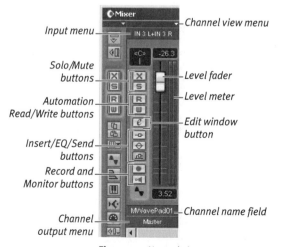

Input menu

Solo/Mute buttons

Automation Read/Write buttons

Insert/EQ/Send buttons

Record and Monitor buttons

Channel output menu

Channel view menu

Level fader

Level meter

Edit window button

Channel name field

Figure 11.4 Normal view

The extended view—which you access by toggling a button on the Common panel (**Figure 11.5**) or by selecting Expanded from the pull-down menu at the top of the panel (**Figure 11.6**)—displays an array of EQ settings, and insert and send effects for each channel, along with the tools provided in the normal view. Neither view is better than the other. Extended view provides more information per channel on the mixer, but takes up nearly the entire vertical area on a 1,024 x 768 screen. Normal view leaves more room for other windows, but limits what can be edited in the Mixer window.

The Cubase mixer display for the extended view is quite flexible. You can choose the way in which you work most comfortably, displaying or hiding effects parameters or displaying them as numerical fields or knobs.

Figure 11.5 The extended view makes the mixer much larger, but shows crucial information.

Figure 11.6 You can also use this pop-up menu to toggle the extended view area on and off.

Figure 11.7 Opening the pop-up menu for the extended view

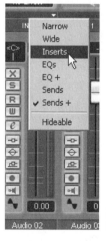

Figure 11.8 Selecting inserts to be viewed

Figure 11.9 The extended view showing different parameters for different channels

To configure the extended view display:

1. Click the small triangle directly above an audio channel's input settings to open a pop-up options menu (**Figure 11.7**).

2. From the menu, select the type of information that you want displayed in the extended view (**Figure 11.8**).

Figure 11.9 shows the extended view for two adjacent channels, one showing EQ settings and the other showing insert effects.

✔ Tip

■ A plus sign (+) next to a menu selection indicates that the view will be displayed with knobs instead of numerical fields.

Viewing All Channel Options Simultaneously

Another handy set of controls lets you change view parameters for every channel in the mixer, providing a quick way for you to see one part of a mix on every channel. For example, you can instantly look at the send effects for all viewed channels or change from narrow to wide view.

◆ The common buttons next to the extended view force each channel to show the same category of information in that view. Clicking the Show Inserts button (the top button on the left), for example, will display inserts for all channels (**Figure 11.10**)

◆ The other buttons, from top to bottom, display EQs, EQs+, Sends, and Sends+ information when clicked.

◆ You can use the drop-down menu at the border between the main and extended mixer areas to change many view settings. For example, selecting Narrow (**Figure 11.11**) forces mixer channels into that view mode (**Figure 11.12**).

Figure 11.10 Click the button under the arrow to display insert effects for all channels in the extended view.

Figure 11.11 This menu controls view parameters for all channels in the mixer.

Choose Your View

Personally, I tend to use the normal view and then the Edit window for the track I want to modify. The Edit window displays many parameters for an individual track and is described later in this chapter. Many people prefer the extended view because it looks and feels more like a hardware mixer, with EQ, send, and insert controls above each channel fader. Use either or both views, according to what works best for you.

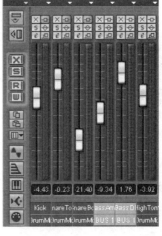

Figure 11.12 Choose Narrow to display all channels in narrow view.

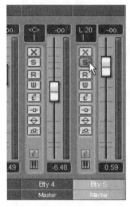

Figure 11.13 Clicking this button solos the channel.

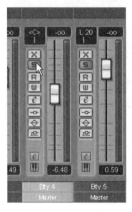

Figure 11.14 More than one track can be soloed at the same time.

Soloing and Muting Mixer Channels

Mixer channels can be soloed and muted just like tracks in the Project window. In fact, wherever you click the button to solo or mute a track, the effect is the same. The following example shows how to solo two VSTi tracks.

To solo a mixer channel:

1. In the mixer channel you want to solo, click the S button (**Figure 11.13**).

   When a channel is soloed, the Solo button becomes red, and all other tracks are muted. The X (Mute) button becomes yellow. Only the soloed track will play back.

2. To hear another track, click its Solo button (**Figure 11.14**).

   Now only these two soloed tracks will be heard.

3. To hear the entire mix again, click the Solo buttons again to deselect them.

   When all of the Solo buttons are deselected, the entire mix will be audible again.

✔ Tips

- Of course, you can individually mute channels by clicking the Mute button for a channel. In truth, soloing a channel mutes every other channel automatically.

- You can also rename mixer channels by double-clicking them and typing a new name, just as with tracks in the Project window.

Working with Audio Channels

Figure 11.15 shows a generic audio channel. It's particularly important to understand audio channels for two reasons. First, most of the features in audio channels are also found in VSTi, ReWire, and Group channels. Second, nearly every project you create will contain at least a few audio channels.

Audio channels have a few basic parts:

Level meter: This is a graphic representation of the volume of the audio track.

Level fader: This controls the level of the track, which is silent when the fader is pulled to the bottom and progressively louder as the fader control is moved higher.

Channel name field: This is where the name of the channel appears. The name can be edited here or in the Project window.

Channel output menu: An audio track can be routed to the master output, a group channel, or an active audio bus. This menu specifies where the audio from the track is sent.

Record and Monitor buttons: These buttons control whether a track is in record or monitor mode.

Insert/EQ/Send buttons: These buttons show the current status of insert effects, EQ settings, and send effects for the track. If they are in use—that is, if an effect has been applied—the button turns blue. You can also use these buttons to bypass each type of processing by clicking on them. if you've bypassed the processing, the button will turn orange.

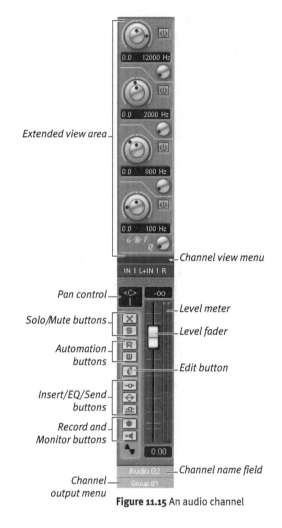

Extended view area

Channel view menu

Pan control

Solo/Mute buttons

Automation buttons

Insert/EQ/Send buttons

Record and Monitor buttons

Channel output menu

Level meter

Level fader

Edit button

Channel name field

Figure 11.15 An audio channel

WORKING WITH AUDIO CHANNELS

Automation Read/Write buttons: Use these two buttons to turn automation on and off. Automation is covered in Chapter 14, "Using Mix Automation."

Solo/Mute buttons: Use these buttons to solo or mute the current track in the mix.

Pan control: This setting controls the relative placement of the track in the stereo field. When the pan control is at the far left, the track will be audible only in the left speaker; when it is at the far right, the track will be audible only in the right speaker; when it is in the middle, the track will be equally loud in both speakers.

Input menu: Use this menu to select a hardware input for the track.

Channel view menu: Use this menu to change the look and visible parameters for the individual track.

Extended view area: If extended view is selected, this area displays additional information about the audio channel, such as EQ settings, insert effects, and send effects.

Choosing an Output for an Audio Channel

By default, audio channels are routed to the master channel and then to the stereo hardware output on your soundcard that is connected to your speakers or headphones. This is a good approach, and it generally routes the audio where it should be, but Cubase provides great flexibility for routing audio tracks to other locations.

Here are some common situations where you may want to route an audio channel somewhere other than the master channel:

Figure 11.16 The channel output pop-up menu shows all available destinations for the channel.

◆ You may want to route the entire channel to an external effect connected to your sound card.

◆ You may want to route the entire channel to an individual performer in a headphone mix.

◆ You may want to route a channel to a group bus to add effects or control it with a single fader.

To choose an audio track output:

1. Click the very bottom of the audio channel.

   A pop-up menu opens (**Figure 11.16**) to show all available busses and groups.

2. From the menu, select the correct output for the audio channel.

   The channel will show where the track is being routed (**Figure 11.17**).

Figure 11.17 Choosing Group 01 will route the Loop01 channel to a group.

✔ Tips

■ The slightly cryptic destination of SurroundPan is also an option on the channel output menu. You will use this only if you are working in some form of surround sound, in which case you should consult Chapter 10, "Surround Sound," in the Cubase manual.

■ The even-more-cryptic Links and Rechts options on the channel output menu are derived from the German words for left and right and they route the channel only to the left or only to the right of the master channel. These options might be in English by the time you read this.

Figure 11.18 Changing the pan setting with the mouse

Figure 11.19 The same channel with slightly different settings

Adjusting Level and Pan

The two absolutely fundamental properties of an audio mixer channel are level and pan. Level is the overall loudness of the channel, and pan is the location of the channel in the left/right stereo field. Both also fundamentally relate to the master channel, because the level and pan of all channels in a mix make up what is controlled by final master channel level and pan controls.

If you have used a hardware mixer, you will find the Cubase mixer interface familiar. Nevertheless, you should be aware of some features unique to a digital mixer. And if you are new to mixers, here is an overview of the basic mixer functions:

◆ The fader is used to increase and decrease volume; the pan control places the channel in the left/right mix. **Figure 11.18** shows the fader at its lowest level, meaning the track is effectively muted, and the pan setting is at the farthest left point. **Figure 11.19** shows the same channel with the fader raised and the pan control set to send the channel more to the right of the master channel than the left.

◆ Pan settings are displayed by the Cubase mixer with somewhat confusing numbers: L64 for fully left and R64 for fully right. We human beings think in decimal numbers (multiples of 10), but computers use binary numbers (multiples of 2). The pan settings in Cubase are a legacy of MIDI, where binary numbers rule.

◆ Clicking either the pan control or fader while holding down the Ctrl (Windows) or Command (Mac OS) key will reset the controls to their default values.

Panning Conventions

There is a somewhat famous story from a very famous record producer about the beginning of stereo. For many years, all playback formats were monaural; a record had only one channel, and every instrument and vocal had to be crammed into that single speaker. When stereo mixing first came along, nobody really knew what to do with it. According to the famous producer, for his first stereo mix he prepared a complete mono mix, as he normally did, and then he put only the tambourine in the other speaker. Imagine driving down the highway and a song comes on the radio with the entire band and all of the singers playing through the right speaker and the tambourine alone playing through the right.

No rule is unbreakable, but in almost all music mixed for stereo, the kick drum, snare drum, and lead vocal are panned dead center. The rest of the drums are usually panned according to some logical spatial rule: either the way the drummer would hear them or the way a person standing in front of the kit would hear them. The bass is generally also in the middle or close to it. Backing vocals are usually panned to a greater or lesser degree away from the stereo center but to both sides of the mix. Other mono instruments such as guitars, percussion, and samples, are usually placed somewhere in the stereo field away from the center. Another common trick is to double a part—to play the same acoustic guitar part twice, for example—and then pan one track fully left and one track fully right. Adjusting the pan of each doubled part can create some interesting soundscapes.

All of these rules can be broken if doing so makes the mix sound better, but they provide a good place to start.

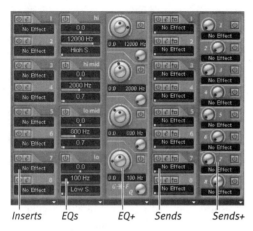

Inserts   EQs   EQ+   Sends   Sends+

Figure 11.20 Extended view for five adjacent audio channels

Working with the Extended View

Figure 11.20 shows the extended view section for five adjacent audio channels. Each channel has the extended view set to one of the possible options, so all of the possible settings are visible in the illustration. Here's a quick explanation of each view and how it is used.

Inserts: This setting displays all insert effects used in that audio channel. Insert effects operate in serial, with each successive insert processing the output of the last one, and usually process the entire audio signal. If you have used a guitar pedal or something similar, you have used an insert effect. Distortion, filters, compression, and sometimes phasers and flangers are usually used for insert effects.

EQs: Cubase includes four bands of equalization, commonly called EQ, for each audio channel. EQ is used to boost or attenuate particular frequencies in the track being played back. The bass and treble controls on a stereo provide very simple EQ effects. The EQs option shows all four bands, with sliders and buttons to control the parameters for each of the four EQ bands.

EQ+: This view shows the same EQ options for the same four bands, but uses knobs instead of sliders for those who prefer to set EQ that way.

Sends: Send effects operate in parallel. In other words, the channel plays back the audio without effects, but splits off part of the audio and routes it to an effect for processing as well. The most common uses for send effects are reverb and delay, where the dry sound is enhanced by the send effect.

Sends+: Like EQ+, this option displays the parameters for send effects, but with a knob instead of a slider.

✔ Tip

■ You can use the Narrow/Wide setting to collapse a channel so it shows only the channel fader, the meter, and a few buttons. Narrow channels take up less room, meaning you can see more of them on the screen, but are they not as easy to edit.

Understanding EQ

EQ, or equalization, is used to change the frequency characteristics of an audio channel. Software-based EQ did not have an easy youth. For years, most digital audio programs had EQ that sounded almost fingernails-on-the-chalkboard bad. To get around this, many people used expensive and CPU-hungry third-party plug-ins or outboard hardware to do the job. Luckily for you, Cubase now includes flexible, good-sounding EQ for every audio channel.

Working with EQ is an art and is a long-time learning experience that can't be immediately explained. All EQ boosts or attenuates sound, which means that EQ can also properly be called filtering. Cubase includes three different filters:

◆ **Peak filters** (usually called parametric filters) boost or attenuate sound at a particular frequency. Peak filters have three main parameters. First, you can set the center frequency for the boost or cut. Second, you can set the amount that the filter boosts or cuts. Third, you can set how far above and below the center frequency the filter is active—in other words, how wide the filter is. Peak filters are very flexible and can be used for broad changes or for very limited corrective EQ.

◆ **Shelving filters** boost or cut everything above or below a certain frequency by the amount that you specify and at a starting point that you define. Shelving filters are not as versatile or precise as peak filters, but many of the most famous, sought-after, vintage EQs are shelving filters. They can be very effective at sweetening tracks with a broader stroke because they usually effect a wider frequency spectrum than a peak filter. Shelving filters are sometimes used on full mixes.

◆ **High/low-pass filters** attenuate audio above or below the specified frequency. They are usually described in terms of how much they cut per octave. A low-pass filter might decrease audio by 6 dB per octave, meaning that one octave above the frequency set for the filter, the signal will be down 6 dB; two octaves above, it will be down 12 dB; and so on. These filters are very useful for removing rumble and hiss from individual tracks.

The Cubase EQ section is designed with four bands of EQ. The middle two bands are always peak filters, and the high and low bands can be peak filters, shelving filters, or pass band filters.

Applying EQ in the Channel Settings Window

There is more than one way to set EQ in Cubase. Although you can use the extended view, virtual knobs, or numeric values to set EQ parameters, the best approach is to use the Channel Settings window. The Cubase Channel Settings window is one of the most powerful features of the mixer. It organizes all settings for an audio channel in a single window, from routing to EQ to inserts and sends. You will hear about the Channel Settings window for other purposes in the rest of this chapter, but it is particularly useful for adjusting EQ because it offers an intuitive, graphical way to see EQ settings. All discussions and examples of EQ here will use this window.

In the following task, you will use the Channel Settings window to add a small peak filter in the high midrange. You might do this in any number of musical situations, such as to add more presence to a guitar sound or to tweak a snare sample to make it more prominent in a mix without raising its overall level.

To apply EQ to a channel with a peak filter:

1. In the channel to which you want to apply EQ, click the *e* (Edit) button (**Figure 11.21**).

   This opens the Channel Settings window for that channel. The EQ settings appear in the center of the window, displayed as knobs, and are also shown in the display above the knobs.

2. Click the virtual power button (**Figure 11.22**) to activate that band of EQ.

   Each active EQ band appears in the breakpoint display above the EQ knobs. The breakpoints are numbered: the point marked 1 will adjust the first band of EQ, 2 will adjust the second band, and so on. This display provides an easy way to adjust the EQ settings.

3. To adjust the EQ settings, click the breakpoint in the display for the band you want to adjust and move it with the mouse.

   Figure 11.23 shows a slight boost in the midrange, around 2 kilohertz.

4. Use the knobs to make finer adjustments to the EQ settings as needed.

   Pay particular attention to the bottom knob for each band. This knob adjusts the width of the band, referred to as the Q of the band. The higher the setting, the narrower the EQ band will be.

Figure 11.21 This button opens the Channel Settings window.

Figure 11.22 Click this button to turn on a band of EQ.

Figure 11.23 Dragging the breakpoint creates a small boost for the third EQ band.

Figure 11.24 The first EQ band is now turned on.

Figure 11.25 The display shows the effect of the shelving EQ.

Using a Shelving Filter

Shelving filters boost or cut all sounds above or below a frequency you set. They are great for gently adding or subtracting bass or treble from a track that doesn't sound quite the way you want it to. For example, a shelving filter would be a good choice for removing unwanted low-end sound from an acoustic guitar, boosting high-end sound in cymbals or percussion, or adding low-end sound to a singer with a slightly thin voice. This task shows you how to cut out unnecessary low-end sound from a track with low-shelf EQ.

To boost or cut with a shelving filter:

1. Click the *e* (Edit) button in the channel that you want to adjust to open its Channel Settings window.

   Only EQ bands 1 and 4 can act as shelving filters; the two middle EQ bands are parametric (peak) filters only.

2. Turn on the bottom EQ band by clicking its power button (**Figure 11.24**).

3. Turn the bottom knob (the Q setting) all the way to the left (counterclockwise).

   The display below the knob says "Low S," which stands for low shelf and refers to the type of filter.

4. In the EQ display above the knobs, click the breakpoint for the first EQ band and drag it to set the EQ.

   The display will show you what the filter is doing, and your ears will guide you to the right settings. In **Figure 11.25**, the shelving filter is set for a significant cut, with its center frequency set at 341 Hz.

✔ Tip

■ You can also click any of the EQ parameters and enter values using the keyboard or the up and down arrow keys. These methods are convenient when you know precisely the frequency you want to use.

Using a High- or Low-Pass Filter

High- and low-pass filters are most often used to remove unwanted sounds from individual tracks. When recording, it's easy to wind up with low-frequency hum and rumble or high-frequency noise and hiss. The low-end junk might be traffic noise, nearby appliances, or ground loops; the high-end noise might be tape hiss or an air conditioner. A high-pass filter can also help when an instrument was recorded near a drum kit; a carefully set high-pass filter can remove most of the unwanted leaked sound from the simultaneous recording of a nearby kick drum.

This next task shows you how to deal with another common scenario. High-frequency noise and hiss can easily work their way into a recorded track. You can use a low-pass filter to get rid of much of this high-frequency content.

When in Doubt, Cut It Out

Nothing pegs a mix as hopelessly amateur like too much boosting with EQ. It's tempting to crank up every value on every track so that each one sounds wicked loud—but usually the song turns to mush instead. Pick your spots for EQ boosting and don't get carried away. Often the only places that need EQ boosts are the parts that should be most prominent in the mix, like the main vocal, an instrument solo, or the snare drum.

On the other hand, you can probably use a lot more subtractive, or cutting, EQ than you realize. If you read the music production magazines, you've read about producers using 128-track mixes and 60 tracks of backing vocals. The only way to keep that many tracks from trampling all over each other is to use a *ton* of subtractive EQ. Producers and engineers use EQ to carve away everything but the smallest part of the audio spectrum for each track. If two instruments seem to occupy the same sonic space, instead of boosting the one you want to be more prominent, try cutting the other one. Often this will help a mix sound a lot better.

Figure 11.26 Click this button to turn on the top EQ band, which can be a low-pass filter.

Figure 11.27 Use the Q knob (the bottom knob for each band) to set a filter as a low-pass filter; the result is visible in the EQ display.

To use a high- or low-pass filter:

1. Activate the fourth EQ band for use as a low-pass filter (**Figure 11.26**).

   Remember that only the top EQ band can be used as a low-pass filter, and only the bottom EQ band can be used as a high-pass filter.

2. Click the Q knob and drag it all the way to the right (clockwise).

   At this extreme position, the band will become a low-pass filter. The Q display will show "Low P" to indicate this (**Figure 11.27**).

3. Click the breakpoint to adjust the location where the filter begins to take effect. You can also use the knob or enter a frequency manually.

✔ Tip

■ Don't be afraid to experiment with low- and high-pass filters on most tracks. Getting rid of excess high- and low-end sound on most tracks can really clean up a mix.

Insert Effects Basics

An insert effect is the simplest kind of effect. The entire audio signal from a channel is fed into the effect, the audio is modified in some way, and the audio with the effect replaces the original track in the mix. The following task uses the simple DaTube plug-in included with Cubase as an insert for an audio channel. This particular plug-in emulates the saturation, overdrive, and compression of an old analog vacuum tube.

To use an insert effect:

1. Use the extended view drop-down menu (click the downward-pointing arrow on the left side of the Mixer window) to display inserts in the extended view area.

2. Click the top effect slot, marked "No Effect."

   A drop-down menu opens showing all installed VST effects and any installed DirectX effects (**Figure 11.28**).

3. From this drop-down menu, choose Distortion; then select DaTube.

   Selecting this plug-in automatically opens its editor window (**Figure 11.29**).

4. Adjust the settings to get the sound you want.

✔ Tips

■ You can also access inserts in the Channel Settings window. **Figure 11.30** shows the inserts for the audio channel in Figures 11.28 and 11.29. Note that the top slot has the DaTube plug-in selected and turned on.

■ Insert Effects are discussed in depth in Chapter 12, "Audio Effect Plug-Ins."

Figure 11.28 This menu shows every installed effect that Cubase can use.

Figure 11.29 The editor window for DaTube.

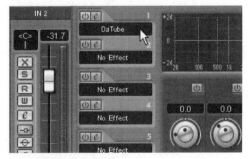

Figure 11.30 You can also use the Channel Settings window for insert effects.

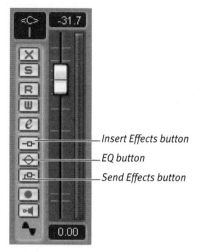

Insert Effects button
EQ button
Send Effects button

Figure 11.31 An audio channel, with each button marked to show its function

Bypassing EQ and Effects for a Channel

As a mix progresses, you'll often want to check to see if your changes are working. For instance, EQ on a bass track might sound great when it's soloed, but not so good in the context of a mix. It's also easy to add so many effects to a sound that the sound gets lost. Cubase offers a quick and easy way to keep track of the effects in use in a channel and to bypass groups of effects. Huddled together next to the channel fader are three buttons with particularly obscure-looking hieroglyphics (**Figure 11.31**). These buttons can bypass all of the EQ settings, insert effects, or send effects for that channel. These three buttons also do more than just bypass EQ effects; they indicate whether any EQ bands, insert effects, or send effects are active on that channel, and they provide important information about the channel no matter what their active status.

The buttons can be white (or clear), blue, green, or yellow, depending on the status:

◆ A white (or clear) button indicates that none of the represented effects are on. In other words, if the EQ button is white, none of the EQ bands for that channel are on.

◆ Blue is used for the send and insert effects. When a send or insert effect is turned on, the appropriate button in the audio channel turns blue. This shows you at a glance whether any effects are active for that channel.

continues on next page

◆ Green is used only for the EQ button. When one or more bands of EQ are active for a channel, the button turns green. **Figure 11.32** shows an audio channel with both the send effect and EQ button active.

◆ Yellow indicates bypassed effects. If a button is blue or green (indicating that EQ or effects are in use), clicking that button bypasses those effects, and the button then turns yellow (**Figure 11.33**).

These buttons are very useful elements of the Cubase mixer. They let you know what is active within an audio channel, and they provide a one-click method for bypassing all of the EQ and other effects for that channel. This capability can be extremely useful, because it's easy to go overboard with effects and EQ. For example, after spending a long time working on a sound, it's good to be able to check the original to see if all of the effects and EQ really are improving things.

Figure 11.32 For this channel, the send and EQ buttons are lit.

Figure 11.33 If effects are bypassed with these buttons, the buttons turn yellow.

MIDI Mixing: Mixed Results

Though MIDI and audio are very different, Steinberg went out of its way to make MIDI mixing feel, as much as possible, like audio mixing. A MIDI mixer channel (**Figure 11.34**) looks in many ways like an audio channel. It has a fader and a pan control, as well as mute, solo, and automation buttons and other buttons and controls.

As much as MIDI channels look like audio channels, the fact remains that they do not deal with the same kind of information. An audio channel plays back files created by Cubase, and those files are stored on a local hard drive. MIDI channels are often used to send instructions and data to hardware and software such as synths, samplers, effects devices, and controllers that may or may not behave as expected. For example, the pan control for an audio channel will work flawlessly every time. With a MIDI channel, the pan control actually sends a MIDI continuous controller message; most devices will respond correctly to this CC, but an older synth or a synth that is filtering CCs will not respond correctly to the pan control in the Cubase mixer.

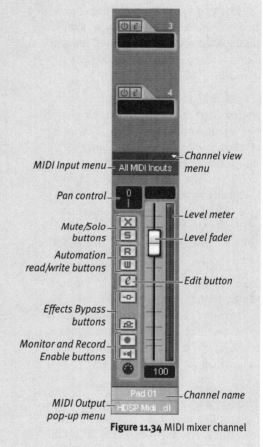

Figure 11.34 MIDI mixer channel

A second level of complexity is introduced by the fact that often MIDI parameters can be set in two places: in the Cubase mixer or in the device receiving the MIDI data. For most synths, the pan location can be stored as part of the sound preset, but it can also be set in the Cubase mixer. Neither approach is necessarily better, but keep these alternatives in mind if the MIDI channel parameters aren't functioning as you expect; the problem might be related to the device that is receiving the MIDI data.

Basic MIDI Mixing

As mentioned previously, MIDI mixing controls in Cubase are very similar to audio mixing controls. This means that many of your audio mixing skills will translate easily to MIDI.

For example, you control both pan and volume for MIDI channels precisely the same way you do for audio channels. **Figure 11.35** shows a MIDI channel with the fader pulled down a bit and the track panned to the right in the stereo field. Keep in mind, though, that what the channel fader really does here is proportionally decrease the velocity of the MIDI notes, and the pan control sends a CC message to the MIDI device.

You also solo and mute MIDI channels in the same way as audio channels. **Figure 11.36** shows two adjacent MIDI channels with the one on the left soloed. It's hard to see in the illustration, but just as with audio channels, when one MIDI channel is soloed, all other tracks are muted.

Finally, Cubase also has a Channel Settings window for MIDI channels (**Figure 11.37**), just as it has one for audio channels. Click the edit button for a MIDI channel to open this window. Most of the examples in the following pages use this Channel Settings window.

Figure 11.35 Simple velocity and pan settings are obvious in this MIDI channel.

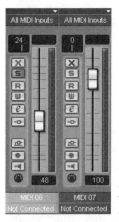

Figure 11.36 Solo and mute controls for MIDI channels work just like those for audio channels.

Figure 11.37 The MIDI Channel Settings window is much like the Channel Settings window for an audio channel.

Figure 11.38 Choosing Inserts to show MIDI inserts in the extended view

MIDI Insert Effects

One of the ways in which Cubase is different from many other MIDI applications (and from previous versions of Cubase) is in the way it processes MIDI. Most applications process MIDI data in something like the Project window or the Key editor. MIDI tracks can be edited in those Cubase windows, but the MIDI channels in the mixer also have their own specialized effects.

MIDI insert effects are similar in some ways to audio inserts. The MIDI data goes into the effect, where it's processed or changed in some way, and then continues through the channel to the fader and output. Again, remember that MIDI isn't audio, so many more parameters, such as note pitch and duration, can be changed with insert effects. Effects are a big part of MIDI mixing; the next few paragraphs describe some of the effects that ship with Cubase and offer ideas for using them in your own music.

To create and edit a MIDI insert effect:

1. If the MIDI channel is not in the wide mode, open the extended view drop-down menu and choose Wide.

2. Open the extended view pop-up menu and choose Inserts (**Figure 11.38**).

   You will see four slots in the extended view area that can be used for MIDI insert effects.

continues on next page

3. Click the top slot, where "No Effect" is displayed, to open the pop-up menu (**Figure 11.39**); then choose an effect.

For this example, select the MidiEcho effect; this both turns on the effect and opens its editor window (**Figure 11.40**). MidiEcho and its parameters are described later in this chapter.

4. Close the effect window when you are finished setting the parameters.

You can reopen the editor by clicking the cursive *e* button, as seen above the MidiEcho slot at the top left of the Figure 11.46.

Figure 11.39 Selecting the MidiEcho effect

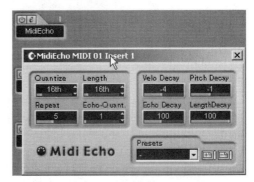

Figure 11.40 The editor window for MidiEcho

MIDI INSERT EFFECTS

268

Figure 11.41 Opening the MIDI effect presets menu; click the button with the plus sign to save the current settings as a preset.

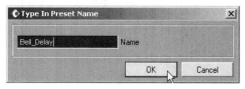

Figure 11.42 Naming the preset in the Type In Preset Name dialog box

Figure 11.43 The new preset is displayed in the preset menu for that effect.

What's a Tick?

You can edit MIDI effects plug-ins with different kinds of values. You can use note values as parameters, such as 8T for tied eighth note or 4th for a quarter note, when you want musically obvious time settings. However, you can also set most parameters to a certain number of *ticks*, which are the smallest time divisions that MIDI uses. Internally, MIDI has a timing resolution of 480 ticks per quarter note, and you can set most tempo-based parameters in MIDI effects to a particular number of ticks. This feature is useful for creating non-tempo-based settings or for creating settings that modulate another parameter slightly. For example, you could set a delay that becomes a few ticks longer with each successive delayed note.

MIDI Effect Presets

Many MIDI effects include preprogrammed settings to help you get started with the effect. When you first use a particular effect, you should check for presets to learn more about how the effect works.

We've already discussed how to save presets for VST instruments, and we'll discuss the use of presets with audio plug-ins later. But MIDI effect presets work a bit differently than either of these. The biggest difference is that a MIDI effect preset is saved within the plug-in, not as a discrete file on your hard disk.

To save a MIDI preset:

1. Open the Effects editor window (click the *e* button). Set the effects parameters exactly as you want them saved in this window. Click the drop-down menu if you want to view the list of current MIDI effect presets.

2. To add a new preset to this list, click the Add button (the button with the plus sign; see **Figure 11.41**).
   A dialog box for naming the preset opens.

3. Type a name (**Figure 11.42**) and click OK. After the preset is saved, you can select it from the drop-down menu (**Figure 11.43**).

✔ Tips

- To delete a MIDI effect preset, select it in the list and then click the Remove button (the button with the minus sign), located just to the right of the button for adding a preset. Be careful, though—you won't get a dialog box that asks if you really want to delete the preset. Once you click Delete, the preset is gone.

- Although you can't save presets as discrete files, you can use your MIDI effect presets in other projects. You can save a preset in one song and use it in another one.

MidiEcho

Cubase SX includes a number of MIDI effects. The next few paragraphs should help you become familiar with them and learn how to modify them to make the sounds you want.

The MidiEcho insert effect (**Figure 11.44**) is a delay effect that acts a lot like an audio delay effect and uses some of the same parameters. As a MIDI effect, though, it also does some things that would be impossible for an audio delay effect, such as changing the length and pitch of the delayed sounds. Keep in mind, too, that the MidiEcho effect works differently than an audio delay. The MidiEcho effect sends additional notes to a synth or sampler, whereas an audio delay repeats a sound after a specified amount of time.

Four MidiEcho parameters are grouped at the top left of the Effects editor:

◆ **Quantize** controls the time of the delay effect. Usually, you will set this to a musical value by clicking the arrows next to the setting, or with the slider below the numerical field.

◆ **Length** determines the duration of the delayed notes. If you set this parameter to its minimum value, each delayed note will be exactly as long as the original. If you set it to another value, you can use this parameter to shorten or lengthen delayed notes.

◆ **Repeat** controls the number of times that a delayed note repeats. This parameter is similar to the feedback control on an audio delay effect.

◆ **Echo-Quant** forces all delayed notes to fall on a quantize grid. Even if the original or delayed note is off of the grid, you can set a note value with Echo-Quant to force all delays to be quantized.

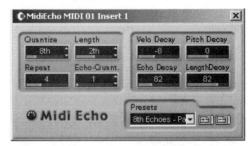

Figure 11.44 Use this window to modify settings for MidiEcho.

MidiEcho also has controls to change or transform the delayed MIDI notes:

◆ **Velo Decay** modifies the velocity of the notes generated by the effect. If the number is negative, each successive note will have a lower velocity and will be quieter. If the number is positive, the delayed notes will have a higher velocity than the original.

◆ **Pitch Decay** changes the pitch of the delayed notes similar to the way Velo Decay changes the velocity. Setting this parameter to −1 will, for example, decreases the pitch of each repeat by one semitone.

◆ **Echo Decay** modifies the length of time between repeats. You can use this control to slightly (or dramatically) speed up or slow down the repeated notes.

◆ **Length Decay** modifies the duration of repeated notes. You can set the repeats so that they are longer or shorter than the original notes.

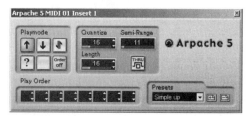

Figure 11.45 You can use the Arpache effect to create arpeggios.

Figure 11.46 The Playmode controls determine the order in which notes are played in the arpeggio.

Figure 11.47 These settings control the nature of the notes in the arpeggio.

Arpache 5

The Arpache effect (**Figure 11.45**) is a powerful arpeggiator for transforming MIDI tracks. An arpeggiator is fundamentally a simple effect; it takes a group of notes played simultaneously and transforms them into an arpeggio (notes played in rapid succession). An arpeggiator has many uses, but most often it is used on synth bass or synth lead lines to create note patterns out of chords. You can use this effect on tracks you have already recorded or to create arpeggios in real time.

Arpache has two main sets of controls. The Playmode set controls the way that the effect orders the notes in the arpeggio (**Figure 11.46**), and the other window controls parameters related to the notes themselves (**Figure 11.47**).

To navigate the Playmode area:

◆ Click the up arrow to create an arpeggio that plays from low to high pitch.

◆ Click the down arrow to create an arpeggio that starts at the highest pitch and proceeds to the lowest pitch.

◆ Click the up and down arrows together to create an arpeggio that ramps up and down in pitch.

◆ Click the question mark button to order pitches in the arpeggio randomly.

◆ Click the Order Off button to turn on the Play Order section of the effect, which lets you set the pitch order of the arpeggio manually.

Creating a Simple Arpeggio

The Arpache effect is difficult to understand in theory, but pretty easy to use in practice. The following shows you how to create a simple effect for a MIDI track that has already been recorded. Remember that the effect can also be used on live MIDI coming from a MIDI controller.

Figure 11.48 Setting the arpeggio to ramp up

Figure 11.49 Setting Quantize to 8 creates an arpeggio with a note played every eighth note.

To create an arpeggio effect with Arpache:

1. Choose a MIDI track with some kind of chord material. Select Inserts from the extended view pop-up menu (on the left side of the Mixer window).

2. Select an Insert slot and, from the pull-down menu, choose the Arpache 5 effect for that MIDI channel.

3. Click the up arrow button (**Figure 11.48**) to create an arpeggio that moves from low to high pitches.

4. Click the arrow in the Quantize setting to determine the number of notes in the arpeggio.

   In this example, the value is set to 8 (**Figure 11.49**). With this setting, the effect will play a note in the arpeggio every eighth note.

Figure 11.50 If you set Length to 32, the effect will play only short thirty-second notes, creating a very staccato sound.

5. Use the Semi-Range value to determine the low and high boundaries of the arpeggio.

   This value is set in semitones. For example, set the value to 24, and all notes created in the arpeggio will be within a two-octave range.

6. Set the Length parameter to determine the length of the notes in the arpeggio.

   If you set this value higher than the Quantize value, more than one note will play back simultaneously; a lower setting will create progressively more staccato arpeggios. A setting of 32, as shown in **Figure 11.50**, creates a very short note length.

7. Start playback in Cubase to hear the effect.

   The track with chords will now play a staccato, ascending arpeggio.

AutoPan

If any MIDI effect in Cubase is poorly named, it's AutoPan (**Figure 11.51**). Anyone seeing the name would sensibly assume that the effect is used to modulate the pan setting for a MIDI device. Although AutoPan certainly can do this, it actually does much more and can be used to generate a huge variety of MIDI continuous controller information. An AutoPan-generated controller can be used not just for pan, but can also generate controller data for nearly any parameter on any MIDI device, such as volume, filter cutoff, and delay time.

AutoPan generates controller data according to the shape you choose for it. Use the buttons at the top of the effect window to make this choice (**Figure 11.52**). You can understand most of them just by looking at the curve shape on the button. The other main parameters in the AutoPan window are as follows:

♦ **Period** specifies how quickly the controller curve changes. You can set the period in ticks or rhythmic values. For example, if you set the period to 4th, the controller will complete its curve every quarter note.

♦ **Density** specifies how often a new controller message is sent; like the period, it is set in ticks or note values. A very small value, such as 30 ticks (the equivalent of a sixty-fourth note), will send a new controller message every 30 ticks. This will create a very smooth curve, but it may pump out so much MIDI data that a synth may have trouble handling it.

♦ **Max** and **Min** set the boundaries for the controller values that are sent.

AutoPan comes with many presets (**Figure 11.53**) to get you started. However, it's a complex effect; it will require—and reward—time spent learning it.

Figure 11.51 The AutoPan editor

Figure 11.52 These buttons set the shape of the controller.

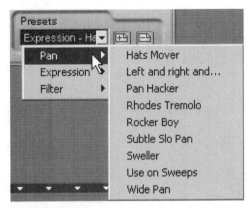

Figure 11.53 Cubase includes a large number of AutoPan presets.

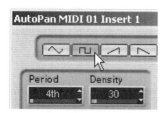

Figure 11.54 A square wave shape will create a strong, pulsing effect.

Figure 11.55 Set the controller to Main Volume to create a tremolo effect

Creating a Tremolo Effect with AutoPan

To see the versatility of AutoPan, we will use it to create a tremolo effect, changing only a few parameters from the defaults. Remember that you can use this effect to modify any continuous controller message.

To create a MIDI tremolo effect with AutoPan:

1. Using a track with some sustained notes or chords (electric piano sounds work great for this), click an Insert slot and select the AutoPan effect as an insert on the mixer channel for the track.

2. Select the square wave (**Figure 11.54**).

   Any of the controller shapes will work for a tremolo sound, but we will use the square wave to achieve a somewhat choppy effect.

3. Click the handle below the Controller setting and use the slider to set the value for the Main Volume controller field (**Figure 11.55**).

   Tremolo is nothing more than modulation of the output volume.

4. Set Density to 30 (it probably will default to that value).

continues on next page

5. Set the period to determine how rapidly the controller cycles. In this case, click the arrows next to the Period value to set it to 2th (**Figure 11.56**), which translates to a half note.

   With this setting, the waveform will cycle through its complete range every two beats, creating a fairly slow tremolo effect.

6. Set the Max and Min values to specify the range of the controller values sent.

   The settings in Figure 11.56 will create a fairly subtle effect, varying the output velocity between 90 and 105. A larger range would create a more pronounced effect.

7. Start playback in Cubase to hear the effect.

   You can change the parameters in real time to get a better understanding how they work.

Figure 11.56 With Period set to 2th, the pulse controller waveform will finish once every half note.

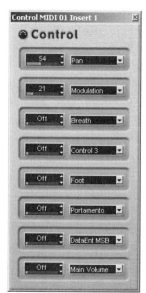

Figure 11.57 The Control effect is a Swiss Army Knife tool for changing any controller parameter.

Other MIDI Effects

The past few sections discussed a few of the MIDI effects that come with Cubase. Here is a quick description of the other MIDI effects you can use. If you want to find out more about them (and you probably should), check the electronic documentation that accompanies Cubase.

Chorder triggers whole chords with a single note from a controller. This effect is useful for one-finger keyboard playing and can be used to create some interesting MIDI parts.

Compress is a simple effect that reduces the range of MIDI velocity values. You can use it to reduce the dynamic range of a MIDI part, much the same way that you can use an audio compressor effect to change the dynamic range of audio.

Control can change up to eight MIDI controllers for a MIDI channel (**Figure 11.57**). You can choose the controllers and values that are sent.

Density thins excessive MIDI data. Some old (and, sadly, some not so old) synths have trouble processing large streams of MIDI data. Symptoms of problems include missing and delayed notes, as well as full lockup of the device. You can use the Density effect to filter out data so the device stops choking on MIDI.

Micro Tuner allows you to change the tuning of any MIDI instrument that supports it. If you are interested in micro tuning and alternate scales, this effect allows you to use both external devices and VST instruments with altered tuning parameters.

continues on next page

Note 2 CC is a simple effect that lets you play notes on a MIDI keyboard to control any controller message. A higher note played on the keyboard translates as a higher controller value. By converting note values to controller values, this plug-in provides another way to send CC data.

Quantizer allows real-time quantizing of MIDI data. Though it lacks some of the quantizing options of the Key editor, it has the advantages of being simple and easy to use.

Step Designer is more than just a MIDI effect. In fact, it blocks note data when it is used as an insert in a MIDI channel. Step Designer is a very powerful step sequencer (**Figure 11.58**). You can use it to program note, velocity, gate, and up to two controller messages at the same time. Step sequencers were the first sequencers created and they're used to create patterns of MIDI data. If you are interested in electronic music, particularly techno or electro, take extra time to learn this MIDI effect.

Track Control gives users of GS and XG synthesizers (you know who you are) graphical control over the specialized parameters for those synths.

Track FX mimics the Track Parameters section of the Project window's Track inspector for a MIDI track. Use this effect if you prefer it to the Track inspector.

Transformer can do nearly anything imaginable to MIDI data. It's a lot like the logical editor that was part of Cubase VST, and you can use it to modify MIDI data by building rules to insert, delete, or modify notes and controllers. It's pretty geeky, and using it feels more like computer programming than playing an instrument, but it's extremely powerful and accurate.

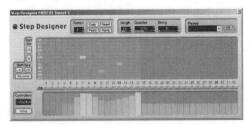

Figure 11.58 Step Designer, for serious step sequencing in MIDI

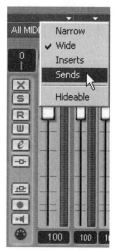

Figure 11.59 Opening send effects in the extended view area

Figure 11.60 Selecting MidiEcho as a send effect

MIDI Send Effects

So far, we've explored MIDI effects for insert processing. An insert effect takes incoming MIDI, routes it through the effect or effects, and takes the output and routes it to the VST instrument or MIDI output for that channel. Send effects operate differently. When you use a send effect, the incoming data is split off from the main data stream and processed in parallel with the original signal. Essentially, the MIDI data is sent to the send effect and also to any insert effects and to the MIDI output for that channel.

Some effects, such as MidiEcho, lend themselves easily to send effects. Others, such as Density, don't necessarily make sense as send effects, because there's no benefit from thinning MIDI data using only part of the data stream.

One very cool feature of MIDI send effects is that they can be sent to their own outputs. This gives rise to some interesting creative possibilities. For instance, the delay from a MIDI track can trigger a different sound than the original MIDI notes.

To use MIDI send effects:

1. From the extended view pop-up menu for the channel to which you want to apply the effect, select Sends (**Figure 11.59**).

2. In the extended view area, click the first send effect slot, which will default to No Effect, and select MidiEcho (**Figure 11.60**).

continues on next page

MIDI SEND EFFECTS

3. Set the parameters of the plug-in as you want and close the editor when you are finished.

4. Click below the name of the selected effect to access a menu that allows you to specify where the output of the effect is routed. In this case, specify where to route the MIDI echoes.

In **Figure 11.61**, the output of the send effect is routed to a third-party VST instrument called PPG Wave 2V.

5. Start playback of the project to hear the original MIDI sound and the echoes.

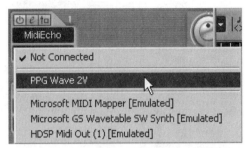

Figure 11.61 A MIDI send effect can route its output to any MIDI device—in this case, to a VST instrument.

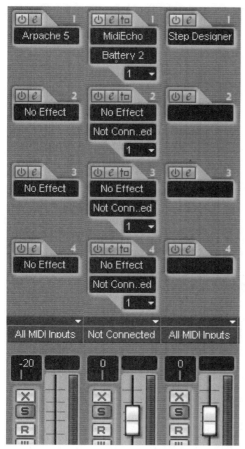

Figure 11.62 Three tracks, all soloed, with MIDI effects and Step Designer

Saving MIDI with Effects

When mixing a project, different people will want to use MIDI effects in different ways. Some people will always want to use the mixer and effects live, with all effects running at the same time. Other people will want to freeze the effects into a distinct MIDI part, so they can play it back later without need for the effects.

If you are familiar with traditional audio mixing, this is akin to what are called printing effects. Some engineers like to add all effects at mixdown so that every sonic decision can be considered and reconsidered. Some prefer to record the effects along with the original signal to tape (or disk) and thereby commit to the sound with the effects. Many people use both approaches. You might want to commit your MIDI effects to new parts for convenience or to have a copy of one attempt to get a good sound, avoiding the trouble of saving and recalling presets later.

To save parts with MIDI effects:

1. Use the mixer, insert effects, and send effects to set up all MIDI channels precisely as you want them. You can do this for one channel or multiple channels.

2. Solo all channels that you want to print to a new part.

   Figure 11.62 shows three channels, with insert and send effects, soloed and ready to go.

3. In the Project window, set the left and right locators to include the area you want to save to a new MIDI part.

4. Still in the Project window, select an empty MIDI track as the location to which you want to save.

continues on next page

SAVING MIDI WITH EFFECTS

5. From the MIDI menu, choose Merge Midi in Loop (**Figure 11.63**).

A dialog box opens (**Figure 11.64**).

6. If you want to print the effects, check Include Inserts and Include Sends.

7. Click OK.

Cubase will process the MIDI and place the new MIDI part on the track you selected in the Project window while leaving the original part intact.

Figure 11.63 This command, Merge MIDI in Loop, makes Cubase bounce MIDI to a new part.

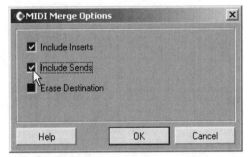

Figure 11.64 Select both of these options to include all MIDI effects in the new part.

VST Instrument and ReWire Channels

VST instruments were explained in Chapter 7, "Using Virtual Instruments" and ReWire will be covered in Chapter 13, later in this book, but in brief, ReWire is a protocol that lets audio applications on the same computer exchange MIDI, audio, and synchronization information.

VST instruments and ReWire applications usually create channels in the mixer where the audio they produce can be folded into a project. **Figure 11.65** shows two mixer channels; the one on the left is a ReWire channel, and the one on the right is a VST instrument channel.

If you say to yourself that these two channels look an awful lot like audio channels, you will be right. In fact, the only difference between an audio channel and a VSTi or ReWire channel is the source of the audio. ReWire and VSTi channels use the same effects, EQ, and mixer settings as described earlier in this chapter for audio channels.

The only situation in which you might trip up with these two types of channels is when they are soloed or muted. Remember that most VST instruments (and many ReWire channels) are triggered by a MIDI channel in the Cubase mixer. It's easy to inadvertently mute the MIDI source for a VST instrument and then wonder why it isn't sending audio to its mixer channel.

Figure 11.65 A ReWire channel (on the left) and a VST instrument channel (on the right).

Using Output Busses

If you have a sound or audio card with multiple outputs, you can activate the additional outputs in stereo pairs to make them available for Cubase. These are called output busses and are used to send audio directly to those sound card outputs instead of to the main mixer. You can use output busses in many ways. For instance, you can send tracks to output busses to create individual headphone mixes for each performer, or you can send tracks to external effects or processing devices connected to the sound card in the computer.

To view and activate output busses:

1. From the Devices menu, select VST Outputs (**Figure 11.66**).

   The VST Outputs panel opens, showing all available stereo pairs of outputs on the sound card installed in the computer. The leftmost fader pair will be the Master channel.

2. To activate any other output bus, click its on/off button (**Figure 11.67**).

   It's a bit difficult to see, but in Figure 11.67 the ModPro bus is turned on and the MoFx bus is turned off.

✔ Tips

■ Busses can be named easily. Simply click the name of the bus to select it and then type a new name (**Figure 11.68**).

■ Always remember that to send audio to a particular hardware output on your sound or audio card, it must be activated as an output bus to make it available in the Cubase mixer.

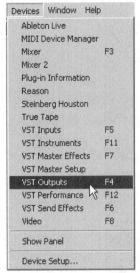

Figure 11.66 This menu item opens the VST Outputs panel.

Figure 11.67 You must turn on output busses by clicking their power buttons.

Figure 11.68 Giving an output bus a descriptive name makes it much easier to figure out what should be routed to it.

Figure 11.69 A group channel, with two insert effects active: Group channels are fundamentally the same as audio channels.

Assigning Group Channels

The final channels in the Cubase mixer are the group channels. A group channel (**Figure 11.69**) is like an audio metachannel. A group channel plays back audio only when another channel (such as an audio, VSTi, or ReWire channel) is configured to send audio to it. Group channels do the same thing that audio bus channels do on more complex hardware mixers, but because they are part of a digital mixer, group channels offer additional flexibility for routing and effects.

One of the main uses for a group channel (or a mixer bus in hardware mixer language) is to control multiple channels with one fader. A carefully recorded acoustic drum kit might have 12 channels or more, with multiple microphones on each drum and many more for cymbals and room ambience. After each channel gets its own tweaks and modifications, usually the full drum mix is sent to a group channel. At this point, it might get additional EQ and effects, before being sent to the final stereo output of the mix. You might also use a group channel when you overdub multiple guitar tracks playing the same part to get a thicker sound. You can send all of those tracks to one group for additional mixing before sending the channel to the final stereo output.

To route multiple channels to a group:

1. Create the group channel, if necessary, and give it a name (**Figure 11.70**).

2. Choose one of the other audio (or VSTi or ReWire) channels that should be routed to this group. At the very bottom of the channel is a pop-up menu that assigns the output of the channel to the master output, to any additional active outputs, or to any group. Open this menu and assign the channel to the group (**Figure 11.71**).

3. Repeat step 2 for each channel you want to route to the group.

    Figure 11.72 shows multiple channels of a drum kit routed to the same group.

✔ Tips

■ When tracks are routed in this way, they are sent to the group channel at the very end of the signal chain. All insert effects, EQ settings, and pan settings will be reflected in the group channel.

■ Remember that group channels themselves can be routed to other group channels or to output buses. This capability can be useful when routing audio to external effects, creating headphone mixes, and performing many other mixing tasks.

■ Group channels have one additional, very important property when the channels are soloed. If a channel is routed to a group, as described in this chapter, when such a channel is soloed, the group to which it is routed is soloed as well. In addition, when a group is soloed, all channels that are routed to it are soloed along with the group.

Figure 11.70 This group channel has been named DrumMix.

Figure 11.71 The output pop-up menu assigns audio channels, in this case to the DrumMix group channel.

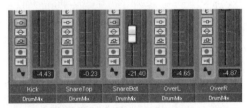

Figure 11.72 A simple multichannel drum mix, with all channels routed to a single group channel

- If you have more than one group channel, you can route a group channel to another group channel, but only in ascending order. That is, you can route group channel 1 to group channel 4, but you can't route group channel 11 to group channel 9.

- Group channels cannot be monaural.

- Group channels contain all of the insert and send effects and EQ capabilities of audio channels. The only difference is the source of the sound.

- You create group channels in a project exactly like you create audio and MIDI channels, by using the context menu in the Project window or by choosing Project > Add Track > Group Channel. You can add more group channels to a project whenever you need them.

A Practical Example

While my editor and I were working on this chapter (and the next chapter about effects), we decided that practical explanation of some of the techniques discussed would be helpful. It's easier to comprehend some of these concepts with audio and screen shots from a particular track than when you simply read about them in the abstract.

To provide these examples, I've created a tutorial at my Web site. You'll find a few pages with ideas and explanations demonstrated with one of my own tracks. You can download an archive of loops and audio clips, and the full mix created with them, at www.thadbrown.com/cubase if you want to see some of these features in action instead of just on the page.

Linking Mixer Channels

Another common approach when working with multiple tracks is to link channels. Two channels that are linked will synchronize their fader moves with each other. If you move the fader on one channel, the level of the other channel will change as well. In fact, the two channels will change levels proportionally, allowing them to be treated as one fader.

One situation in which linked channels are very useful is when you are working with multiple sounds from the same instrument. For instance, a bass might be recorded on two tracks: one with a microphone on an amplifier and one plugged into the sound card after a direct box or a preamplifier. After you set the relationship between the two tracks to achieve the sound you want, you can link the channels together and edit them as a group.

What Should Your Listener Hear?

Much of the art of mixing involves leading your listener to the parts you want heard. A song can have dozens of instruments and hundreds of tracks, with each one being important to the final mix, but a complex mix can easily become confusing.

Assume that you are mixing a song completely on your own and can make all of the decisions. When starting to mix the song, try to identify the two or three most important and highest-quality parts of the song (and hope that they are the same). If you are mixing a hip-hop tune, for instance, the bass line and the vocal may be what matter most. For an acoustic jazz record, you might decide that the soloists and the ride cymbal are most crucial. With a singer-songwriter recording, you might have only a guitar and a vocal, so you don't have much of a decision to make.

After you've identified the crucial elements of a song, check yourself every now and then while you are mixing to see whether you have made changes that enhance or detract from these critical parts.

LINKING MIXER CHANNELS

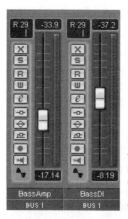

Figure 11.73 Two channels that together create a single bass sound. The direct (or DI) sound is louder, and the amp adds texture.

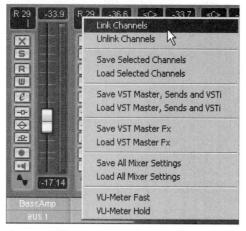

Figure 11.74 Select both channels and then use this menu to link them.

Figure 11.75 The fader on the right is being moved; the fader on the left follows automatically.

To link mixer channels:

1. Set the relative levels of the two tracks so they sound correct to you (**Figure 11.73**).

2. Click the name at the bottom of one channel and hold down the Shift key while clicking the other channel.

   This will select the channels to be linked.

3. Right-click (Windows) or Control-click (Mac OS X) any selected channel to open the context menu and select Link Channels (**Figure 11.74**).

4. Click either fader to change the level of one channel, and the other will follow (**Figure 11.75**).

✔ Tip

■ To unlink channels, select them and choose Unlink Channels from the same context menu as shown in Figure 11.74.

Learning from Masters

One of the best ways to learn about mixing is to listen to great mixes. Don't listen as a fan or a musician, but try to figure out what kind of panning, level, EQ, and effects techniques were used to create the mix. Try to figure out what the mixer did to make the mix sound good. And don't listen only to types of music that you like, but try to learn from a variety of styles.

Here is a purely subjective list of albums that I find provide insight into mixing techniques and that you might want to listen to get ideas.

Rock/Pop

AC/DC—Back in Black: An extremely simple approach to a two-guitar rock band with bass, vocals, and drums. Drums are in stereo, guitars are panned fairly hard right and left, and vocals and bass are right up the middle.

Ministry—Filth Pig: Nobody crams sonic information into a track like Ministry. Every single slice of the frequency spectrum is used, often as abrasively and aggressively as possible.

Verve—Urban Hymns: An expertly mixed, lush pop record. The vocals are always prominent, but other instruments are still present and forceful.

Acoustic

Buena Vista Social Club: An expertly recorded and mixed record of rediscovered Cuban music legends. Producer/engineer/guitar genius/legend Ry Cooder creates a very believable space with a stereo mix.

Grant Green—Idle Moments, RVG Edition: RVG stands for Rudy van Gelder, the engineer behind the classic Blue Note records from the 1950s forward. He remastered this eerily present and real-sounding 60s classic.

Electronic

Madonna—Ray of Light: Pop superstar gives big-budget access to dream shopping list of British/European dance music producers.

Thievery Corporation—Richest Man in Babylon: American downtempo duo brings mixing techniques from hip-hop, dub, pop, and R&B to a single record. Expert use of effects.

AUDIO EFFECT PLUG-INS

Audio effects date back to the earliest days of recording, and many different effects are used today in all styles of music. You probably have spent at least some time with effects if you have done analog recording previously.

Steinberg pioneered the use of software effects, usually referred to as plug-ins. These run completely inside the computer and comprise an amazing advance for computer audio users. Now, instead of having to learn a whole new application to apply reverb or chorus to a track, you can use effects to accomplish everything within Cubase itself. We take this for granted today, but it was not always so.

In this chapter, you will begin by learning about the types of plug-ins you can use in Cubase. You will also learn about the basic kinds of audio effects available and about some of the plug-ins included with Cubase. Once you are familiar with some of the tools, you will learn more about routing audio to effects and creative ways to combine effects using groups.

Supported Plug-in Formats

In an enlightened world, every audio application would work with all effects from every developer. Sadly, this is not the world we live in, and not every plug-in will work with all programs. Steinberg was a pioneer in the software effects arena, and their VST format is probably the most popular on the market, so as a Cubase user you have one of the widest selections of plug-ins from which to choose. Still, it is important to remember that (depending on your platform) only one or two plug-in formats are supported in Cubase.

Cubase supports the following plug-ins formats:

◆ **VST** plug-ins naturally are supported by Cubase. Steinberg created the VST format, and one of the greatest attractions of the first VST versions of Cubase was the wide range of effects plug-ins for the program. VST plug-ins are supported on both PCs and Macs.

◆ **DirectX** (usually referred to in shorthand as DX) is the Microsoft-supported and blessed format for multimedia development in Windows. For years, installing a new version of DX had an effect on computer stability and performance roughly akin to pouring gasoline on the CPU, setting it on fire, and then throwing the machine from a third-story balcony. Luckily, things have improved greatly, and DX on Windows XP works quite well. DX plug-ins are for PCs only. You can select them at the bottom of the drop-down menu in each effect slot (**Figure 12.1**).

Figure 12.1 A list of installed VST plug-ins, with DirectX plug-ins in a submenu

Cubase does *not* support the following plug-in formats:

◆ **RTAS** and **TDM** are proprietary formats designed by Digidesign and work only within its hardware/software systems.

◆ **Audio Unit** is part of the new system-level multimedia toolkit from Apple. As this is written, Cubase does not support Audio Units, but Audio Unit plug-ins for use with Cubase may be available in the future.

◆ **MAS**, or the MOTU Audio System, is a proprietary format used only by Digital Performer, a Mac-only digital audio sequencer from Mark of the Unicorn.

Four Kinds of Effects

You probably have heard of dozens of different kinds of effects over the years. It can seem overwhelming at times to keep track of all of the different names and types of effects. However, nearly every effect can be considered a member of one of four groups.

♦ **Filters** change the harmonic or timbral content of a sound. The simplest filters to use, such as shelving EQ, will modify, mask, or highlight bass or treble frequencies in a sound. If you have ever used an analog or virtual analog synthesizer, you know that synths also have filters, which are often more dramatic and aggressive in their sonic characteristics, but they basically perform the same functions.

♦ **Dynamics** includes compressors, limiters, and expanders. These effects modify the volume, or level, of a sound. A compressor, for example, lessens the dynamic range of a sound by reducing the volume of the signal when it passes a defined level. Usually the compressed track is then turned up a bit in the mix to increase its overall perceived volume.

♦ **Delay** is used to create repeats of a sound, which are offset in time as the sound is sent through the effect. In some instances, delays are used to mimic sound bouncing off of walls, and in some instances, they are used for much less natural effects. Very short delay times can thicken a sound without sounding like an effect at all.

♦ **Modulation** effects are technically a subset of delays but work so differently from delays that they are best considered on their own. Very short delay times (from less than a millisecond to a few milliseconds) are used to create effects like chorus, flanging, and phase shifting. When a slightly delayed sound is mixed back with the dry, nondelayed sound, various comb-filtering, doubling, and phase-shifting effects result. Often the length of the delay is modulated in some way—thus, the general term *modulation* effects.

It helps to keep in mind that all effects are some variation on these four basic sound modifiers. The legendary voltage-controlled filter in a Mini-Moog is just a versatile and great-sounding low-pass filter. A ridiculously expensive vintage Echoplex is simply a great-sounding delay unit that uses magnetic tape to generate the repeats. Even a trippy effect like a vocoder is still just a number of narrow-frequency-band filters that can be modulated.

Insert and Send Effects

An insert effect is the simplest kind of effect. The audio enters the effect, is modified, and then is routed to the fader for that channel and to whatever output that channel feeds.

With send effects, the audio is split and routed to two paths. The audio sent to the "normal" path (which can include insert effects and EQs) runs directly to the channel fader. Audio routed to the send path is processed by the send effect and then normally sent to the master output, but it does not have a fader to control the level of the signal processed by the send effect. Often an audio channel in the mixer will have both send and insert effects, and some effects lend themselves specifically to being send or insert effects. Others can work quite nicely in both contexts.

The fundamentals of creating and using insert effects have already been covered, but before you learn about the effects included with Cubase, you ought to know the basics of creating and using send effects.

To use a send effect:

1. Select Devices > VST Send Effects (**Figure 12.2**) to open the VST Send Effects window.

2. In the window, click the top effects slot (which is probably marked "No Effect") to open a drop-down menu of the installed effects. (Your options will not be exactly like mine.) From this menu, select Reverb > Reverb A (**Figure 12.3**).

Figure 12.2 This menu opens the Send Effects virtual rack.

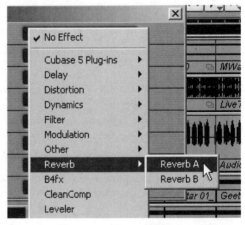

Figure 12.3 Adding a reverb plug-in as a send effect

Figure 12.4 To route sound to a send effect, you need to select Sends in the Extended View/Change Track View menu.

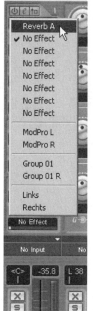

Figure 12.5 Selecting the Reverb A send effect

Figure 12.6 The amount of sound sent to the effect is controlled by the blue-green slider (under the mouse pointer here).

3. Open the Cubase mixer and find a channel to which you might want to add reverb. Click the Extended View (also known as Change Track View) pop-up menu—the down-pointing triangle in the dark gray band between the channel fader and the effects slots—and select Sends (**Figure 12.4**).

4. Click the top effects slot (in the vertical row of effects slots, above your selected channel in the Mixer) to open the menu of available Send effects. Select Reverb A for that slot (**Figure 12.5**).

This will allow you to use the first slot to send audio to the effect.

5. Drag the blue-green slider, which is below the name of the effect, to adjust the amount of the signal that is sent to the effect (**Figure 12.6**).

You can use up to eight send effects simultaneously, and as you will learn later in this chapter, you can also use group channels for send effects. The following pages describe the effects included with Cubase, and then you will learn more about how to use effects to create better-sounding mixes.

INSERT AND SEND EFFECTS

DoubleDelay

Delays, as noted previously, are effects that repeat an audio signal. Delay effects have the following fundamental parameters:

♦ The length of time for the delay, usually expressed in milliseconds or in tempo divisions.

♦ The amount of the delayed signal that is fed back into the delay effect. This creates more than one repeat with the effect and is usually called feedback.

♦ The mix between the unaffected dry signal and the effected "wet" signal.

The DoubleDelay plug-in included with Cubase SX (**Figure 12.7**) is fairly simple looking but is actually a quite powerful delay. As its name indicates, it's really two delays in one plug-in, and it has some parameters beyond those mentioned in the preceding list. Each delay can have independent settings for the delay time and each also has a pan setting for the delayed audio, but the amount of feedback is set globally for both delays. The following example uses DoubleDelay as a send effect.

To use DoubleDelay:

1. From the Devices menu, select VST Send Effects.

2. In the panel that opens, click the first slot labeled "No Effect." In the drop-down menu that opens, select Delay > DoubleDelay (**Figure 12.8**).

   When the editor for the DoubleDelay plug-in opens, you will set a number of parameters.

Figure 12.7 The editor panel for DoubleDelay

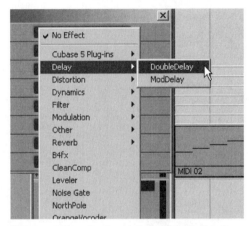

Figure 12.8 Choosing DoubleDelay from the list of available plug-ins

Figure 12.9 Click this button (under the mouse pointer here) to set the DelayTime parameter to TempoSync.

Figure 12.10 Use this drop-down menu to select the delay time in note values.

Figure 12.11 The send effect slot set to route audio to the delay effect

Figure 12.12 Use the slider to determine how much audio is sent to the effect.

3. Set the Mix slider all the way to the top, to 100%.

Because send effects run in parallel, you will usually want only the effected signal (without the dry signal) to come out of the effect.

4. Turn on tempo sync for both delays by clicking the white button above each DelayTime knob (**Figure 12.9**).

Most likely, the defaults for the delay times will be just as shown in Figure 12.9, where 1/4 means a quarter-note.

5. Click the setting for DelayTime2 and select 1/8 from the menu (**Figure 12.10**). Leave the other parameters at their defaults.

6. Close the DoubleDelay editor and open the Cubase mixer.

7. Find a channel to send to the delay. A percussive sound or drum loop will let you hear the delay clearly. Most likely, DoubleDelay will be selected in the first slot of the Sends section in the extended view area (**Figure 12.11**) above the channel. If it is not, click the first send slot to select it.

8. Turn on the send slot by clicking its power button at the top left of the channel (if it's not already lit and activated). Click and drag on the green slider in the Send slot to add more or less of the signal to the Send effect (**Figure 12.12**).

9. Play the project to hear the effect.

DOUBLEDELAY

Using Tempo-Synchronized Delays

DoubleDelay is one of many plug-ins with parameters that can be set to note values that automatically synchronize with the project tempo. Because so many plug-ins have tempo-based parameters, including many third-party plug-ins that are not covered in this book, it's worth looking at these a bit more closely. Most plug-ins use the same basic settings:

◆ Straight, or "normal," settings are simply the note values shown: 1/4 means a quarter-note, 1/8 means an eighth-note, and so on.

◆ Dotted note values add half again to the duration of their note value. That is, a dotted eighth note sets the parameter value to the duration of an eighth-note with a sixteenth-note tacked on the end of it.

◆ Triplet settings result in a duration that is a third of the note value set. That is, a quarter-note triplet setting will set the parameter value to one-third the duration of a quarter-note.

If you don't read standard musical notation and this is all mumbo-jumbo to you, don't worry; you can hear these changes easily when working with a plug-in. Here is a way for you to hear the tempo-synced parameters using another delay plug-in bundled with Cubase.

Using Delays

Delay is used in nearly every kind of music, for all kinds of effects. If you listen to the original Sun Studios Elvis Presley tracks, you will often hear a clearly audible, very short single delay on the vocals and guitars. This prominent delay is usually called slapback and is characteristic of lots of early rockabilly and rock'n'roll. Guitar players have used delay effects for years to thicken their guitar sounds, usually less prominently than on the rockabilly tracks, and usually with a few more repeats.

Rock music often uses a combination of delay and modulation effects on snare drums, vocals, and guitars, all with the goal of fattening the sounds of the instruments. Only rarely are the effects obvious enough that average listeners can hear them.

To really hear a delay in a mix, electronic music and Jamaican music are the best place to listen. In fact, a CD by one of the '70s dub pioneers from Jamaica like King Tubby or Lee "Scratch" Perry is almost a master class on creative delay techniques.

Figure 12.13 The ModDelay editor panel

Figure 12.14 The bundled VST plug-ins all use these buttons to turn on TempoSync.

Figure 12.15 Selecting a tied eighth note as the delay time

To hear tempo-based delays:

1. Find a track with percussive content. Even a simple snare drum will do. Avoid full drum loops or vocal or string tracks because delays on these types of tracks can be difficult to hear. In the mixer channel for this track, select Inserts from the drop-down Change Track View triangle between the channel fader and the effects slots.

2. In the first insert effect slot, select Delay > ModDelay.

3. In the setting window that appears, set the Mix slider to 25%, Feedback to 30%, and Delay Mod to zero (**Figure 12.13**).

4. Click the small box next to the DelayTime setting to turn on tempo synchronization (**Figure 12.14**).

5. Start the project playing and click the DelayTime setting to open the drop-down menu (**Figure 12.15**). Select some of the tempo settings to audition the straight, dotted, and triplet time delay settings.

✔ Tip

■ The TempoSync setting, to the right of the DelayTime setting in Figure 12.14, is a multiplier for the tempo sync. That is, if DelayTime is set to 1/8 and TempoSync is set to 3x, the resulting delay time is the duration of three eighth-notes.

Varying Pitch with ModDelay

ModDelay is useful for more than just learning about tempo-based parameters or creating simple repeats. The *Mod* in ModDelay stands for modulation, which plays a significant role in many different kinds of effects. Modulation is the automatic changing of the value of a particular parameter over time. A simple modulator is the speed setting on a tremolo effect: the volume of the signal is changed more slowly or quickly according to that speed setting.

ModDelay uses pitch modulation to add to what the effect can do. Classic delay units, like tape delays and analog chip-based delays, change the pitch of the delayed signal if the delay time changes. This makes sense in the example of a tape delay; one way to change the delay time of a tape delay is to speed up the tape, which, of course, will temporarily increase the pitch of the repeats.

Figure 12.16 The ModDelay plug-in set to allow you to hear how it works

Figure 12.17 Dragging the Delay Mod knob adds pitch modulation to the delays.

To use ModDelay:

1. Using the same sound as in the previous example with DoubleDelay, open ModDelay as an insert in the channel by selecting Delay > ModDelay in the first insert slot.

2. In the ModDelay window, set the Mix slider at 25%, set Feedback to 30%, turn on TempoSync with the square button above and to the right of the DelayTime knob, and select 1/16 (**Figure 12.16**).

3. Start playback of the project to hear the delay effect on the channel. You might want to solo the channel as well.

4. Drag the Delay Mod knob to increase its value (**Figure 12.17**).

   You'll hear the pitch of the delays change as you increase this setting.

VARYING PITCH WITH MODDELAY

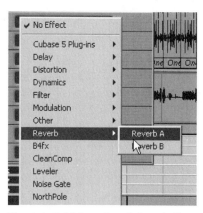

Figure 12.18 Adding a Reverb A send effect

Figure 12.19 Selecting the Large preset for the Reverb effect

Reverb

Reverb, of course, is short for reverberation. A sound in an enclosed space will take part of its quality from the space in which it occurs. Reverb is really nothing more than an extremely complex set of delays that simulate the effect of distance and reflection on a sound as it bounces off the walls, floor, ceiling, and any other objects in the room, over and over again. The delays are so close together that our ears perceive them as a wash of sound instead of distinctive delays.

The characteristics of reverb vary widely, depending on the room (its size, shape, composition, number of objects inside it, and so on), the position of the sound generator and the listener, and even factors such as the temperature and humidity of the air. Reverb is almost always used as a send effect and is used at least some of the time on every instrument in every type of music, for every style of mix. Cubase includes two distinct-sounding reverb plug-ins.

To use reverb:

1. Open the Send Effects panel by clicking the Devices menu and selecting VST Send Effects.

2. In an open effects slot, select Reverb > Reverb A (**Figure 12.18**).

3. In the Reverb A window that opens, click the presets menu at the bottom and select Large; then drag the Mix slider all the way to the bottom, to 100% wet (**Figure 12.19**).

continues on next page

REVERB

4. In the Cubase mixer, find a track to test the reverb and select Sends from the Change Track View triangle midway on the channel strip.

5. Click an open effect slot and select Reverb A from the drop-down list.

6. Drag the blue-green slider in the effects slot to the right to send part of the signal from that channel to the reverb effect (**Figure 12.20**); then play the project.

7. Go back to the Reverb A editor panel and audition some of the other presets to become more familiar with the way that they modify the sound.

Figure 12.20 Adding the reverb effect with a send slot for an audio channel

REVERB

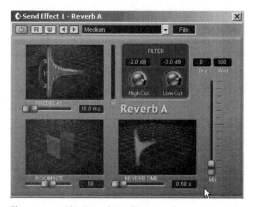

Figure 12.21 The Reverb A editor panel

Reverb A Settings

Cubase's Reverb A plug-in (**Figure 12.21**) includes parameters common to most digital reverb effects. If you take the time to become familiar with how it works, and how the parameters change the sound of the reverb, you will have an easier time understanding lots of other reverb effects.

◆ **Predelay** mimics one of the characteristics of reverb in an actual room, where there is usually a slight delay between the sound being created and the start of the reverb. This delay occurs because the sound has to travel to at least one wall or other surface and then travel back to our ears before we hear the start of the reverb. This delay can be anywhere from a couple of milliseconds in a smallish room to much longer in a big room.

◆ **Filter** changes the timbre of the reverb. The High Cut filter is used to make the "room" sound more or less bright. A room with deep shag carpet on the floor and curtains on one side will sound different than a brick-walled room with a hardwood floor. Using High Cut to filter out the high-end will make the reverb sound more like the carpeted, "darker" room. The Low Cut filter is useful for cutting out low-end rumble that usually sounds pretty bad when fed to a reverb.

◆ **Roomsize** controls the character of the reverb by mimicking the timbre differences between larger and smaller acoustic spaces.

◆ **Reverb Time** controls the length of time the reverb lasts. The Reverb A plug-in can range from very short to very, very long reverb times.

✔ Tip

■ Reverb B, the other reverb plug-in included with Cubase, uses many of the same parameters, but with a more knob-oriented interface. It also sounds a bit different and uses somewhat less CPU bandwidth to run.

REVERB A SETTINGS

Using Reverb

Few topics in the audio world create more catfights than the use of reverb. Beauty is as much in the eye (or ear) of the beholder with reverb as it is with anything related to music. The earliest reverb units were what are now called reverb chambers. A fairly small, bright (lots of flat surfaces to reflect sound), enclosed space was set up with a speaker on one side and a microphone on the other side; the reverb send on the mixer routed audio to the speaker in the reverb chamber, and the microphone in the chamber picked up the sound with its added reverb effect and returned it to the mixer. One famous '50s engineer drove around the country-side yelling into empty water tanks until he found one he liked the sound of; then he bought the tank, outfitted it with a speaker and a microphone to create a reverb chamber, and buried it behind his recording studio.

Even in the '50s, not many recording studios could or would go to that trouble, so other methods of artificial reverb were created over time. Usually they used some kind of trans-ducer to translate sound waves into energy that would move a metal spring or plate, and the resulting back and forth motion of the metal would produce a reverberating effect on the sound. The reverb tanks in guitar amplifiers and some electric pianos descend from those artificial reverb units. Eventually, effects designers put reverb on computer chips, giving birth to digital reverb.

Reverb can be used on pretty much every instrument in a mix, though this does not mean that it needs to be slathered on everything in sight. As with the overuse of EQ, a huge wash of long reverb on every instrument in a mix positively screams "novice mixer." When you are working with a mix, try creating two reverb sends with different sounds and then send very slight amounts of grouped tracks to one or the other. For example, if you have multiple acoustic guitar tracks, applying a little reverb will make them sound like they are from the same acoustic space and can really flesh them out. The same can be done with horns or backup singers or some other part of the mix. Often one or two very prominent parts, like the snare drum or the vocal, will have their own reverb sound parts.

A very personal note: I love digital sound, digital recording, digital synths, and electronic music. My life often seems to be a riot of the digital—but most digital reverb sounds awful to me. Because of this, I tend to use very low-tech, low-fidelity spring reverbs from the '70s and '80s when I use reverb at all. Until my landlords agree to let me tear up the parking lot behind my house and bury a water tank underneath it, that's really my only option. You may find reverb plug-ins that you think sound great, but take a look at some of the hardware units, both digital and analog, to see if one better fits your sonic needs.

Chorus

Chorus is a modulation effect used to add thickness and oftentimes audible pitch modulation to a signal. The name derives from the fact that a chorus of four singers, no matter how skilled and prepared, cannot sing the same part in exactly the same way and at exactly the same pitch. A chorus effect takes the signal, splits off a very short delay line, pitch modulates the delayed signal (or signals in a stereo chorus), and then mixes the delayed signal with the original. The modulation is from a low-frequency oscillator, or LFO. Like a lot of modulation effects, chorus sounds show up everywhere, from very inexpensive stomp boxes, to vintage analog devices, to high-end digital multi-effects hardware boxes.

Chorus can do a lot of things. As an insert effect, it can thicken sounds by adding a subtle doubling effect, like two players playing the same part. Because it pitch modulates the delays, it can also offer a good way to add stereo ambience to a mono signal. To do this, chorus needs to be used as a send effect, because applying an insert effect to a mono channel produces only mono output. The following example uses chorus as a send effect.

CHORUS

To use chorus:

1. Open the Send Effects panel (Devices > Send Effects) and select Modulation > Chorus.

2. In the Chorus settings editor panel, set the Mix slider to 100% and drag the Frequency knob to a setting slightly below 1.00 Hz. Set Delay to about 1.5 ms and set Stages to 2 (**Figure 12.22**).

3. In the mixer, find a channel that you want to send to the chorus effect. Using the Extended View/Change Track View drop-down menu, select Sends.

4. Click the drop-down menu in the top send slot in the channel strip to select Chorus if it isn't already selected. Turn on the power button for the send slot and use the green slider in the settings window to adjust and send audio for the chorus effect (**Figure 12.23**).

5. Play the project to hear the effect.

✔ Tips

- The Stages setting in the settings window controls how thick the chorus sounds. Each progressive stage adds another delay to the effect.

- The Shapes buttons in the settings window control the shape of the LFO that is modulating the pitch change in the effect. The default sawtooth waveform is very common for effect modulation, but the other two waveforms produce interesting results as well.

Figure 12.22 The Chorus editor

Figure 12.23 Adding chorus via a send slot

CHORUS

Figure 12.24 The Dynamics editor

Figure 12.25 You can use these buttons to change the order of the three effects in the Dynamics plug-in.

✔ Tip

■ The Routing section (**Figure 12.25**) is used to change the order of the effects. By default, the plug-in routing path is Compressor-Autogate-Limiter, but you can use the Routing buttons to reorder the effects.

Dynamics

Dynamic effects alter the level, or volume, of audio and can perform all manner of tasks. For instance, they can perform compression to reduce the dynamic range of audio, perform expansion to increase the dynamic range of audio, and set limits to establish the absolute maximum level for a signal. Cubase includes plug-ins that can accomplish all of these tasks and a good many more. The main plug-in covered here is the Dynamics plug-in (**Figure 12.24**).

The Dynamics plug-in is actually three plug-ins in one, with distinct sections for three different dynamics control jobs:

◆ **Compress** is the compressor section. A compressor reduces the dynamic range of an audio signal by reducing the level of that signal after it rises above a certain value.

◆ **Autogate** is an audio gate effect. Gates are normally used for noise reduction; a gate silences the channel when the level reaches a specified value. In other words, below a certain volume, a gate mutes the channel. Gates can be useful for controlling tracks with unwanted sounds such as background noise and hiss.

◆ **Limiter** is a little like a compressor but is a more heavy-handed effect. A compressor reduces the signal when it passes a certain level, but a limiter is a brick wall and will not let a signal sound beyond a certain level.

You turn each of the three effects on or off by clicking its name at the top of its section of the editor.

DYNAMICS

Compressor

The Compressor section (**Figure 12.26**) of the Dynamics plug-in is probably its most used component. The controls and parameters for this effect are pretty standard. If you have used hardware compressors, you should be able to negotiate this section immediately. If you are not familiar with compression, here are the parameters and what they do:

Figure 12.26 The compressor effect in the Dynamics plug-in

◆ **Threshold** determines at what level the compressor starts to act on the signal. Audio below the threshold passes through unchanged.

◆ **Ratio** controls how much the audio above the threshold is compressed. For example, a 3:1 ratio means that for every increase of 3 decibels in the signal, the compressor will increase the level by 1 decibel. The higher the ratio, the more pronounced the compression effect.

◆ **Attack** is used to change how quickly the compressor takes action once the signal is above the threshold. Short attack times clamp down on the audio quickly, while longer attack times allow more of the front edge of a signal to pass through the compressor before it starts to change levels.

◆ **Release** is the flipside of attack. It controls how long the compressor takes to stop compressing when the signal drops below the threshold.

◆ **Mode** determines how the compressor looks at the incoming signal, using the RMS and Peak buttons. RMS responds to the average level, which is usually best for legato instruments and vocals, and Peak responds more to transients and is generally better for transient-heavy material like percussion.

Figure 12.27 The Autogate effect in the Dynamics plug-in

Autogate

The second section of the Dynamics plug-in is Autogate (**Figure 12.27**). The main use of gates is to mute channels that have excessive noise or hum, so they don't clutter up the sound of a mix. You can also use gates to create dramatic and obvious stuttering audio effects. Autogate is a very complex tool, and a lot of people don't use it much, but it's still good to understand how it works in case you do find the need for the effect. Here's what the settings do:

◆ Three of the bottom four knobs, **Threshold**, **Attack,** and **Release**, act in the same way as in the Compressor section. Threshold sets the level at which the gate is opened and the level below which the channel is silenced. Attack controls how quickly the gate opens when the signal passes the threshold level, and Release controls how quickly the gate closes when the signal goes below the threshold setting.

◆ **Hold** governs how the gate closes, because when you use a gate as a noise-reduction tool, it often makes a sound when it opens and closes, and this sound usually sounds bad. The Hold setting simply holds the gate open for a specified amount of time when the signal gets below the threshold. When that time has passed, the Release parameter takes over. Use Hold if you have a good gate setting that closes a little too often, such as when a horn player is breathing.

continues on next page

DYNAMICS

- **Trigger Frequency Range** is an even more advanced method for noise gating. This setting, modified by the slider, limits the part of the signal that the gate watches to see when it should open. By limiting the frequencies that can open the gate, you can keep out unwanted sounds like low-frequency rumble or high-frequency tape hiss. **Figure 12.28** shows a very narrow range, and **Figure 12.29** shows the full audio spectrum.

Figure 12.28 A narrow frequency range for triggering the gate

Figure 12.29 A wide range

Limiter

The third section of the Dynamics plug-in is the **Limiter** (**Figure 12.30**). Limiters are devices that set an absolute ceiling on how high (loud) the level of an audio signal is allowed to go. Limiters are particularly useful with digital audio, to keep ugly digital distortion from being introduced later in the processing chain.

Figure 12.30 The Limiter section has only a few adjustable parameters.

The parameters for the Limiter in the Dynamics plug-in are very simple. **Threshold** sets the ceiling for the limiter; audio will not be allowed to exceed the level set here. **Release** controls how quickly the limiter lets go of the signal when the level falls below the threshold. You can click the **Auto** button in the Limiter settings window to enable the plug-in to find a setting based on the kind of audio passing through the plug-in. You'll know when the Limiter is engaged and acting on the signal when the red Limiting light is on. The light can help you gauge how much the Limiter is changing the signal.

Analog limiters have a very difficult job. Usually a limiter is supposed to grab transients (the beginning, percussive milliseconds of a note produced by some instruments) and pull down their level, but most transients are short and sudden. It takes a real expert to properly set a hardware limiter to act as a brick wall for audio. For digital audio, though, the limiter can peek ahead to see what is coming down the audio pipe.

Figure 12.31 Selecting Dynamics as an insert plug-in

Using Dynamics

As with EQ, using compression is an art, and your skills will get better with practice. If you already know a good bit about compression, the controls for the Dynamics plug-in should be transparent. If you're not familiar with compression, spend some time working through the presets and practice with different kinds of audio material.

Compression is nearly always used as an insert effect. The point of a compressor is to control the dynamics of a sound, and routing only part of a channel to a compressor will not give full control over its dynamics. A compressor used as a send effect and set to reduce the transient pluck part of a bass sound will do so for only part of the signal. Only an insert effect will fully control that part of the sound. The following example shows you how to compress an electric bass track to bring it out more in the mix.

To compress a track with Dynamics:

1. For the channel you want to compress, set the Extended View/Change Track View menu to show inserts.

2. Click the top insert effect slot to open its drop-down menu and then select Dynamics > Dynamics (**Figure 12.31**).

3. Play the project to hear the track.

4. Click the Compress button in the settings editor window to activate compression in the plug-in. The button will turn yellow to indicate that it is active. If either Autogate or Limiter is selected, unselect them.

continues on next page

5. Drag the Threshold knob until the Gain Reduction meter begins to show that the compression is taking effect (**Figure 12.32**).

   The lower the threshold, the more the signal will be compressed.

6. Adjust the Ratio setting if the compression sounds too strong or not strong enough.

   Higher compression ratios force the level of the sound into a smaller range.

7. Adjust the Attack parameter if the compression is acting too quickly; this will take away the transient of the instrument being compressed.

8. Using the Gain Reduction meter as a guide, increase the MakeUp Gain knob (**Figure 12.33**) so that the effect of the plug-in is roughly equal for the overall level of the channel.

Figure 12.32 The meter is showing gain reduction of about 4 dB.

Figure 12.33 Adding back the gain that has been taken away by the compressor

Thinking Compression

Compression is not easy to understand, and the graphical tools for editing the parameters of an effect are not necessarily the easiest to use for an effect. Delay time is a comparatively easy parameter to figure out, but release for a compressor isn't, and editing release with a knob is not terribly intuitive. When learning to work with compressors, think about each sound as having three dynamic parts. The first part is the *transient*: the pluck of a guitar string, or the sound of the stick hitting a drum. Next is the *sustain* of the sound: the guitar string in its full resonance moving the wood of the guitar, or the sound of the full drum as it resonates. Last is the *decay*: where the string or drum stops moving and where the ambience of the room is heard. If you think of a sound as having these three main parts, it's easier to understand how dynamics control works.

Each of these dynamic components takes place over time, but every instrument is a bit different in how these three dynamic characteristics are manifest. If you think of a sound in terms of these three factors, it becomes easier to work with compression. For instance, the previous task, "To compress a track with Dynamics," discussed how to set a compressor for a bass. **Figure 12.34** shows a quick-and-dirty compressor setting for this bass. I wanted to keep the transient of the bass sound (the finger plucking the string) prominent, so I used a fairly slow attack. The threshold was set low, but the ratio was not too high. The compressor will compress a lot of the bass sound, but it won't compress it too much. I turned off the auto release and set a fairly long release time, to help smooth the transition from the compressed to the uncompressed part of the signal. In the end, what this setting does is raise the level of the middle, sustained part of the bass line, leaving the transient mostly untouched. There is little decay in the bass sound anyway, so the long release allows the action of the compressor to be very smooth.

Figure 12.34 A setting that I created quickly to compress a bass channel

Other Cubase Audio Plug-ins

The electronic documentation that comes with Cubase SX includes a PDF file containing parameter lists for the rest of the plug-ins included with the program. Here is a short description of each of the other effects:

◆ **SPL DeEsser** is an effect used to remove *s* sounds from vocals.

◆ **Bitcrusher** reduces the fidelity of the audio that plays back in Cubase. This effect is often used to mimic older, lo-fi samplers.

◆ **DaTube** emulates the saturation and compression characteristics of vacuum tubes.

◆ **StepFilter** combines a multimode resonant filter, as might be found on a virtual analog synthesizer, with a step sequencer. The sequencer can control both the frequency of the filter and the resonance (**Figure 12.35**).

◆ **Ringmodulator** is a classic synthesizer effect, generated by finding the sums and differences of two audio signals.

◆ **Rotary** emulates the sound of a spinning speaker, like the Leslie speakers used with Hammond B3 organs.

◆ **Vocoder** creates incredibly versatile and interesting effects. A vocoder uses two banks of identical filters, one of which modulates the other. A different signal is fed to each filter, and the filters of one of the signals are used to control the filters of the other signal (**Figure 12.36**).

◆ **VST Dynamics** adds a few features to the Dynamics plug-in discussed in this chapter. However, it also operates at a slightly higher latency and can use more CPU bandwidth.

Figure 12.35 The StepFilter plug-in combines a synth-style filter and a step sequencer.

Figure 12.36 The bundled Vocoder plug-in

Figure 12.37 Tranceformer allows any channel to be ring modulated.

◆ **QuadraFuzz** is a multiband distortion plug-in. The audio spectrum is divided into four bands that you can modify, so you can change the level of each band before processing with the distortion effect.

◆ **Flanger** derives its name from the effect produced by running two tape recorders with the same sound in sync and then slowing down or speeding up one recorder by dragging or pushing on the flange of the tape to create a doubling and filtering effect that modifies the sound. This plug-in mimics that effect digitally.

◆ **Symphonic** is a stereo-enhancement plug-in.

◆ **Phaser** is a phase-shifting plug-in used to generate a swirling, filtering effect somewhat like a flanger.

◆ **Overdrive** attempts to emulate the effect of a guitar amplifier and speaker combination.

◆ **Chopper** combines a tremolo effect and an autopanned effect to produce effects from subtle tremolo to stuttering audio.

◆ **Metalizer** is a filtering/modulation plug-in that applies to the audio a metallic-sounding band-pass filter that can be modulated.

◆ **Tranceformer** modulates the audio in the channel with its own, internal, oscillator (**Figure 12.37**).

◆ **Grungelizer** is another lo-fi effect used to mimic the static, pops, clicks, and noise found on old vinyl records.

◆ **Mix6to2** is used to quickly control the levels in a six-channel surround mix when mixing a stereo version from the surround version.

OTHER CUBASE AUDIO PLUG-INS

Pre-Fader Send Effects

Effects are most often used in the ways described up to now: as either insert effects or as send effects, where a percentage of the signal is sent in parallel to the send effect. There are other options for effects, though, and the last few pages of this chapter will explain some of them. For instance, effects can use a pre-fader.

To understand what a pre-fader is, it's important to remember how send effects work in the default post-fader method. By default, the blue-green slider that controls the level of send effects is actually just a ratio control. If the channel fader is moved up, more signal goes to the send effect, and if the fader is moved down, less signal goes to the send effect. The ratio between the two stays the same. With a pre-fader send effect, the same blue-green slider controls the amount of signal sent to the send effect regardless of where the channel fader is set. It no longer just sets a ratio, but acts almost like a second fader controlling the level of the send effect. The following task lets you hear the difference.

Figure 12.38 The audio channel with the send effect selected and the fader at zero

To hear a pre-fader send effect:

1. Open the send effects panel (Devices > VST Send Effects) and create a send effect. For this example, use a delay or reverb plug-in, because they are easy to hear as pre-fader send effects. Whatever effect you use, set the mix slider to 100%.

2. Choose a channel for testing the effect, solo the channel, and set the channel fader to zero.

3. Select send effects via the Extended View/Change Track View triangle and choose the send effect you just created.

   The channel strip should look something like **Figure 12.38**.

Figure 12.39 Adding the delay send

Figure 12.40 Clicking the Pre-fader button changes the send effect to pre-fader.

4. Play the project and drag the green slider for the send effect slot halfway or so to engage the send effect (**Figure 12.39**).

5. Drag the channel fader up until you hear both the channel and the send effect to be sure everything is working.

6. Drag the fader back to zero

   You will hear both the dry and effected signal fade out.

7. Click the Pre-fader button in the send effect slot (**Figure 12.40**).

   The button turns orange when it's selected. After this button is clicked, you will hear the send effect, even though the channel fader is set to zero.

8. Move the green slider left and right to hear the effect change.

When to Use Pre-Fader Send Effects

The most accurate answer to the question of when to use a pre-fader send effect is whenever you need control over the level of the effect independent of the channel fader. Here are a few situations where a pre-fader send effect is useful:

- Some effects, such as gates and vocoders, work by one sound triggering or modifying another sound. If you don't want the dry signal at all, you can use a pre-fader send effect.

- For some special effects, you might want the effect louder than the dry signal. For example, you might want a lead vocal to be very dry, with the backing vocals very low but soaked in reverb. A pre-fader send effect lets you control how much of the backing vocals go to the reverb effect.

- You can use pre-fader send effects to create headphone mixes for multiple musicians.

These are only a few of the situations where pre-fader send effects can be useful. Keep this capability in mind as you work with the Cubase mixer, and you'll find more places where pre-fader effects work for you.

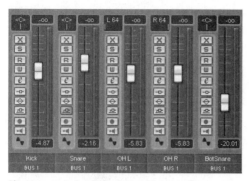

Figure 12.41 A simple five-channel drum mix

Figure 12.42 Selecting the group channel as the output for one of the tracks in the mix

Group Channels and Effects

Most people use effects mainly as either insert or send effects, but Cubase provides another way to work with effects: using group channels. Chapter 11 included a brief discussion of how to control the volume of multiple channels by assigning the channels to one group. You can also put insert and send effects in the group channel to add routing and effects flexibility. The following task shows how to apply an effect to a group of tracks at the same time. Putting a compressor across the stereo drum mix is standard operating procedure for rock and pop drums, but the same basic approach works in many other situations as well.

Applying an effect to multiple tracks with a group:

1. Create a group using the Project menu; select Add Track > Group Channel.

2. Name the group channel by double-clicking the name in the mixer and typing a new name.

3. Find the channels you want to route to the effect and add any individual effects, EQ, and inserts for the individual channels.

   Figure 12.41 shows a simple five-channel drum mix.

4. Click the bottom of each channel to open the pop-up menu for routing the channel. Route each channel to the group.

   In **Figure 12.42,** a channel is being routed to the DrumMix group.

continues on next page

5. After all channels in the drum mix are routed to the group, navigate in the mixer to find the group, drag the fader to zero, and make inserts visible with the Extended View/Change Track View triangle.

6. Click the first insert effect slot and add the Dynamics plug-in by selecting Dynamics > Dynamics.

7. Play the project; then display the group channel fader and use the Dynamics plug-in on the full stereo drum mix (**Figure 12.43**).

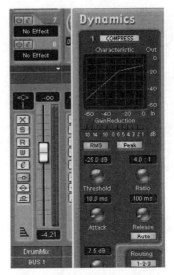

Figure 12.43 The DrumMix group and the compressor section of the Dynamics plug-in: This plug-in compresses the whole drum mix, and the single fader can control its level.

Figure 12.44 Two effects as inserts on the group channel

Figure 12.45 Selecting the group channel PhaseDelay as the destination for this send effect

Figure 12.46 Adjusting the amount of audio that goes to the group and is processed by the effects

Chaining Effects Using Groups

You can also use group channels to chain send effects in a series. For example, you might want to apply a phaser to the delays, or you might want to put a gate after a reverb sound. The easiest way to do this is with groups, because the send effects on mixer channels can be routed to any active group. The audio is sent to a group, which can include up to eight insert effects, allowing the audio to be processed in serial by multiple plug-ins. In the following task, a phaser is placed after a delay plug-in, and audio is sent to the serial effects.

To create serial send effects with a group:

1. Create a group using the Project menu; select Add Track > Group Channel. Name the group.

2. Using the Extended View/Change Track View triangle, set the group channel to display insert effects; add a DoubleDelay effect to insert 1 and a Phaser effect to insert 2 (**Figure 12.44**).

3. Edit the effects panels for both effects. Apply tempo sync on the delays to create a quick setting that sounds good.

4. Choose the stereo channel that you want to use as the source for the effect and set it to display send effects in the extended view.

5. Click a send effect slot and, in the drop-down menu, select the group (**Figure 12.45**).

6. Play the project. Adjust the amount of signal sent to the group with the green slider, as with any other effect (**Figure 12.46**).

Third-Party Plug-ins

Much of the fun of being a Cubase user comes from the ability to choose from the huge list of cool VST plug-ins available. As with VST instruments, Cubase users get all of the really cool stuff first, and it usually works best in the Cubase program. There are lots of resources on the Web for obtaining free or shareware plug-ins, some of which are as good as their more expensive commercial brothers. Here's a list of a few of my favorite plug-ins from the major groups of effects. This selection is purely subjective, but it should give you a start in finding the right stuff for you.

Filters: I actually use the VST EQ a good bit, but the kind of music I do involves fairly little EQ. I also use the Cubase Step Filter on occasion in my own music. For synth-style filtering, I usually use hardware, though the Prosoniq North Pole plug-in (www.prosoniq.com) is a very good free synth-style filter. German hardware synth manufacturer Waldorf (www.waldorf-music.com) also makes D-Pole, a digital multimode filter patterned after its hardware filters. I also use vocoders a good bit, and Orange Vocoder from Prosoniq is one of the finest ever made.

Dynamics: Mixer and speaker manufacturer Mackie distributes the Universal Audio UAD-1 card (www.mackie.com/uad1/), which is a hardware/software plug-in combination that works great on PCs (though, as of this writing, not with Mac OS X). The package includes a PCI card that performs the calculations, so adding the amazing sound compressors places almost no hit on the CPU. The plug-ins include fantastic-sounding emulations of the super-famous (and super-expensive) LA-2A limiter and 1176N compressor. I use the UAD-1 or the PSP Audioware (www.pspaudioware.com) Vintage Warmer for full mixes.

Delay: I'm a delay fanatic, so I use everything, from the Cubase delay plug-ins to old guitar pedals. One of my favorite plug-ins is Ohm Boyz from Ohm Force (www.ohmforce.com) software. It's a really powerful delay with an easy-to-use interface. Another great plug-in is the PSP 84 delay (also from PSP Audioware), which was inspired by a famous early digital Lexicon delay. Both sound great and have a lot of modulation possibilities. A final option is the Karlette plug-in from Steinberg. If it didn't come with your copy of Cubase, you can download this emulated tape delay from the Steinberg Web site (www.steinberg.net).

Modulation: I've spent a lot of money and time collecting a good number of funky old hardware flangers and phasers, and I do a lot of my modulation effects with them, but there are plug-ins that sound great. Mobilohm from Ohm Force is an extremely versatile phaser plug-in, and again the plug-ins included with Cubase are pretty good, too.

ReWire
and Cubase

Cubase is designed to be a complete audio and MIDI music production system, and you can use it to take many projects from beginning to end. Even so, there are some situations where additional tools might make a project better or easier, and Cubase has developed formats such as VST instruments, which make it easy for developers to create software-based sound generators that work within it. To help you incorporate some additional tools, you can also use ReWire.

ReWire is a protocol developed by Propellerheads software (www.propellerheads.se) and Steinberg. Its original purpose was to enable Propellerheads' synthesis and sampling applications (such as the very successful Reason and Rebirth) to work seamlessly with other music applications—such as Cubase—and with each other. Today, ReWire is supported by many applications from companies other than Steinberg and Propellerheads.

In this chapter, you will learn how to configure Cubase as a ReWire master application and how to configure other ReWire-savvy applications as slaves and then share audio and MIDI with them. To illustrate the use of ReWire with Cubase, this chapter uses two third-party programs—Reason and Live—as examples. The discussion applies equally, however, to other ReWire applications you might use with Cubase.

What Does ReWire Do?

ReWire allows multiple music applications to share audio, MIDI, and tempo information. When two applications are "ReWired" together, they almost act as one big application, leveraging the capabilities of the separate applications into (one hopes) a more creative and productive whole.

Many applications support ReWire in one form or another, but two applications commonly linked to Cubase via ReWire are Propellerheads' Reason (**Figure 13.1**) and Ableton Live (www.ableton.com) (**Figure 13.2**). Reason is an integrated sequencer/sampler/synthesis application, and Live is a performance and recording tool for working with audio loops. This chapter includes examples of these two applications, but the basic rules apply to any ReWire-savvy program.

You may be asking why ReWire would be necessary. Cubase, after all, has its own set of software synthesis and loop tools, so why use anything else? The answer is nothing more than that there is more than one way to skin a cat, and some are quicker, easier (for us of course, but about the same for the cat), and more productive. Reason, for example, includes a boatload of cool pattern-sequencing options that no other program has. And with ReWire, instead of creating tracks in Reason, exporting loops or MIDI files, and then importing them to Cubase, you can run everything together in real time.

Figure 13.1 Reason is an integrated sequencer/sampler/synth application that supports ReWire.

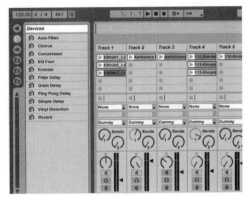

Figure 13.2 Live is a powerful looping and performance application that supports ReWire.

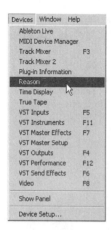

Enabling a ReWire Application in Cubase

When a ReWire-capable application is installed, it becomes available to Cubase, but you have to activate it in Cubase before Cubase and the ReWire application can work together. When the ReWire application is enabled, Cubase creates ReWire channels in the mixer and allows the ReWire application, like Reason, to connect with Cubase. If the application is not ReWire-enabled in Cubase, it will simply open as a stand-alone application, unaware that it ought to be synced with Cubase and sending MIDI and audio data back and forth.

Figure 13.3 ReWire applications are treated like devices and need to be activated in this menu.

Figure 13.4 Clicking any button will activate that audio channel for a ReWire program.

Figure 13.5 Reason now has six channels of audio that can be routed to Cubase.

To enable a ReWire application:

1. With Cubase open but with the ReWire application closed, open the Devices menu in Cubase and select the application you want to configure (**Figure 13.3**).

   The ReWire configuration panel (**Figure 13.4**) for the selected application opens, showing available and active audio channels.

2. Click the green buttons to activate as many ReWire audio channels as you want (**Figure 13.5**).

3. When you have finished, close the window and open the Cubase mixer to see the ReWire channels.

✔ Tip

■ Up to 64 audio channels can be activated for *each* ReWire application. That's usually more than you'll need, but it's nice to know that you have them. Between 8 and 16 channels is usually enough for me, and selecting a number in this range makes the Cubase mixer less cluttered.

Starting and Closing ReWire Applications

ReWire applications need to be started and stopped in a particular order to work correctly. This is because one ReWire application will always be the master (telling other applications when to play), and all others will always be slaves to that master application. The ReWire slaves get their tempo and synchronization information from the master application, and the first ReWire application opened will always be the master. Most of the time, you will want Cubase to be the master, with the other applications slaves to it, so you should follow this sequence when working on a Cubase/ReWire project:

◆ Start Cubase.

◆ Start the ReWire applications.

◆ When you are finished working, close the ReWire applications.

◆ Close Cubase.

If you try to close Cubase with any ReWire applications active, Cubase will display an error window and refuse to quit (**Figure 13.6**).

Some ReWire applications (including Cubase) will work only as a ReWire master, and some will work only as a ReWire slave (Reason, for example). Others (such as Live) will work as either a ReWire master or ReWire slave; Live can be slaved to Cubase, or it can be the master with Reason slaved to it. However, if Live is the master application and Reason is slaved to it, then Cubase can't use ReWire with either of them. This can sometimes get confusing; just remember that only one application can be the master, and all others must be slaves to it.

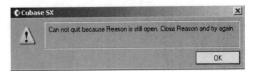

Figure 13.6 This error message appears when ReWire master and slave programs are not closed in the correct order.

Transport Controls and Looping

One very convenient benefit of using ReWire is that when you use it, the Transport bar of any application can be used to control the others. For example, if you are editing a part in a ReWire slave application and move the left and right locators and start playback, the controls will all move transparently in the master application. This feature can save you a whole lot of mouse clicking, window hiding, and general messing around when you're working with ReWire applications.

Figure 13.7 The Cubase and Reason transport panels, set to 87 beats per minute

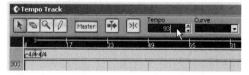

Figure 13.8 You can enter a new tempo manually in the tempo track editor by typing a number in the Tempo field.

Figure 13.9 After you change the setting in the tempo track editor, both the ReWire master (Cubase) and the ReWire slave (Reason) show the new tempo.

✔ Tips

■ A fair number of ReWire applications have the annoying habit of sending Cubase a tempo change when they start. The result is that the Cubase tempo track is turned off. It's not a huge problem—just click the Master button on the Transport bar and all is well, but it is a drag.

■ There's a lot more to the tempo track and its editor than is discussed in this book. If you have music with tempo changes, you should research the tempo track in the Cubase electronic documentation.

Tempo and ReWire

There are two ways to set tempo in Cubase. One is to simply type a setting for the project on the Transport bar. The other way is to use the tempo track in Cubase, which is turned on and off using the Master button on the Cubase Transport bar. The latter is the better way to go when you're working with ReWire applications. (The tempo track was discussed in Chapter 3, "Starting a Project.")

If you are using a tempo track, you should make all tempo changes for your project in Cubase. If you make changes in tempo with a ReWire slave application, it will turn off the tempo track and reset the tempo in Cubase. The following example uses the tempo track to change the tempo for both Reason and Cubase.

To change the tempo for Cubase and ReWire applications:

1. In Cubase, click the Project menu and select Tempo Track.

   You will be changing the tempo for both Cubase and the ReWire application—in this case, Reason. **Figure 13.7** shows the Cubase and Reason Transport bars. Note that the tempo for both is 87 beats per minute.

2. When the Tempo Track editor opens, double-click the Tempo field and type a new tempo (**Figure 13.8**).

   When you check the ReWire slave, you will find that the tempo has changed to match the Cubase master tempo (**Figure 13.9**).

Using Multiple ReWire Applications

Cubase can use more than one ReWire application simultaneously. Using multiple ReWire applications helps you keep everything running together in real time, as long as you don't get confused working with a lot of open windows and applications. There are only a few points to remember:

◆ You need to enable audio inputs for each application (**Figure 13.10**).

◆ If you are using Cubase it must be the ReWire master, so it must be started first, before any of the ReWire slave applications are opened.

◆ Don't forget to open the ReWire applications (and the projects in those applications) the next time you work on the project in Cubase.

Figure 13.10 Two ReWire programs enabled

Multiple Displays for Multiple Applications

If you use a lot of ReWire applications, you might want to consider upgrading your studio by adding another monitor or two. Many modestly priced video cards have dual outputs and can drive two monitors. Digital videographers and graphic designers have long used multiple monitors to extend their workspaces so they spend less time showing, hiding, and moving application windows.

Using two or more monitors with Cubase provides a lot of flexibility. In Cubase-only projects, the project window can be stretched across both monitors, or one monitor can show the project window while the other displays the mixer. For a project including Reason, one monitor can display the Reason rack while the other shows Cubase. Most people have limited budgets for studio upgrades, but a few hundred dollars for a new or additional video card and monitor can make your time in Cubase a lot more fun and productive.

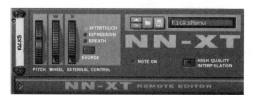

Figure 13.11 One module in a Reason project: a sampler with multiple kick drum samples mapped across the keyboard

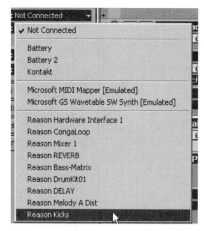

Figure 13.12 Selecting the Reason Kicks sampler in Cubase

✔ Tip

■ Note also that using this method of MIDI routing lets you play a ReWire instrument directly from Cubase, even if it has its own sequencer. You might prefer this approach to working in the sequencer included with the ReWire slave application.

Sending MIDI via ReWire

Most, though not all, ReWire programs are synthesis applications. Some include their own sequencers, while others work exclusively with MIDI data sent from a ReWire master application. In either case, it is usually possible to send MIDI to the ReWire sound generators, regardless of whether the ReWire slave includes a sequencer to generate its own MIDI.

Reason, for instance, has a built-in sequencer that is linked via ReWire as a Cubase slave, and it can also receive MIDI directly from Cubase.

To send MIDI from Cubase to a ReWire slave:

1. Open both Cubase and the other application with ReWire enabled; for example, open both Cubase and Reason.

2. Set up the ReWire synth or sampler as you want.

   Figure 13.11 shows a Reason sampler named Kicks that includes a number of kick drum samples.

3. Returning to Cubase, click a MIDI file to select it and open the Track Inspector for that track.

4. In the Track Inspector, open the MIDI output drop-down menu and make a selection.

   In addition to the MIDI hardware and VST instruments, all possible Reason MIDI destinations are also visible. **Figure 13.12** shows the Kicks sampler being selected.

5. Start playback in the project to trigger the ReWire instrument.

Sending Audio via ReWire

The first two ReWire audio inputs in Cubase are almost always dedicated to the full mix coming from the ReWire application. When you use Live with Cubase, for example, the master two-channel output from the program will be routed by default to ReWire inputs 1 and 2 in Cubase. That's fine for many situations, but part of what makes ReWire so great is its multichannel capability. If you want to apply EQ to one Live loop in Cubase or to bus a synth sound from Reason to a group with other VSTi synth sounds and a delay insert, ReWire lets you. Not every ReWire slave application manages this routing in the same way, but all will work somewhat like the following example, which uses Live.

Saving ReWire Projects

One of the great advantages of a software system like Cubase is that when a project is saved, every element is also saved. This includes not just audio files, but mix settings, plug-ins, software synths, and everything else that makes a project a song. When you start using ReWire applications, you bring an extra layer of power and complexity to your workflow and project file management.

Here are some keys to help you master file management.

First, always save all ReWire slave projects in the same folder as the Cubase project. This makes finding your files later easier.

Second, if you import samples or loops to the ReWire slave application, make a folder inside the Cubase project folder and copy all of the imported files into that folder. If you move the project later, you won't miss any of the files if you keep them together with your project.

Last, include something in the file name of the Cubase project to indicate that it uses a ReWire application. For example, I include an R for Reason in the name, so WhirlingDub.cpr becomes WhirlingDub_R_.cpr.

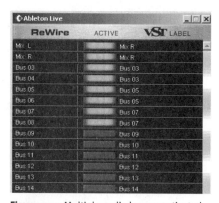

Figure 13.13 Multiple audio busses activated for Live in Cubase

To route audio from a ReWire slave application:

1. Configure Cubase and Live to work via ReWire and enable more than one pair of ReWire inputs in Cubase (**Figure 13.13**).

2. Switch to Live. Each channel strip in Live has a drop-down menu for routing its output (**Figure 13.14**). Open this menu and select Bus 3/4.

3. Return to Cubase and open the mixer. Start playback of the project.

   The audio from the ReWire slave will play back on the channel selected in the slave application (**Figure 13.15**).

✔ Tip

- Name your ReWire mixer channels right away, because they don't have even slightly descriptive channel names like VST instruments do.

Figure 13.14 Selecting a particular output bus in Live

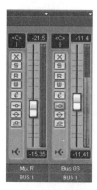

Figure 13.15 The left ReWire channel has the mix output from Live, but the second stereo pair is playing back the audio from the channel in Figure 13.14.

Stand-alone Versus ReWire Applications

Many ReWire applications can be used either as stand-alone music-creation tools or as ReWire slaves. There are advantages to both, and the two methods are not mutually exclusive. Here are some pros and cons.

Stand-alone application

◆ Usually, stand-alone applications can use ASIO drivers directly, making routing audio to and from external hardware easier than when using Cubase and ReWire.

◆ Stand-alone applications may have some features that are unavailable when they're in ReWire slave mode. Live, for example, can use VST effects when the application is run alone, but it cannot use them when it's slaved via ReWire.

◆ Switching between stand-alone applications can become tiresome.

ReWire application

◆ The Cubase mixer is generally much more powerful and flexible than the mixer that comes with most ReWire applications, such as Live or Reason.

◆ Cubase is a top-quality audio recording and editing platform and is far superior to ReWire applications for adding overdubs and new audio.

◆ Audio from ReWire applications that do not support VST effects can be routed through those effects in Cubase when slaved.

◆ Cubase mixer automation, which is both powerful and easy to use, can be applied to ReWire channels. Many ReWire applications alone do not have the same quality and complexity of mixer automation.

✔ Tip

■ Here's one approach to working with ReWire: I often start songs in Live or Reason and then slave them to Cubase only after the first bits are ready. I record new tracks in Cubase and mix in Cubase, leaving the ReWire applications running as slaves. When a song is finished, I always archive all of the ReWire sounds and tracks with the rest of the project.

14

AUTOMATING A MIX

One theory of mixing holds that the only proper way to mix is with a board. If sounds are recorded correctly, according to this theory, all you need to do is push the faders up to unity gain and then leave things alone. You might get lucky with a track every now and then and that will be enough, but usually when you listen to your song with the levels about right, there will be some parts that you want to change.

Mix automation is the ability to record your mixing moves and play them back automatically, rather than having to move the controls yourself every time you play the track. Instead of changing the level of the vocal track manually, Cubase can record your changes to the fader and play them back automatically.

In this chapter, you will learn the two ways of creating automation in Cubase: by recording your actions in the Cubase mixer, and by creating automation manually in the Project window. You will learn about the tools available for manually creating automation, and how to view and edit automation as efficiently as possible.

Why Automate Mixes?

For most of the time that music has been recorded and mixed, actual human beings had to perform all of the changes to a mix in real time. Mixing, though, is like many areas of endeavor in that human solutions have become less prominent while technological solutions have expanded.

The simplest reason for automating a mix is that it makes it easier for you to mix by yourself. Before the era of full-featured mixer automation, many studios had a team of mixers to set up and practice a mix and then perform each action at the right time. If one guy shanked and forgot to mute the shaker after the second chorus, the only options were to live with the mistake or redo the whole mix. Mixer automation allows you to find such a mistake and quickly change it, and to make precision changes to your mix, such as fading a track, without having to move the faders yourself each time you play the mix.

One of the great advantages of working with software and digital mixers is that they usually have very deep and powerful mix automation. If you learn the automation features of Cubase and listen carefully, you will be able to add a great deal of polish to your mixes, because the program has world-class tools.

Writing Automation with the Mixer

Cubase offers two primary methods for creating automation. One is using the mouse or a remote controller and the Cubase mixer; the other is writing automation directly to automation tracks in the Project window. Most jobs can be accomplished about as well using either method, and you might prefer one method to the other. Manually writing automation is a bit less intuitive for some people, though it has the advantage of providing visual access to the audio waveform. You can start learning about automation by using the mixer, which makes automation obvious and graphical.

In the following example, you will automate a fader or two in a project. First, you'll start writing automation in Cubase and then move channel faders in the mixer. Cubase will be able to make those moves automatically if Read is turned on. Automation can be tricky to understand at first, so you might want to start with an empty project or a backup copy of a recorded project. Of course, you can undo or erase automation after the fact, but it's a bad idea to start learning automation on an important track. Always begin work on a copy.

To write automation with the mixer:

1. Open the mixer by selecting Devices > Track Mixer.

2. Click the Write button to activate it if it isn't active already. With Write turned on, Cubase will write automation.

   The Write button is at the far left of the mixer; it is the button marked with a W (**Figure 14.1**).

3. Make sure the Read button is *not* active, by clicking it if necessary.

   The Read button appears above the Write button and is labeled with an R.

4. Start the project playing and move a few of the faders in the mixer to create your automation (**Figure 14.2**).

5. Stop the project and rewind to where you began writing automation.

6. Click the R button (**Figure 14.3**) to activate reading of all automation.

7. Play the project.

   You will see the faders move just as you moved them when you wrote the automation in step 4.

Figure 14.1 This button turns on write automation for all channels in the mixer.

Figure 14.2 The faders are being moved with write automation enabled.

Figure 14.3 Turning on read automation for all mixer channels

Figure 14.4 Select this menu to see all automation in a project.

Viewing Automation

Cubase has top-quality tools for viewing and editing automation in the Project window. You'll learn more about editing and creating automation graphically later in this chapter, but seeing the automation in the Project window is a good way to start getting a better understanding of how automation works.

The easiest way to see automation for a project is to click the Project menu and select Show Used Automation (**Figure 14.4**).

- In the track list, all tracks with automation applied to them will display a new automation subtrack for each automated parameter.

  Figure 14.5 shows two tracks (this is an empty project). Audio 01 has no automation, while Audio 02 has one parameter automated.

- The name of the automated parameter appears on the automation subtrack; in Figure 14.5 the parameter is Volume.

- A line appears in the Event display showing the value of the automated parameter and any changes in it over time.

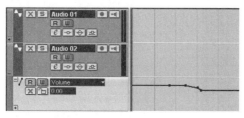

Figure 14.5 Automation as it appears in the Project window

✔ Tip

- You can also show and hide automation on a per-track basis. Right-click (Windows) or Control-click (Mac OS) the track in the track list for which you want to view automation. Select Show Used Automation (**Figure 14.6**).

Figure 14.6 Showing all automation used for a single track

Mixer Automation Modes

Not every setup or individual will write automation in the same way. Because of this, Cubase writes automation from the mixer in three different modes, which you can select in the Project window (**Figure 14.7**). Here is an explanation of each mode, with a few suggestions for using each one:

◆ **Touch Fader** mode will start writing automation when you click a control, and it will stop writing when you release the mouse. Touch Fader is usually the best mode for writing automation when using the mouse and the Cubase mixer.

◆ **Autolatch** mode will start writing automation when you click a control, and it will continue writing automation until you deactivate it manually or stop the transport. You need to use Autolatch if you're using one of the supported external controllers for Cubase, such as a Steinberg Houston controller, a MIDI fader box, or an external digital mixer that can send MIDI. You should also use Autolatch when you want to write over a large amount of previous automation.

◆ **X-Over** mode works like Autolatch mode, except that when you cross a line of previously written automation, writing is turned off. This mode is great for making small tweaks on previously written automation that is not quite as you want it to be.

✔ **Tip**

■ Over the course of a mix, you often will use more than one mode. You might write a first pass in Touch Fader mode, then make some tweaks in X-Over mode, and then decide you want to redo everything for one particular track; for that track, you would probably use Autolatch to write over all previous automation.

Figure 14.7 The three modes for writing automation from the mixer

Figure 14.8 Turning the send effect off before writing automation

Figure 14.9 Changing parameters in the plug-in while writing automation

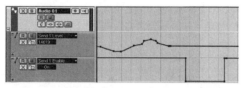

Figure 14.10 The result of the plug-in automation in the Project window

Writing Plug-in Automation

By now you might be asking, "What can I automate?" The answer is just about everything in the mixer, including fader level, pan, EQ, send and insert effects, and send/insert effects parameters. A good way to see the options available is to automate the amount of the signal sent to a send effect. This can be used to add different amounts of the effect to a track over the course of a song.

To write plug-in automation:

1. Create a send effect in the Send Effects rack and select the send for a track to be automated. For now, click the power button to turn off the send effect on the track (**Figure 14.8**).

2. Activate Write automation for all channels by clicking the W button on the left of the Cubase mixer. Deactivate read automation if it is active.

3. Set the automation mode to Touch Fader or Autolatch.

4. Start playing the project; then turn on the effect send and drag the blue-green slider to adjust the amount of the signal that goes to the send effect (**Figure 14.9**).

5. Stop playback to stop writing automation.

6. Turn off Write automation and turn on Read automation.

7. Rewind the project and play it back to see the automated moves, or look in the Project window to see the automation graphically represented (**Figure 14.10**).

Automating Effects Parameters

While automating the on/off status of an effects send and its level for one track is certainly useful, you can do much more with effects automation. Any parameter in a VST effect can be automated. While mixing, you might want to change the feedback on a delay plug-in, increase the depth of a phase shifter, or change the dry/wet ration in a vocoder. In the following example, an insert effect is automated on an audio track.

To automate effects parameters:

1. For the channel you want to automate, select and activate an insert effect.

2. Activate Write automation for all tracks, and deactivate Read automation if necessary.

   Figure 14.11 shows a plug-in ready for automation.

3. Begin playing the project and change the effect parameters as you like; stop the project when you are finished.

4. Turn off Write automation and turn on Read automation.

5. Rewind the project and play it back to see your automated moves.

   You can also look in the Project window; insert effects automation will be visible in automation subtracks for the track that has been automated (**Figure 14.12**).

✔ Tip

■ Unfortunately, only VST plug-ins can be automated, so PC users with DirectX plug-ins are out of luck.

Figure 14.11 The Write button is active, so this plug-in will write automation when its parameters are changed.

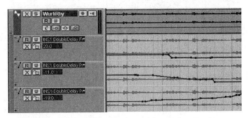

Figure 14.12 Automated insert plug-in parameters viewed in the Project window

Figure 14.13
Automation
subtracks for an
audio channel

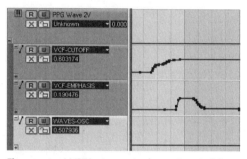

Figure 14.14 A VST instrument, when automated, has its own track and automation subtracks.

Figure 14.15
Master automation
automates the
master fader and
output busses.

How Automation Is Displayed

By now, you've probably figured out that to automate anything in Cubase, you need to enable write automation, make whatever moves you want as the track is playing, enable read automation, and play back the project.

You can view all automation data for a project in the Project window, but what is being automated determines where in the Project window the automation data appears.

- **Channel strip** automation—including automated fader, pan, EQ, insert effects on/off status and parameters, and send effects on/off status and amount—is visible in automation subtracks under the automated track. **Figure 14.13** shows one audio channel with automation subtracks. Automation for MIDI tracks also is visible in subtracks below the track in the Project window.

- **VST instruments**, when automated, appear on their own automation tracks, with automation subtracks for each automated parameter. **Figure 14.14** shows a VST instrument that has been automated.

- **Send effects**, when automated, appear much like automated VST instruments. Each send effect has its own automation track with subtracks below it.

- **ReWire** automation is just like audio track automation and is viewed on automation subtracks below the ReWire channel on the Project window.

- **Master automation** is viewed in much the same way as VSTi and send effect automation. The master fader and all active output busses have automation tracks with subtracks. **Figure 14.15** shows master automation active.

Writing Automation for a Single Track

Up to now, all of the examples have involved turning on write automation for the entire project and then turning on read automation for the entire project. This is often the best way to work; when you are creating a first take of a mix, for example, you might want everything you touch to be recorded.

Later in a mix, though, it's common to want to change or write automation for a single track (or a few tracks) instead of for the whole project. A solo part may need to be carefully tweaked while the rest of the mix sounds great, or a part may need to be muted for certain sections of a song. Cubase allows you to turn automation reading and writing on and off on a per-track, per-effect, or per-instrument basis. The following example shows how to write automation for one track while reading previously created automation in the rest of the project.

Reading and Writing Automation at the Same Time

One of the tricky aspects of working with automation, particularly when changing automation already recorded, is figuring out when to read, when to write, and when to do both. The nice thing about having read and write active at the same time is that you can watch a track that is automated and then grab it whenever you want to try something new. The tricky part is what happens when you let go of that control.

Suppose, for example, that you want a sound that is panned hard left to move in a little bit during a mix. If you enable read and write, you can hear everything happening on that track and then just snag the pan control when you want to move the sound closer to center. If you are in Autolatch mode, once you touch the pan control you will keep writing until you turn off writing or stop the project. If you are in Touch Fader mode, though, as soon as you let go of the pan control, it will snap back to hard left.

If you find this confusing, the best approach is to use Autolatch mode with read turned off to write new automation for a track. Another option for tweaking an automated track is to make the finer changes using the graphical tools, which are covered next in this chapter.

Figure 14.16 This button turns on write automation for this track only.

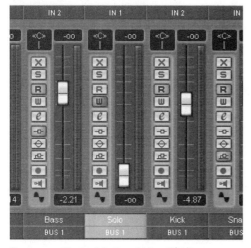

Figure 14.17 The track in the middle will write new automation, and the other tracks will read automation.

To write automation for one track:

1. Open the Cubase mixer and find the channel strip you want to automate. Click the Write button for that channel (**Figure 14.16**).

2. Click the Read button on the far left of the mixer to set all tracks to read automation.

3. You probably want to create all new automation data for your chosen track, so click the Read button for that channel to turn off Read automation for it.

   Figure 14.17 shows a few adjacent channels set to read automation, with the Solo channel set to write it.

4. Start playing the project and write new automated actions on the channel you want to modify.

5. Stop playback when you are finished.

6. Turn off write automation for the channel you just wrote. Then turn on read automation for that channel.

   Now when the project plays, you will hear the new automation.

WRITING AUTOMATION FOR A SINGLE TRACK

Writing Automation Manually

Almost any action in Cubase can be done by hand, graphically, in the Project window, including writing automation. Many of the tools used to write automation are like those used in MIDI continuous controller editing, so if you know about them, you already know a good bit about the tools for creating and editing automation. In the next task, you will create a simple ramp-up in volume.

To write automation manually in the Project window:

1. Find the track in the Project window that you want to automate. Display the automation subtrack by clicking the small plus sign at the lower-left corner of the track (**Figure 14.18**).

2. In the automation subtrack, click the drop-down menu (**Figure 14.19**) and select Volume if it is not already selected.

   Your choice in this menu determines what parameter is viewed and edited in that automation subtrack.

3. On the toolbar, on the Draw tool, click the small arrow to open a drop-down menu to select the mode for this tool. Select Line (**Figure 14.20**).

4. Using the Line tool, drag in the automation subtrack, creating a line from low to high (**Figure 14.21**).

   When you release the mouse, a new automation line will be written (**Figure 14.22**).

5. Turn on read automation and play the track to hear the result. The track will ramp up in volume.

✔ Tip

■ The snap setting and value determine the granularity of the data created when writing automation in the Project window.

Figure 14.18 Clicking the small plus sign opens the automation subtracks.

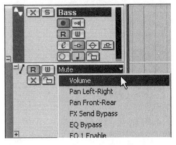

Figure 14.19 This menu sets the parameter to be viewed in the subtrack. In this case, Volume is selected.

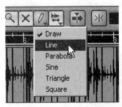

Figure 14.20 Selecting the Line tool on the toolbar

Figure 14.21 Drawing a line of automation to write a volume change

Figure 14.22 The result after releasing the mouse

Figure 14.23 Selecting the Eraser tool

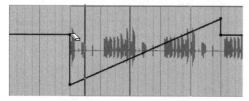

Figure 14.24 Clicking this breakpoint with the Eraser tool will remove the breakpoint.

Figure 14.25 After you remove the breakpoint, the volume change will begin from the correct value.

Deleting Automation Breakpoints

If you examine the results of the previous task, you can see one of the pitfalls of writing automation manually. You can see in Figure 14.22 that the ramp-up in volume probably isn't going to sound right with the sudden drop before it starts and the drop when it ends. Automation breakpoints indicate a change in direction or a change in value. In Figure 14.22, there are two breakpoints that need to be deleted for the automation to produce the desired sonic results.

To delete automation breakpoints:

1. Using the toolbar (**Figure 14.23**) or the context menu (right-click Windows, Command-click Mac OS), select the Eraser tool.

2. Click the breakpoint you want to delete to remove it (**Figure 14.24**).

✔ Tip

■ **Figure 14.25** shows the automation for this track after the first breakpoint is erased. Keep in mind that the first automation breakpoint determines the initial value for the parameter, and the last automation breakpoint for a track sets the value extending to the right for the duration of the project. Sometimes a stray, forgotten breakpoint will cause all kinds of confusing results with automated parameters.

Other Breakpoint Operations

You can move automation breakpoints manually, just as you can move breakpoints and change curves when editing objects such as MIDI controllers. Here are a few operations you can perform on breakpoints using the Object Selection (or arrow) tool:

◆ You can move any breakpoint simply by dragging it (**Figure 14.26**).

◆ You can double-click with the Object Selection tool to create a new breakpoint you can move (**Figure 14.27**).

◆ You can use the Object Selection tool to select a group of breakpoints (**Figure 14.28**). You can then use the same tool to move these breakpoints as a group (**Figure 14.29**).

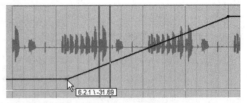

Figure 14.26 You can use the Object Selection tool to manually move automation breakpoints.

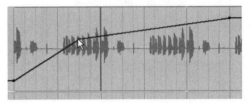

Figure 14.27 Moving a newly created breakpoint

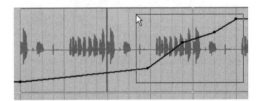

Figure 14.28 Selecting multiple breakpoints with the Object Selection tool

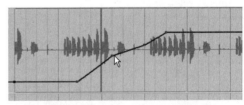

Figure 14.29 With multiple breakpoints selected, you can move them as a group by dragging any one of them.

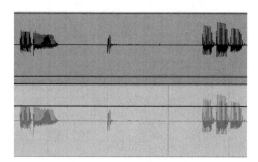

Figure 14.30 The blip in the middle of this event needs to be silenced.

Figure 14.31 Selecting the Draw tool in the correct mode

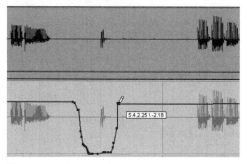

Figure 14.32 This automation, created with the Draw tool, will effectively remove the section from the song.

Writing Automation with the Draw Tool

One of the most useful tools for writing automation is the Draw tool (or pencil). It's particularly powerful because it's very visual—you can see the audio as you are making the changes to the mix. There are tons of applications for this tool, but this example and the next one show two of the more common ones.

Musicians often play an extraneous sound or inadvertently hit an instrument or microphone while performing. You can deal with this problem in a couple of ways, but mixer automation is one of the easiest and most visual approaches.

In **Figure 14.30**, the piece of the waveform in the middle of the illustration is the sound of the bass being hit unintentionally. In the Project window you can see exactly where in the waveform the mistake occurs, so you can fix it right there.

To write automation with the Draw tool:

1. Zoom in so you can easily see the section of the project that you want to automate.

2. Select the parameter to be automated on the automation subtrack. In this example, we are automating volume.

3. On the toolbar, click the small triangle on the Draw tool and select Draw (**Figure 14.31**) if it is not already selected.

   The mouse pointer will turn into a pencil.

4. On the track you want to automate, drag around the part of the track that you want to remove (**Figure 14.32**).

5. Turn on read automation for the track and play the project to hear the results of the automation.

✔ Tip

■ The Draw tool has more than one mode. If you want to explore the Draw tool more, choose the other modes and write automation with them to see how they work.

Selectively Boosting a Part

Another common use for graphical, manually written automation is to selectively boost a small part of a track. Often mixers refer to this as "pushing" a certain part of a track. A syllable may be a little too quiet in one word, or a particular word may need to be emphasized in a vocal; in either case, you can use manual automation to boost the sound.

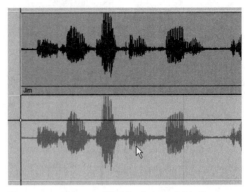

Figure 14.33 One word in this phrase, right above the mouse pointer, is too low in comparison to the rest of the event.

To boost part of a track with the Draw tool:

1. Zoom in to see the section of the track that you want to automate (**Figure 14.33**).

2. From the toolbar, select the Draw tool as described in the previous task.

   The mouse pointer will change into a pencil when you have the right tool selected.

3. Drag to create a small volume boost where the word should be more prominent (**Figure 14.34**).

4. Activate read automation for the track and play the project to hear the results of the automation.

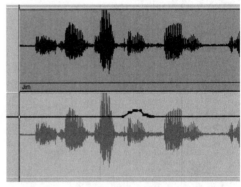

Figure 14.34 After writing with the Draw tool, only the one word in the phrase will be boosted.

✔ Tip

■ Pushing a track like this is very common in rock and pop productions. Often most tracks will be carefully automated to bring out notes or words that are a bit weak. You may not want to go to that extreme, but if you do, you can use the method described in the preceding task.

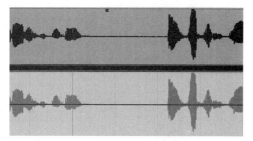

Figure 14.35 The stretch of silence in the middle of this vocal can be muted automatically.

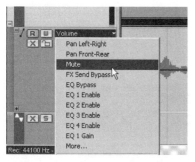

Figure 14.36 Select Mute to be shown on the automation subtrack.

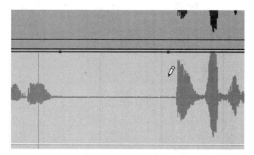

Figure 14.37 Two automation breakpoints have been created.

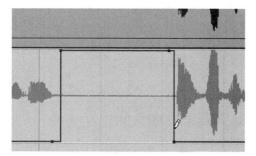

Figure 14.38 The completed mute automation

Automating Mutes

Many people recording or mixing at home don't take advantage of an easy way to improve the sonic quality of their mixes: muting unused parts. Microphone input always has some hiss and room noise, no matter how careful the recording process, and as the number of microphones multiplies, so does the sonic trash.

Cubase has more than one way to get around this problem; the audio events themselves can be edited, for example. A common and simple approach, however, is to automate mutes.

To automate mutes:

1. Zoom in close enough to see the part that you want to mute.

   Figure 14.35 shows a stretch of relative silence between words that can be muted.

2. Turn off Snap.

3. Open an automation subtrack for the track if one isn't already open.

4. Select Mute from the drop-down menu to select the parameter you want to automate (**Figure 14.36**).

5. Using the Draw tool in pencil mode, click the top half of the automation subtrack to turn on muting where the silence begins and ends (**Figure 14.37**).

6. Click the bottom half of the automation subtrack at about the same places to finish the muting (**Figure 14.38**).

7. If you need to adjust where the muting starts and ends, you can use the Object Selection tool to drag the breakpoints to move them.

Viewing and Automating Other Parameters

The examples in this chapter have used only a few of the available parameters. Of course, you are not limited to these parameters when creating automation. You can always open more automation subtracks to view additional parameters, but this procedure can get cumbersome and clutter the Project window mightily. As an alternative, you can set any automation subtrack to show any parameter for automation.

To view additional automation parameters:

1. Open an automation subtrack for the track you will be automating.

2. Click the drop-down menu (**Figure 14.39**) to see some of the more common parameters and select the one you want.

3. If the parameter you want is not in this list, select More (**Figure 14.40**).

4. In the window that opens, select the parameter you want to automate (**Figure 14.41**) and click OK.

   When you return to the Project window, that parameter will be selected for that automation subtrack, and you can edit it as you wish.

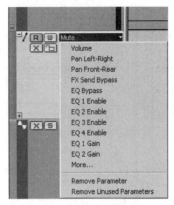

Figure 14.39 The automation parameters initially available for an audio track

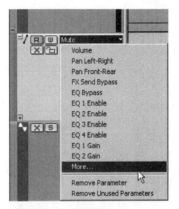

Figure 14.40 Select More to see more possible automation destinations.

Figure 14.41 Some of the additional parameters, any of which can be viewed on any automation subtrack

Non-Audio Channel Automation

The examples in this chapter have focused on audio channels, and these will probably be the most commonly automated tracks in a mix. But remember that you can automate any track in the mixer. Here are the other types of automation that you might want to use in a mix:

◆ **MIDI** channels are automated nearly identically to audio tracks. The only differences are which parameters can be automated and the location of the automation subtracks under the MIDI tracks.

◆ **ReWire** channels are automated exactly like audio channels. You can create automation for them using all of the same tools as for audio channels.

◆ **VST instrument** channels are also automated like audio channels. One thing to remember when working with a VSTi, though, is that it's usually triggered by a MIDI channel. You can automate the level of a VSTi both by writing automation on the MIDI channel that triggers it and by writing automation on the VSTi output. This can sometimes create some confusion because the same result can come from two different places. The volume of a VSTi, for example, could be changed by automating the fader for the VSTi output or by automating the fader on the MIDI channel triggering the VSTi.

◆ **Group** channels use all of the same tools and parameters as for audio tracks.

Two Types of Parameters

You probably noticed that Mute automation looks different than Volume automation. This makes sense if you remember that some parameters (mute, effect on/off, bypass) are either on or off, while other parameters (volume, pan, filter cutoff, delay feedback) can vary continuously.

On/off parameters are sometimes a little harder to see and edit manually. A parameter like Mute, since it has only two settings, is shown in the automation subtrack as set either fully to the top or fully to the bottom of the track. If the line is at the bottom of the track, the setting is off, and if it is at the top of the track, it's on.

Another quirk is that because all automation values start with an initial value, you sometimes need to add a breakpoint. In the previous example, the initial value was set to off, which is what we wanted. If you create the first breakpoint as on, that value will be used for all the time following that first breakpoint. If you are editing on/off values, remember that you may need to create a breakpoint with an initial value established at the start of the track and remaining in effect until the first time you change it.

An Example of Mix Automation

Everyone mixes and writes automation differently, but here are a few more suggestions based on how I generally do it.

I usually start out mixing a song with automation completely turned off. I have an external hardware controller for Cubase, so I start by adjusting the levels and basic EQ, compression, and effects settings so that the mix sounds good to me. If tracks need to go to groups, I set them up early so that all of the necessary mixer channels exist. I rarely automate EQ or compression at any stage in a song, and I often go back and change them throughout the mixing process.

Then I turn on write automation for all of the tracks and get the basics of the mix correct. I change fade and pan on the tracks that need modification and make whatever special changes I need to make. I do all of this in one pass; if it's a train wreck, I erase all automation for the track and start over.

Once I have a complete rough take, I turn on read automation for the whole mix and listen to it. Usually, there are obvious places where things aren't right, and in that case, I will usually redo the entire automation for that one track, writing to it while reading the other tracks. All of this, of course, is done with my hardware controller; you might want to try the same thing using the mouse and Cubase mixer.

The last thing I do with the hardware controller is muting. Usually I make a pass or two just writing mutes to any track that needs them, and in that case, I have both read and write automation turned on for all tracks.

With the mix in that state, normally I then switch to the Project window to do any final exacting tweaks. I might more carefully control the level of some tracks or add specific automation to a soft synthesizer or automate the effects sends. For those tweaks, I turn off write automation for all tracks and turn on read automation for all tracks.

After I finish working in the Project window, the mix should be finished. Once I start writing automation manually, though, I rarely go back to the mixer or my hardware controller. I find switching back and forth to be confusing, and once I make the break into the Project window and begin manually writing automation, I usually stay there for the duration of the mix.

USING
EXTERNAL EFFECTS

One of the best things about using Cubase is the wealth of really interesting software plug-ins—including the very good plug-ins bundled with the program and a massive collection of third-party VST plug-ins—that you can use with Cubase.

That said, you might already own some hardware processing equipment you really like and want to keep using. Maybe you have a favorite external digital reverb box, a super high-quality outboard EQ/compressor, or an early 80s analog stereo phase shifter that sounds heavenly. You certainly don't want to be forced to choose between your digital recording system and your collection of favorite (and expensive) external hardware. Cubase doesn't force you to do so, as long as you have a few extra outputs on your sound card and are willing to spend a little time learning how to get the job done.

In this chapter, you'll learn how to set up Cubase to use external signal processors as both send and insert effects. You'll discover some of the options for monitoring hardware effects as you work with them and also learn how to include external effects in your final mix.

Routing External Effects

Using software effects is certainly easier than working with external hardware. If you are using VST or DirectX effects, all of the routing and processing happens right inside the computer, and all of your parameters and settings are saved with the project. Cubase even manages the plug-in latency for you in some circumstances.

Using external effects is a bit more cumbersome than using software, but it's not all that difficult once you understand how it works. This is the basic procedure:

1. The audio from a channel or send is routed to one of the hardware outputs on your sound card.

2. The signal travels from the sound card output to the input of the effect unit and is processed by the effect.

3. The processed signal is routed back from the output of the external effect unit to an input on your sound card. From there it can be monitored in (or recorded with) Cubase.

As you can probably guess, you usually need at least four outputs on your sound card to do all of this. The two main outputs are for monitoring your mix, and the second pair can be used to route audio to the external effect. If you use many external effects devices, you'll need to assess the number of I/Os you'll need on your sound card.

15.1 This button activates a VST hardware output.

15.2 You should name outputs if you can. If the effect connected changes, you can give them generic names like FX1, FX2 and so on.

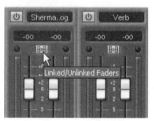

15.3 Use this button to unlink faders if you need individual control of the level sent to two mono effects.

Using VST Outputs

To use an external effect, you'll need to have the correct VST outputs active, and you should name them if possible.

To configure VST outputs for external effects:

1. From the Devices menu, select VST Outputs.

   The VST Outputs panel that opens includes all available physical outputs on your sound card.

2. Turn on as many outputs as you want by clicking the power buttons (**Figure 15.1**).

3. If you want the external effect permanently attached to a particular hardware output, click the name of the VST output and give it the name of the effect (**Figure 15.2**).

4. Click the Link Faders button (**Figure 15.3**) to lock the faders together permanently. Leave the faders linked for a stereo effect, or click the button to unlink the faders if you will use the output for a pair of mono effects.

Creating an External Send Effect

The simplest way to create an external send effect is to use the available send effects on the channel strips to route audio to the VST outputs. The process is the same whether you route your audio to external hardware or to internal send effects or groups. A channel—whether audio, VSTi, or ReWire—can route a signal to any active send effect in the VST Send Effects rack, or to any active group channel. Each send on the channel strip can also route to any active VST outputs. To use an external effect, you need to make the VST outputs available using the Devices menu.

To create an external send effect:

1. Be sure that your VST hardware outputs are configured to route audio correctly to your external effect.

2. On the mixer channel that will be the send source, click the drop-down menu above the input setting and select Sends (**Figure 15.4**).

   The Send effects are listed in the extended view area.

3. Click one of the effects slots and, from the drop-down menu, select the hardware output for the external effect.

   Figure 15.5 shows MoFx being selected for a send slot.

4. Adjust the blue-green slider to control the amount of the signal from the channel that is fed to the external effect (**Figure 15.6**).

15.4 Select Sends to make send effects visible in the extended view area for the channel.

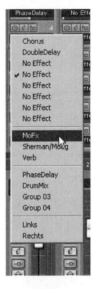

15.5 Selecting one of the VST outputs, in this case one named MoFx, as the send destination

15.6 Adjusting the amount of the signal sent to the external effect

15.7 To use an external effect as an insert effect, you must route the whole track to the VST output.

Creating an External Insert Effect

In my experience, when people work with digital systems, they tend to use more external send effects—like outboard reverb, delay, or modulation units—than external insert effects. The common insert effects like EQ and compression are usually created with plug-ins or applied to the signal on its way to the computer before it's recorded. Still, there is no reason why a track can't be run through an external insert if you want to do so. If you have a special synth filter or a borrowed "magic pixie dust" compressor or EQ that you want to use on a track, it's no more difficult to use this than a send effect. The MoFx unit used in the previous send effect example also has a great tremolo effect; the following example uses the same effect unit as an insert.

To create an external insert effect:

1. Be sure the hardware outputs are properly configured and active.

2. For the channel you want to send through the insert effect, click the very bottom of the channel strip. In the pop-up menu that opens, select the correct hardware output.

   Figure 15.7 shows MoFx being selected again.

ReWire and VSTi Effects

Always keep in mind that in Cubase, you can do anything with a ReWire or VSTi channel that you can do with an audio channel. This includes using external effects as both sends and inserts. You can run your favorite Reason synth through a funky old analog delay, route a VSTi synth through an external synth filter, or run your samples triggered in a software sampler through an external reverb unit.

Monitoring the Effect Results

The previous two examples show you how to route audio to the proper locations, but you have to be able to hear the result of the external effect. There are several ways to do this using either external hardware, or through Cubase.

◆ You can use an external hardware mixer to mix the effected signal with the master output from Cubase.

◆ If your sound card has a mixer control panel, you can often use this instead of an external hardware mixer.

◆ Depending on the latency of your sound card, you may be able to monitor with Cubase by selecting the inputs on your sound card for a channel that is record enabled.

Although all three monitoring options have their advantages and disadvantages, you should monitor the effect return through Cubase if you can. This approach gives you more options at mixdown, such as a fader to quickly turn the effect return up or down in the mix, and the ability to record the effect return to its own track for archiving or for further mixing. You can also automate a Cubase channel, but then you may not be able to automate an external hardware mixer or the mixer control panel for your sound card.

15.8 The VST Inputs panel, with some of the effects returns named to make it easier to set up monitoring

15.9 Toggle the Stereo/Mono button to change the track used as an effect return to the correct mode for the return.

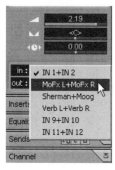

15.10 Selecting the stereo return from a stereo effect

To monitor an effect return through Cubase:

1. Route whatever channels you want through the external effect.

2. Note which of the inputs on your sound card takes the signal back from the external effect. If necessary, turn on that input by selecting Devices > VST Inputs and clicking the buttons to activate each stereo pair.

   Figure 15.8 shows the inputs on my sound card; note that I've named the effects returns on some of the inputs.

3. In the project window, find an empty track.

4. If necessary change the track from stereo to mono or vice versa (**Figure 15.9**).

5. In the Track Inspector, select the sound card inputs that receive the signal from the external effect (**Figure 15.10**).

6. Record–enable the track to monitor it in the mix.

Using Groups for External Effects

In Chapter 12, "Audio Effect Plug-ins," you learned how to use group channels for effects. Groups are convenient because they use one fader to control the levels of multiple tracks, they can apply a single effect to more than one source track, and they can chain multiple effects. The same actions can be applied to groups and external effects. For example, some reverb units sound horrible when too much low-end sound is fed to them; using groups, you can apply a high-pass filter to the low-end sound out of the signal before it is sent to the external reverb. You could also have a delay plug-in as an insert on the group and then feed the delays to an external chorus, reverb, or phase-shifting effect.

To use an external effect via a group channel:

1. Choose a group channel, add any insert effects or EQs to it that you want, and name it (**Figure 15.11**).

2. Click the bottom of the group channel to open the pop-up menu and choose the hardware output (**Figure 15.12**) connected to the external effect.

3. Choose a track to use as a source for sending a signal to the group and external effect. View Sends in the extended view area.

4. Choose an empty send effect slot and click it to open the drop-down menu. Select the name of the group from the list (**Figure 15.13**).

15.11 If a group channel has a good, descriptive name, it's easier to set up send effects to it because the send effects drop-down menu will have a recognizable name.

15.12 Choosing the hardware output for the group channel

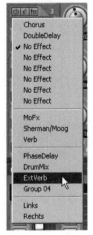

15.13 On the channel with the send, the group channel can be selected as the send destination.

5. Adjust the blue-green slider for the send effect to send more or less of the signal to the group/external effect.

6. Repeat steps 3-5 for any additional channels you want to send to the group/external effect.

✔ **Tip**

■ You can even use groups to route multiple tracks through an external effect as an insert if you want to get really nutty.

Stereo Versus Mono Effects

One of the few things that I don't like about Cubase is the way it deals with mono channels and effects. The mixer allows effects sends to be either pre-fader or post-fader, but they cannot be post-pan and post-fader. This is a minor limitation unless you happen to perform very complex effect routings, such as sending multiple mono channels to an external stereo effect. You're out of luck if you want to maintain the pan position of the mixer channel at the output; you can only choose either the left or right channel of the hardware outputs on your sound card.

Let's say, for example, that you have three tracks: one each panned left, center, and right. If you want to send them to an external stereo effect and keep their pan positions for the effect, you can only select either the left or right output on the sound card. The only option is to copy the tracks to three new mono tracks, route them to a group, and send the group to the external effect. The routing of the entire channel is post-fader and post-pan. The process is cumbersome, but it works.

Pre-Fader and External Effects

External effects, more than software plug-ins, can have problems interfacing with line-level equipment such as a computer and sound card. Some older effects are designed for much lower input levels than current gear, and you may wind up using crazy effects like guitar distortion pedals or vocoder inputs. Because of these potential problems when using external effects, you may particularly want to be able to control the level sent to an effect by making it pre-fader.

Pre-fader send effects allow you to send any amount of the signal to the effect, no matter where the channel fader is set. The fader may be set to zero, with the track not playing in the mix, but a pre-fader send will still route the signal to the effect.

To use an external effect pre-fader:

1. Configure the VST outputs to route audio to the external effect.

2. In the Cubase mixer, find the track that you want to send to the external effect pre-fader and select Sends from the drop-down menu to view send effects in the extended view area.

3. Click a send effect slot and select the output that connects to the external effect (**Figure 15.14**).

4. Click the button to make the send a pre-fader effect (**Figure 15.15**). When the button is selected, it turns orange.

5. Adjust the blue-green slider (**Figure 15.16**) to control the amount of the signal that is sent to the effect.

   Because the effect is pre-fader, this slider alone will control the level sent to the effect, regardless of the setting on the main channel fader.

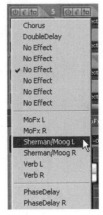

15.14 Selecting the VST output, just as you would for a post-fader effect

15.15 This button makes the send a pre-fader effect. The button turns orange when it is selected.

15.16 Adjust the amount of the pre-fader sent to the external effect.

Mixing with External Effects

There are a couple of serious differences between mixing with external effects (or a combination of external effects and plug-ins) and mixing in a purely software environment. The biggest difference is probably that, when working only with plug-ins, you can bounce, render, and process audio offline, at a time of your choosing. When external effects are introduced, though, all mixing and processing will usually happen in real time.

The process gets most complex when you have to create a final mix. How do you include your external effects, such as delays and reverbs, in the main mix? The answer has a great deal to do with how you are monitoring. If you are monitoring with an external mixer or your sound card mixer control panel, probably the best approach is to record to another computer or hard disk recorder.

If you are monitoring your external effects through Cubase, you have two options. First, you can record the master output to another machine, as you would if you were using an external mixer. Second, you can record all of your effects returns to audio tracks. Then, using the recorded effects returns as audio tracks within Cubase, you can bounce and render mixes in much the same way you would in a software-only effects setup.

I recommend you use this last option if you can, recording your effects returns to a track in Cubase. This requires only one pass through the song, makes creating a final mix easy, and also gives you an archive of the output of your external effects.

EXPORTING & RENDERING TRACKS

When you work in Cubase, you'll spend most of your time working with audio and MIDI files within the program. Sometimes, though, you will need to create a file that will be played back outside of Cubase: for instance, when you want to create a final stereo mix for mastering, or when you want to generate a file that can be streamed over a Web server.

You may also sometimes want to create a stereo track from a larger group of tracks in the course of a project. Once you have a multitrack drum mix sounding good, for example, it may be easier to work with as a single stereo file. Or you may want to save the output of a VST instrument or a ReWire track to an audio file for further mixing or manipulation.

All of these situations require the same fundamental processes, as you will see in this chapter. In this chapter, you will learn how to bounce multiple audio events and parts to a single file. You will also learn how to print effects and EQ to a track by rendering a new file with the effects included. You will also learn how to create a final mix of your song, both as an uncompressed, full-bandwidth audio file and using a number of compressed audio file formats.

Bouncing, Exporting, and Rendering

When people talk about the various ways that Cubase can save, combine, and output audio files, they often use multiple terms interchangeably, even though they refer to slightly different processes. This can be quite confusing. This chapter focuses on rendering, but you may also hear people use the terms *bouncing* and *exporting* to refer to the same process. Here are some definitions to help you understand how the processes differ.

◆ **Rendering** is the process of saving a new version of a track or tracks with effects, fades, mixing moves, and other processing included in the rendered file. In other words, the real-time changes in the sound are printed to the new file.

◆ **Bouncing** refers to a technique used with analog tape decks when a project needs more tape tracks than are available. On a four-track system, for example, music recorded on the first three tracks might be mixed onto the empty fourth track. This freed the original three tracks for more recording. Believe it or not, many classic recordings were made using just this process.

◆ **Exporting** a sound or track saves it in a new format, but the piece sounds the same. For instance, you might export WAV files as SoundDesigner II files for use in another program, or you might export a loop or sound to a new format to load it into a hardware sampler.

Most of this chapter focuses on rendering—creating a new file with mix or effects processing included in the saved file—but you will also learn a bit about bouncing and exporting.

Figure 16.1
Selecting all events
on a single track

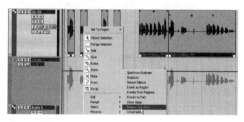

Figure 16.2 Choose from the context menu to bounce the selected events to a new file.

Figure 16.3 The result of the bounce; compare this result to the separate events in Figure 16.2.

Bouncing a Track

Bouncing in Cubase terms means something slightly different than bouncing in analog tape recording. In Cubase, bouncing involves taking discrete parts and events on a track and combining them into a single event. A heavily edited vocal line or guitar part, for example, can be bounced to a new file that includes all of the edits. You can use bouncing to make it easier to see an edited file in the project window or to create a file that is easier to import into another program for further editing or processing. The following task shows you how to bounce all of the events in an edited track to a new file and event.

To bounce an audio track:

1. Select the parts and events you want to bounce. You can select them manually or open the context menu for the track in the track list (**Figure 16.1**) and choose Select All Events.

2. With the events and parts selected, open the context menu by right-clicking (Windows) or Command-clicking (Mac OS) an event or part. Select Audio > Bounce Selection (**Figure 16.2**).

   A status bar shows the progress of the bounce, and a dialog box opens when the file has been created.

3. Choose Replace to place the bounced file on the track to replace the audio selected for the bounce.

   Figure 16.3 shows the result of the bounce.

✔ Tip

■ Notice that the bounce here involves a bit of rendering. The last event in Figure 16.2 includes changes made to the level and fade with the handles, and those are included in a bounce; however, other effects and processing are not included.

BOUNCING A TRACK

Bouncing Multiple Tracks

You may encounter a problem if you record in Cubase but want to mix your song in another program, such as Pro Tools or Digital Performer, or on another system. One way to eliminate the problem is to bounce every track in your project. Doing this chews up hard disk space quickly, but you will finish with a discrete file for each track that is exactly the same length, which then can be imported into another application for mixing.

To bounce more than one track:

1. Set up events and parts with all edits, fades, and crossfades just as you want them.

   Figure 16.4 shows a group of four tracks that will be bounced.

2. From the toolbar or context menu, choose the Range Selection tool.

3. Using the Range Selection tool, select the intended range for the tracks that you want to bounce (**Figure 16.5**).

4. Open the context menu and select Audio > Bounce Selection.

5. In the dialog box that opens, select Replace.

   The bounced tracks will replace the originals (**Figure 16.6**). As you can see in Figure 16.6, the new file names are shown in the events. In this case, the four tracks created are named Bounce_CongaLoop 16 through 19. Those files can be imported to another platform for mixing.

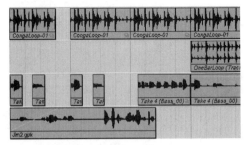

Figure 16.4 Four tracks before a bounce

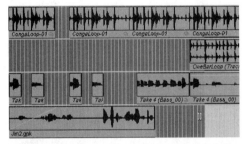

Figure 16.5 The Range Selection tool selecting all of the tracks

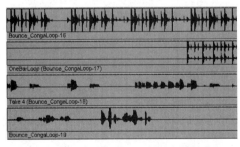

Figure 16.6 After the bounce, each track is continuous and includes the edits and fades from the original events.

Figure 16.7 Setting the channel fader

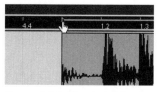

Figure 16.8 Setting the left locator

Rendering a Track with Effects

To render audio, you follow a basic set of instructions, described here and used in the rest of this chapter. Cubase has the ability to spit out an exact digital copy of whatever appears at its master outputs, and the file can include insert effects, send effects, automation, and EQs. The following task shows you all of the steps, including how to print the compression and EQ settings on a track.

To render a single track with effects:

1. Set the EQ and compression as you want for the track.

2. Set the channel fader to 0.00 (**Figure 16.7**), unless you want the rendered file to be louder or softer than the original. Raise or lower the fader to make the rendered file louder or softer.

3. Open the mixer and set the master fader to 0.00, again unless you want the output to be louder or softer than the original. Raise or lower the fader to make the rendered file louder or softer.

4. Set the left and right locators (**Figure 16.8**) at the boundaries of the part of the track that you want to render.

5. From the File menu, select Export > Audio Mixdown.

continues on next page

6. In the Export Audio Mixdown dialog box, set the options you want for the file being rendered.

   Figure 16.9 shows the file name set to BassCompFX and specifies creation of a mono, 24-bit, 44.1-kHz WAV file. The Pool and Audio Track buttons are selected, so the rendered file will also be brought back into Cubase on another audio track.

7. After you set all of the options in the dialog box as you wish, click Save.

   A status bar will show the progress of the export process.

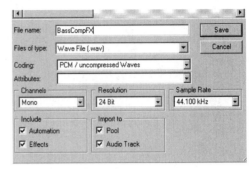

Figure 16.9 The Export Audio Mixdown dialog box: These settings will create a new mono 24-bit file.

RENDERING A TRACK WITH EFFECTS

Track Rendering Versus Audio Processing

Rendering a single mono or stereo track (as described in this chapter) and processing audio (as described in Chapter 9, "Advanced Audio Editing") are somewhat similar operations. In previous versions of Cubase (and many other audio programs), the only way to print effects and EQ to a track was to use a render and import file operation. In Cubase SX, you can use either rendering/importing or audio processing, and there are advantages and disadvantages to each method.

Rendering and importing gives you a few options that aren't available with audio processing. One example is applying EQ to a track. You can print VST EQ when rendering, but the only way to apply EQ to a track with audio processing is to use a plug-in. You can also use groups for send effects when rendering, and you can export multiple tracks, or a full mix, to a single file; neither of these operations are possible with audio processing.

However, you can undo, edit, and rearrange audio processing after the fact, whereas if you want to change a rendered file later, you have to render it again. Audio processing is also a little quicker and more intuitive.

My advice is to use rendering for the situations where it's necessary, like creating mixes and printing send effects to a track, and to use audio processing the rest of the time. In any case, it's important to learn how to do both well.

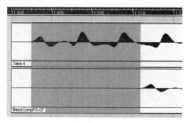

Figure 16.10 The selected range shows the offset in an exported file.

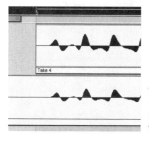

Figure 16.11 The bottom, rendered, track has been moved manually back to match the timing of the original.

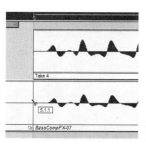

Figure 16.12 With Snap on, the file can be snipped easily.

Figure 16.13 The Delay parameter in the Track inspector can also be used to correct the offset.

Workarounds for Timing Offset

Rendering a track sometimes produces an offset in timing within the exported file. If the timing on your rendered track seems a bit off, one possible cause is that plug-in latency may not be correctly factored in. In addition, some people report that certain combinations of ASIO cards and computer hardware generate this problem.

Figure 16.10 shows a timing offset. The Range Selection tool is highlighting about 25 milliseconds of silence incorrectly inserted at the beginning of the rendered file. The first rise in each waveform should happen at the same time. There are two primary ways work around this problem:

◆ Turn off Snap and manually line up the files (**Figure 16.11**). Then turn Snap back on and use the Scissors tool to snip the beginning of the file (**Figure 16.12**).

◆ Open the main tab in the Track inspector for the rendered track and enter a negative delay setting equal to the offset. **Figure 16.13** shows 27 milliseconds entered for that parameter.

Of course, this offset problem may not occur in your work, so don't worry about it unless it shows up visually or audibly in your projects.

Rendering Multiple Tracks

The same basic rules used to render a single track apply when you need to render more than one track. Set up all of the tracks, with effects if you want them, so that the master output sounds exactly as you wish; then render to a new file. Rendering multiple tracks is useful in many musical contexts. For instance, you may want to create a single stereo file of a multiple-microphone drum part, or if you have multitrack backing vocals that you have edited, tuned, and tweaked to sound just right, you may want to create a single stereo file so you can control all of the backing vocals in the mix with one fader.

To render more than one track:

1. Set each track, including pan, level, and send and insert effects, so the master output sounds as you wish.

2. Solo all of the tracks you want to include in, or mute all tracks you want to exclude from, the rendered file (**Figure 16.14**).

3. Check to see that the master fader is set to 0.00 (**Figure 16.15**), unless you want the overall level of the rendered file to change.

4. Set the left locator where you want the rendered file to start, and set the right locator where you want the rendered file to end.

5. From the File menu, select Export > Audio Mixdown.

6. In the Export Audio Mixdown dialog box, type a name for the rendered file and set the options you want. In this example, change the Channels setting to Stereo Interleaved to create a single file with two channels of audio (**Figure 16.16**).

7. Click Save to start the file rendering process.

Figure 16.14 A group of soloed channels ready to be rendered

Figure 16.15 Setting the master fader to 0.00

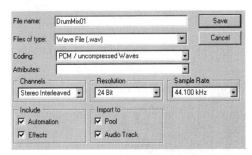

Figure 16.16 Because a stereo drum mix is being exported, it is important to create a stereo file.

Figure 16.17 The MIDI file and ReWire channel, both soloed

Rendering ReWire Tracks

Track rendering is also very convenient when you are working with ReWire applications—for instance, when you create a loop in Live, program a beat using the pattern sequencers included with Reason, or trigger a synth sound in another ReWire application. Working with these applications in real time is great, but when a track is ready to be mixed, the easiest approach often is to print everything to an audio file in Cubase. This approach both simplifies the mix process and frees processing bandwidth for audio plug-ins in Cubase.

To render ReWire tracks:

1. In the Cubase mixer, solo the ReWire tracks you want to render. If a MIDI track in Cubase is triggering the ReWire application, be sure to solo that MIDI track at the same time (**Figure 16.17**). Set the MIDI and ReWire channels if necessary.

2. Set the master channel to 0.00, unless you want to change the level of the rendered file. Move the fader up or down if you want the rendered file to be louder or softer than the original.

continues on next page

Rendering with Groups

There are many situations where you may need to include a group in a rendered file. For instance, you may have used a group to apply a single effect (such as a compressor) to multiple tracks, or you may be using a group to chain together send effects. (Both of these examples are described in the sections on "Group Channels" and "Chaining Effects Using Groups" in Chapter 12.)

Cubase is smart enough that you don't really need to worry about using groups most of the time. If you solo a track that is routed to a group, the group is automatically soloed as well; however, when you use a group to stack send effects you need to manually solo the group along with the tracks that will be using it as a send effect.

Usually it will be obvious if effects are missing, but it's always a good idea to check manually when you are rendering tracks that involve groups.

3. Set the left and right locators at the beginning and end of the section you want to render (**Figure 16.18**).

4. From the File menu, select Export > Audio Mixdown.

5. In the Export Audio Mixdown dialog box that opens, name the file to be rendered and set any other parameters you want.

Figure 16.19 shows the dialog box configured for rendering a drum loop in stereo.

6. Click Save to render the new file.

Figure 16.18 Setting the left and right locators

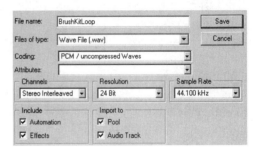

Figure 16.19 The dialog box ready to render the new stereo file

Rendering VST Instruments

VST instruments are rendered just like ReWire tracks, so you need to be sure you solo any MIDI channels that trigger VST instruments along with the VSTi channels. Also note whether a VSTi is routed to a group or uses a group for send effects.

Figure 16.20 Selecting the Export option

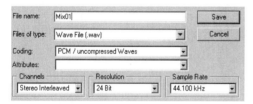

Figure 16.21 Naming the final mix Mix01

Creating a Final Mix

After all of the recording, editing, and mixing is finished, you need to create a final stereo mix of your song. If you are using external effects or triggering hardware synths and samplers, you will have to record the final mix in real time. If, on the other hand, all of your files are inside Cubase and all of the effects still in use are software plug-ins, you can render the final mix.

To render a final mix:

1. Configure the full mix to play precisely as you want it, including mixer automation, effects, VSTi, and ReWire tracks.

2. Set the left locator a bit before the song begins, and set the right locator a bit after the song ends.

3. From the File menu, select Export > Audio Mixdown (**Figure 16.20**).

4. In the Export Audio Mixdown dialog box that opens, name the file (**Figure 16.21**) and set other parameters as you wish.

   When rendering a final mix, you should choose at least 24 bits for the output file. You should also decide whether you want to import the final mix back into the project (where you can solo it and listen to it), or—if you are sure that you're happy with it—export it as a new, separate file.

5. Click Save to render the mix.

CREATING A FINAL MIX

Bits, Floats, and Rates

Cubase supports a number of options for exporting files, both individual tracks and loops or full mixes. You can export files with a sample rate from 8 to 96 kHz and with a bit depth of 8, 16, 24, or 32.

When choosing the sample rate, you need to consider the sample rate of the project itself and the sample rate of the delivery format. If you plan to deliver the mix on CD, for example, at some point the mix will have to become a 16-bit, 44.1-kHz file because that is the only kind of file that an audio CD can use. More often than not, your CD projects will have been recorded at 44.1 kHz, so this will not be an issue. If for some reason your project was recorded at another sample rate, such as 96 kHz, you can export to 44.1 kHz from within Cubase, or you can keep the final mix at 96 kHz and create the 44.1-kHz file later. In general, you should export the stereo mix at the project sample rate. This gives you a file with the highest fidelity possible, and you can use it to create a CD-compatible audio file if you need it.

For bit depth, use 8 bits only in situations where file size is critical. Most situations where you would consider an 8-bit file are better served by using one of the compressed file formats described later in this chapter, such as MP3 or Ogg Vorbis.

Use 16-bit files if you are exporting a file to create a CD or to load into a hardware sampler, or for any situation where you know you need a 16-bit file.

Cubase can use both 16- and 24-bit files in the same project, and in this case, you should render to a 24-bit file, to preserve as much of the fidelity as possible.

To create an even higher-resolution file, you can use 32-bit float, but not many programs can read these files; use this setting only if you plan to bring the rendered file back into Cubase or another application that you know reads 32-bit float files.

You should consider a number of factors when deciding whether to create 32-bit float files. Internally, Cubase (and nearly all VST plug-ins and instruments) work with 32-bit float audio. When Cubase writes audio to disk or sends audio to the sound card for conversion to analog format, the audio is turned back into a 24- or 16-bit file. Exporting or rendering 32-bit float files keeps absolutely the highest resolution available in the project. However, 32-bit float files are large—twice as large as a 16-bit file, and a third again as large as a 24-bit file—and, as mentioned earlier, fewer programs can open them. Check with your own ears and assess your own equipment to weigh the trade-offs.

Figure 16.22 Choosing MP3 as the output file type

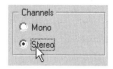

Figure 16.23 Normally, you should create a final mix in stereo.

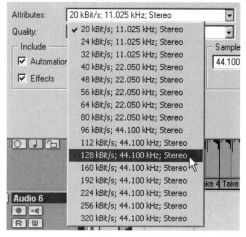

Figure 16.24 The options for exporting a stereo MP3 file: The higher the kBit/s value, the higher quality the audio.

Creating an MP3 Mix

The Web has spawned a group of compressed file formats for audio. A CD-ready, 16-bit, 44.1-kHz stereo file consumes about 10MB of disk space per minute of audio. At some future date, that size will no doubt seem small, but not many people today want to stream 45MB of data from a server to play a four-and-a-half-minute song. MP3 has become the most prominent compressed audio format on the Web because it lets you create files that are fairly small and can sound pretty decent.

Never export your final mix, or even a loop, as an MP3 file. All of the compressed file formats discussed here should be used only for creating files that you put on the Web or distribute in some way other than on a CD. In other words, create your final mix in an uncompressed file format—then create a mix in a compressed format if you like. You use the same methods in Cubase to create an MP3 file that you use to create a WAV or AIFF file, but when you select MP3 (**Figure 16.22**), you have another set of options for the file you will create:

◆ The **Channels** radio buttons let you select stereo or mono output (**Figure 16.23**). In Cubase, you can create higher-resolution files only with this option set to Stereo.

◆ Use the **Attributes** menu to choose a resolution for the MP3 file that you are exporting (**Figure 16.24**). The higher the bit-rate, the better the audio quality, and the larger the file created.

◆ The **Quality** setting determines whether the MP3 file is created more quickly or with higher quality. Most of the time, you should set Quality to Highest to get the best-sounding MP3.

Creating an Ogg Vorbis Mix

MP3 files are by far the most common type of compressed audio files in the world, but not everyone likes everything about them. One potential problem with MP3 files is that the format is patented and subject to license fees in some circumstances. Ogg Vorbis is an open-source, patent-free alternative for compressed audio. If you want more information about Ogg Vorbis files, a good place to start is www.vorbis.com.

The process for creating an Ogg Vorbis file in Cubase is almost exactly the same as for creating an MP3 file. Prepare the mix exactly as you wish, set the locators, choose File > Export > Audio Mixdown, and select Ogg Vorbis File from the drop-down menu (**Figure 16.25**). You then have the following options:

◆ As with MP3 files, you can create either mono or stereo files. You'll almost always want a stereo file when creating a final mix (**Figure 16.26**).

◆ Click the **Quality** drop-down menu to choose among three options (**Figure 16.27**). Normally, you should choose Highest to get the best audio quality, but if you need a smaller file, you can choose Fast or Medium.

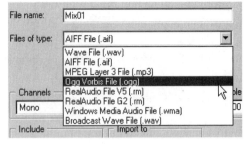

Figure 16.25 Choosing Ogg Vorbis as the file type

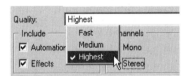

Figure 16.26 Selecting Stereo for the Ogg Vorbis file

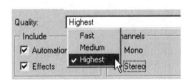

Figure 16.27 Ogg Vorbis files have only three quality options.

Figure 16.28 RealAudio files can be one of two types: V5 or G2.

Figure 16.29 The options for V5 files: V5 files are small and generally of low quality.

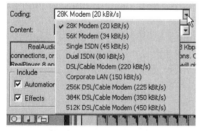

Figure 16.30 With G2 files, you can choose the speed of the connection you stream to.

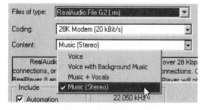

Figure 16.31 G2 files also allow you to choose the source audio to be compressed.

Creating a RealAudio Mix— PC Only

Another common Web-centric audio format is RealAudio. This format was created by RealNetworks (www.real.com), and the files have the extension .rm. RealAudio files are attractive primarily because they are very small and thus are easy to stream over a variety of types of network connections. Generally, they are not great-sounding files, so you may not want to choose RealAudio files if you are after the highest fidelity.

You can use Cubase to create two kinds of RealAudio files: RealAudio V5 files and RealAudio G2 files (**Figure 16.28**). RealAudio V5 files are usually smaller than G2 files, and they are also lower fidelity. After you've set the mix, locator, and export parameters, you can choose between two sets of options for creating RealAudio files:

◆ If you create a **V5** file, the Coding menu (**Figure 16.29**) contains all of your choices. The options with the larger Kbps values will create smaller files with lower fidelity.

◆ A **G2** file has two sets of options. Use the Coding menu (**Figure 16.30**) to choose the kind of network connection you expect will be used by the person playing back the file. Use the Content menu (**Figure 16.31**) to describe the source material of the mix, to give the compression algorithm an idea of how to compress the file for the best results.

As of this writing, the Real Audio export option is not available for Mac users of Cubase SX.

Creating a Windows Media Mix—PC only

Windows Media files are created in a proprietary format written by Microsoft. They are usually quite small but maintain decent audio quality. They have the file extension .wma. Usually, people create WMA files to stream them over a Windows media or web server. There is only one drop-down menu for creating a Windows Media mix. Use the **Attributes** menu (**Figure 16.32**) to choose the network connection speed of the computer that will be downloading the file. Choosing a faster network connection speed will create a larger file with higher-quality audio.

Unfortunately, only the Windows version of Cubase SX offers export options for creating Windows Media files.

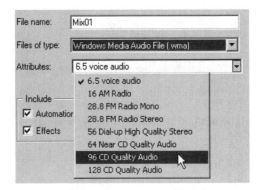

Figure 16.32 The options for creating a Windows Media file

Streaming Format Considerations

Usually, the kind of compressed audio file you create will be an obvious choice. Compressed audio is normally used for streaming over a Web or media server, and the kind of server will usually determine the kind of file you want to create. Some Web servers can stream only RealAudio files, while others can stream only Windows Media files.

To create fairly good-sounding, small files for sharing with friends over the Web or burning to CDs, you should probably choose MP3. Pretty much every computer in the world these days can play back an MP3 file, so you cast the widest net with MP3. If you are an open-source advocate, Ogg Vorbis files offer a patent-free alternative to MP3. You should use the other formats only when the particular streaming technology demands it.

17

MASTERING

In the old days, mastering referred to the arcane and difficult process of making a master disc from analog tapes. This master disc was sent to a duplication plant where it was the template for pressing vinyl records. A mastering engineer was the person who prepared tracks to get consistent level and sound, while also being sure that the needle wouldn't skip out of the groove on the finished product. It was a one-shot, real-time process, and if the cut master didn't sound right or a fade was too early, another master had to be made.

The digital era changed this. Duplication houses have been taking burned CDs for years now, so in theory anyone with a CD burner can make a CD master. Mastering engineers tend to be rather smart fellows, and they converted quite effectively from vinyl jockeys to digital gurus. Because anyone can now make a master CD, professional mastering engineers make their money by making your CD sound as good as possible.

The techniques in this chapter will help you understand what goes on in a professional mastering session, and you can use the same techniques to master your own songs. You will learn how to create a mastering project, how to sequence tracks, create fade-ins and fade-outs, and control the level and sound of each song, and how to export the final 16-bit files to burn to a CD.

The Case for Professional Mastering

If you are releasing a CD on a commercial label or plan to print CDs in large quantities to be sold for profit, you should seriously consider hiring a professional mastering engineer. Top mastering engineers have the experience, ears, and gear to make your mixes sound fantastic. They spend their lives listening to full program material and getting it to sound its best, and they are paid handsomely to do so. A good mastering engineer can make a huge difference in the sound of your tracks and can be worth every penny he or she charges.

There are also bad mastering engineers, just as there are bad recording engineers, bad drummers, and bad kissers. You should avoid all of them with equal determination. It's entirely appropriate to ask for a sample from a mastering engineer, and be sure to ask for—and listen to—"before" and "after" tracks before agreeing to a deal.

Even if you decide to have your tracks mastered by a professional, you can still be a more informed and productive client by mastering on your own in Cubase. Think of your work as a rehearsal mastering session. Armed with the information in this chapter about fades, song sequencing, and the sound of tracks, you should have a better experience at your mastering sessions.

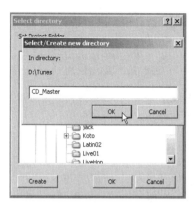

Chapter 17.1 Creating a new folder for the mastering project

Creating a Mastering Project

The first thing to do when mastering your own music is to get all of the songs in the proper form at the highest quality possible. When you talk to your mastering engineer, ask him or her what types of files work best in the mastering studio. Usually you will be asked to create 24-bit AIFF or WAV files at the sample rate of the project. The mastering engineer will make all of the sonic changes necessary and then create the 16-bit, 44.1-kHz files necessary for burning a CD. Here's how to create those files and how to start your own mastering project.

To start a mastering project:

1. Using the techniques discussed in Chapter 16, "Exporting and Rendering Tracks," create stereo files of all of your songs with at least 24-bit resolution. Render those stereo mixes to a separate, distinct folder.

2. Start Cubase and create a new, empty project by selecting File > New Project and selecting the empty template.

    You will be prompted to select a folder for the project in the Select Directory panel.

3. Navigate to the folder where you keep your Cubase projects and click the Create button to make a new folder. Name the folder and click OK to create it (**Figure 17.1**).

4. Click OK again in the Select Directory panel to dismiss it.

    You will be returned to the Cubase Project window.

5. In the new, empty project, click the File menu and select Import > Audio File.

continues on next page

6. In the Import Audio panel that opens, find and select all of the mixes you want to master (**Figure 17.2**) and click Open to import them.

7. In the Import Options panel, make sure Copy Files to Working Directory is checked and click OK (**Figure 17.3**).

8. Save the Cubase project by clicking the File menu and selecting Save.

✔ Tip

■ By using the techniques in this task, you've left your original mixes alone. You're working on copies made in the working directory for the project. Any changes you make will be on those copies, and you can take the originals to the mastering studio by burning a CD of those original files.

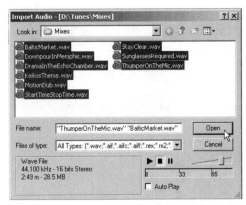

Chapter 17.2 You can use the Import Audio dialog box to import multiple tracks simultaneously.

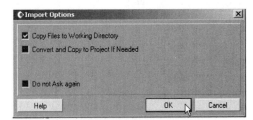

Chapter 17.3 If you check the Copy Files to Working Directory box, you will leave your original mixes intact and work only on copies.

Chapter 17.4 A mastering project with nine songs imported

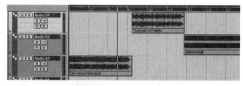

Chapter 17.5 Each song is on its own track, so it's easy to move the songs around and try different sequences.

Chapter 17.6 This menu changes the mode for Snap. Events + Cursor is a particularly good choice when mastering.

Sequencing Songs

If you create a project for mastering as described in the previous task, you will wind up with something that looks like **Figure 17.4**. One of the great advantages of this approach is that you will have each song on its own stereo track in Cubase, and the events created will have the name of the song.

With this approach, you can experiment easily with the sequence of songs for your project. Simply drag the files to change the order. **Figure 17.5** shows three tracks set up so that track 3 plays first, then track 1, and then track 2.

✔ Tip

■ When you're sequencing a dozen tracks, your project may last an hour. You will have to be zoomed out very far to view all of these tracks, and snapping edits to the closest bar won't really be effective. Here's a useful trick when you're zoomed out really far in a project: Change the way Snap works. Click the Snap menu and select Events + Cursor (**Figure 17.6**), which will make any object you move snap to the location of the cursor either at the beginning or end of any other event.

Adding Fades

Fades are used in mastering for two main purposes. The first is to fade-out the end of a song that doesn't naturally stop at a particular point. Rock songs with long instrumental codas are commonly faded out this way. The second reason to use a fade is to fade one track out while fading the next track in. DJs have long done this live. It's called cross-fading, and it's often used in electronic and pop music to create one long piece of music with some or all tracks joined.

Regardless of how you will be using fades, you will be in a much better position at your professional mastering session if you have a good idea when you want fades to start and stop. The following example will note both the fade-in and fade-out points for a track.

To find fade-in and fade-out points:

1. If Event Infoline is not turned on, turn it on by clicking its button on the toolbar (**Figure 17.7**).

2. Click the track in the Project window to select it.

   Figure 17.8 shows a selected song and the Event Infoline information for it. Note the Length, Fade-in, and Fade-out numbers.

3. Use the handles—the blue triangles at the start and end of the event—to set the fade-in and fade-out times.

4. Use the Event Infoline values to determine when fades should start and stop.

   Figure 17.9 shows the track with both a fade-in and a fade-out. Doing a little math, you can see that the fade-in will finish about 20 seconds into the track, and the fade-out will start at about 2:35 seconds into the track.

Chapter 17.7 The toolbar button for Show Event Infoline

Chapter 17.8 Some of the information displayed on the Event Infoline when an audio event is selected

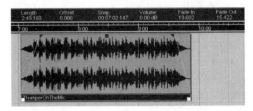

Chapter 17.9 With a fade-in and fade-out set, the Infoline can be used to calculate when fades start and stop.

✔ Tips

- You should write down your guesses on fade-in and fade-out times to report to your mastering engineer. He or she will be very excited you've even thought about such things, and you'll look like you really know what you're doing. You might wind up deciding to change the fade points, but at least you'll have an idea where to start.

- If you think this is all kind of irritating and nonmusical, you're right. You can always hire someone else to do all of this.

ADDING FADES

Chapter 17.10 The Channel Settings window is great for mastering. You can see all of your effects and edit EQ graphically.

Master or Mix

If you're mastering on your own or prepping songs for a professional mastering session, you may find situations where a track sounds more than a little bit off. Problems that didn't seem worth fixing, like a bad edit or an instrument that is clearly too loud, can become frighteningly obvious when you're listening carefully at a mastering session. It's often hard to see the big picture when mixing each individual track, and sometimes an obvious problem will crop up in a mix when mastering the finished mixes.

This is a great argument for doing at least a first pass at mastering a CD yourself. You can always go back and make a few changes in the final mix if the synth pad is too loud or the acoustic guitars disappear in the chorus. Part of finishing a CD is deciding it's really done, since you don't want to spend 10 years on one CD, but if mastering reveals a flaw in a mix, you can usually fix it fairly quickly if you know exactly what the problem is.

Applying EQ

One of the main reasons to pay for professional mastering is to gain access to bending-end EQ and compression hardware. A good mastering house may have EQs modules pulled from famous British consoles, modern EQs specifically created for mastering full mixes, and a collection of famous old compressors worth more than a nice house. Your mastering engineer ought to have some really special units available to tailor the sound of your tracks. EQ can be used in a huge variety of ways when mastering, but there are usually two main reasons for using EQ.

First, a song may be generally weak in high-end or low-end sound. This may not be obvious when mixing each individual track, but one or two may stick out sonically in a way that is unpleasant when they are compared as a group.

The second situation where EQ may be necessary is for making small corrective EQ changes. One part of the frequency spectrum may be a bit too pronounced, making one instrument stick out too much. With luck, good ears, and good equipment, a mastering engineer can make the kinds of changes needed.

When working in Cubase, you may want to use the Channel Settings window (**Figure 17.10**) to test some of these actions on a track. If you find that some EQ changes help the sound of a track, write down the settings you use and take them to the mastering session.

Applying Compression

Compression, which controls the level of a signal, was discussed in Chapter 12, "Audio Effect Plug-ins." In that chapter, you learned how to use compression on an individual track, such as a vocal or bass track. Compression on a full mix is a very different concept, because the compressor may be working with a mix that includes dozens of different instruments. Each instrument has its own characteristics, and it is very difficult to set a compressor to work with full program material.

The solution to this problem is to use multiband compression. A multiband compressor divides the frequency spectrum into two, three, four, or more slices. Each slice has its own settings for the typical compression

parameters of attack, decay, and release. This keeps a strong note in the bass, for example, from triggering a compressor to decrease the level of the whole track.

Unfortunately, Cubase doesn't ship with a multiband compressor. **Figure 17.11** shows Multiband Maximizer, a third-party VST plug-in that includes a multiband compressor. The middle section of the plug-in is one kind of multiband dynamics control. If you are preparing for a professional mastering session, all you can do is try to get a general idea of which songs sound the loudest and softest. If you plan to master at home, you probably should invest in a multiband compressor plug-in.

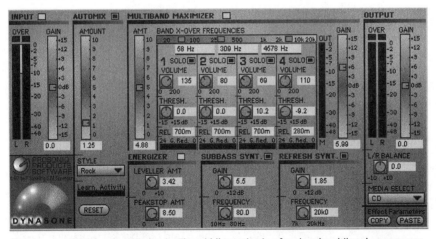

Chapter 17.11 A third-party VST plug-in: The middle section is a four-band multiband compressor.

Chapter 17.12 Click this button to display the master fader.

Chapter 17.13 The eight effects slots above the fader are insert effects that process the sound of the full mix.

Applying Master Effects

So far, when you've applied effects like EQ and compression, they've been used on individual tracks. These will be the most common kinds of effects that you'll apply when mastering, but sometimes you'll want to include an effect for all tracks. The easiest way to do this is to use master effects.

Master effects are very much like insert effects on a mixer channel, but instead they apply to the full mix sent to the master fader. You should use a master effect when you want to apply a change to every track on a CD. You may want to put a final bit of gentle compression on all songs, or you may want to have a limiter plug-in to control stray peaks that occur in a song. If you are getting ready for a professional mastering session, write down any master effects you use and the settings that you think sound the best so you can explain to your mastering engineer what you heard in the effect that improved the songs.

To apply a master effect:

1. Open the Cubase mixer by selecting Devices > Mixer or by pressing F3.

2. In the Cubase mixer, click the Show Master button (**Figure 17.12**) to show the master fader.

3. Above the master fader are eight effects slots (**Figure 17.13**). Click any of the slots to add an effect.

✔ Tip

■ Master effects slots 7 and 8 are different in one important way from the other slots: They are applied after the master fader. Usually these slots will be used for effects that are involved in file exporting—things like sample-rate conversion or conversion of a 24-bit file to a 16-bit file.

APPLYING MASTER EFFECTS

Do-It-Yourself Mastering

The previous sections of this chapter assume that you're taking your songs to a professional engineer for mastering. If that's your plan, you can use this chapter to help create a set of detailed notes that you can take to the mastering session. You will know when tracks should be faded in and faded out, you'll have a good idea about which tracks need EQ to make them fit into the whole CD, and you'll have some ideas about other changes that might need to be made.

While a top-flight mastering engineer will truly make a dramatic difference in the sound of a final CD, there are situations where the best idea is to master your own CD. For example, you may not be able to afford mastering, you may be putting together only a rough CD to use for promotion, or you may be making a CD just to send to other musicians to help them learn material. If you decide to master your own songs, you have a few more steps to complete:

◆ You will need to export each song as a new file, including insert effects such as compression and EQ.

◆ You may need to apply master effects to each song on the CD.

◆ You must create files that can be used by your CD-burning application to make a CD. Usually this means 16-bit, 44.1-kHz AIFF or WAV files.

Most of these processes are described elsewhere in this book, but when exporting mixes, there are a few small tricks to make the process a bit easier. Set up each mix exactly as you wish, including EQ, compression, and level settings, and follow the steps described here.

Chapter 17.14 This option sets the left and right locators to the boundaries of a selected event.

Chapter 17.15 Selecting Audio Mixdown to render a mastered track

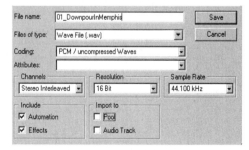

Chapter 17.16 Naming the track and setting the parameters for the track to create a 16-bit, 44.1-kHz, stereo file

To create mastered files:

1. In the Project window, click the first track of the CD.

2. Right-click (Windows) or Control-click (Mac OS) to open the context menu and select Transport > Locators to Selection (**Figure 17.14**).

   This will set the left and right locators at the beginning and end of the selected event.

3. Click the File menu and select Export > Audio Mixdown (**Figure 17.15**) to render a new file of the track.

4. In the Export Audio Mixdown dialog box that opens, name the track.

   A good approach is to name the tracks with a number so the sequence will be obvious. In **Figure 17.16**, the track has been renamed and begins with a number.

5. Select Stereo Interleaved, 16-bit, 44.1-kHz in the Export Audio Mixdown dialog box, as in Figure 17.16.

6. Uncheck the Import to Pool and Audio Track options, as in Figure 17.16. Normally, you will not want or need to import the final 16-bit songs back into the master project.

7. Click Save to render the new file.

8. Repeat steps 1 through 7 for each track of the CD.

✔ Tip

■ If you choose Stereo Split rather than Stereo Interleave in the Audio Mixdown dialog box, it will split the stereo into separate left and right mono files.

A Tale of Two Masters

I don't call myself a mastering engineer because I'm not one. One of the things I do in my studio, though, is what I call CD post-production. I take files or tapes from bands or record labels and make sure the levels are right and the fades are done properly, and I produce a CD with a cue sheet that can be sent to a duplication facility. If asked, I'll also compress and EQ the tracks. The reason I don't call this mastering is because I don't think I'm brilliant at it, I don't have proper mastering gear in my studio, and I just don't like the loaded nature of the term.

I started doing this when a band I had known and liked for years brought me their newly mastered CD. This band plays very clean, quiet rock—very much in the style of "Candy Says"-era Lou Reed and early R.E.M. They had spent two years, working a few weekends a month and a few full weeks a year, in an all-analog recording studio located in a barn. The band recorded to two-inch analog tape and mixed with very few effects and no automation on a big old analog mixing board. The first trip the audio made into the digital domain was when the mixes were recorded to a DAT tape.

Armed with this DAT tape, the group went to a quite expensive mastering house in New Jersey. They came to me after the session because they just didn't think the final CD sounded right, and they wanted my opinion. Listening to the DAT versus the mastered CD was unbelievable. The original DAT mixes had sections so quiet and delicate that you could hear birds chirping outside the barn, and the mastered CD sounded overly compressed, like a Celine Dion record broadcast over AM radio. The mastered CD was loud, for sure, but did a horrible job representing the sweat and time the band had put into their songs.

The band was pretty much drained of cash from the recording and mastering costs, but they were all friends of mine so I told them I would give their songs a shot. I took their mixes, loaded them into Cubase, and used a third-party multiband compressor and a little EQ. The songs held together well and had a consistent sonic thumbprint, so it was easy to get a general idea of what small changes to make to get them sounding nice and buffed.

I wouldn't be telling this story if the band didn't print the CD using every one of my mastered mixes. This doesn't mean I'm a super-brilliant mastering engineer—I'm not. What it does mean is that even if a guy has a $40,000 Pro Tools rig in an anechoic chamber in an industrial park, he still might squash your acoustic jazz trio CD until it has the dynamic range of a Metallica record. If you hire a mastering engineer, make sure you are prepared to speak your mind and get the results for which you are paying.

Chapter 17.17 The UV22 dithering plug-in: This version dithers only to 16 bits.

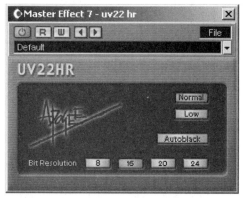

Chapter 17.18 The UV22HR plug-in does the same thing as the UV22 but includes options to create other than 16-bit files.

Using UV22 Dithering

There are lots of factors that can make digital audio sound terrible, including clipping, bad converters, and bad levels from the analog source. Those mistakes can be avoided by recording with care, but some processes that can cause audible problems in digital audio are unavoidable. One of these is conversion of a 24- or 32-bit file to a 16-bit file. For complex mathematical reasons, this process creates an inevitable amount of low-level audio trash.

You are better off recording at 24 bits in your Cubase projects, but at some point you will need to create 16-bit files that can be burned to a CD. This will create some of that sonic trash, and the way to deal with this is a process called dithering. Dithering puts a tiny amount of noise in the converted file, and this low level of noise masks the sonic junk introduced in converting the 24-bit file to 16 bits.

The minutiae of various dithering algorithms and the particular type of noise used in the dithering process are the kinds of details that generate almost never-ending debate among audio geeks. You're in luck, though, because Cubase includes a very high-quality dithering plug-in called UV22. There are two versions of the plug-in: the UV22 (**Figure 17.17**) and UV22HR (**Figure 17.18**). Both do the same thing and differ only in that the UV22HR version allows you to specify the bit depth of the file whereas the UV22 automatically dithers to 16 bits.

continues on next page

- You select the dithering algorithms by clicking the **Normal** or **Low** button. Normal will work for nearly all situations; Low will introduce the smallest amount of dithering noise.

- **Autoblack** creates true silence during sections that are so quiet that the dithering noise is more likely to be noticed.

- **Bit Resolution** (UV22HR only) sets the output to 8, 16, 20, or 24 bits. This option is available only in the UV22HR plug-in. When exporting, you should be sure that the setting in the UV22HR plug-in matches the resolution you are rendering in the final mix.

USING UV22 DITHERING

GLOSSARY

ASIO: Steinberg developed ASIO as a cross-platform protocol for transferring multiple channels of audio to and from an audio interface at very low latencies. Always use the ASIO driver for your audio interface when working with Cubase.

Audio Event: Events are the smallest building block in Cubase SX. An audio event is a single audio clip or part of a clip that is displayed in the Project window. More than one event can be contained in an audio part, and much confusion about events arises from this fact. An event is the audio itself, the part is a container in Cubase to hold one or more events. See also, Audio Regions.

Audio Interface: The hardware used to get audio in and out of the computer is called the audio interface. Audio interfaces can use USB or Firewire to connect to the computer, or they can be PCI cards that install inside the machine.

Audio Part: (see *Part*)

Audio Region: An audio region is a part of an audio clip (event). When an audio file is recorded with Cubase SX, it creates an audio clip to represent that file for editing and processing. Parts of a clip can be designated as independent audio regions, which can then be easily converted to additional events in the project window, or exported and processed into new discrete audio files. Audio regions are almost always created and edited in the Sample Editor.

Automation: Moves and actions performed in the Cubase mixer can be automated. After writing automation, the mixer can reproduce the moves automatically when the project is played.

Bit Depth: When an analog audio is sampled to create digital audio (see *sample rate*), each sample can be of greater or lesser resolution. Cubase can record 16, 24, or 32-bit samples. The bit depth for an audio file or project is the resolution of the recorded samples—for example, a CD uses 16-bit samples—therefore it has a bit depth of 16.

Breakpoint: When a parameter is displayed graphically, and its setting changes over time, Cubase often will use breakpoints to show a change in direction or value for the parameter. Breakpoints are used extensively for things like setting a fade-in or fade-out curve, or for editing automation data.

CC Data: (see *MIDI Continuous Controller Data*)

Comping is taking multiple passes at the same musical part or phrase and selecting the best parts of each to create a new performance. Cubase has extensive tools for creating comps in the Audio Part editor.

Core Audio is the system-level multimedia toolkit that ships with Mac OS X that includes a driver type and plug-in format. Most Mac Cubase users will use ASIO drivers and VST effects, but other applications (and perhaps Cubase in the future) might use Core Audio.

Crossfade: When two audio parts or events are immediately adjacent to each other or overlap, the transition between them will often sound unpleasant. A crossfade quickly fades one out while fading the other in, smoothing the transition between the parts or events.

Cycle Recording: It's possible to record in Cubase when looping the project over the same section repeatedly. This is called cycle recording, and can be used to create MIDI and audio by combining the results of more than one pass over the same section of the project.

DirectX is the system-level multimedia toolkit that ships with Windows, which includes driver types and a plug-in format. Usually shortened to DX, these tools are used to support system level audio and MIDI transfer. Most Cubase users will rely on ASIO drivers, but many will have some DX plug-ins and perhaps a DX-supported MIDI interface.

Event: Events are the smallest building blocks in Cubase SX. An event can be a MIDI note or a sound sample or a recorded piece of audio. In the Project window, every event is contained in a part, and parts contain one or many distinct events.

Group Channel: A group in the Cubase mixer is a specialized channel that is used to mix other channels. A group receives audio from the other channels in the mixer, instead of from an audio track, ReWire channel, or VST instrument.

Insert Effect: An insert effect processes the entire signal for a channel. The entire audio signal from a channel is fed into the effect, the audio is modified in some way, and the audio output with the effect is fed to the rest of the mixer channel.

Mixer Channel: Each channel in the mixer controls an audio signal or a MIDI track. The audio signal can be from a VST instrument, a ReWire application, or an audio track in the Project window. MIDI channels control MIDI data from a track in the Project window.

MIDI stands for Musical Instrument Digital Interface. MIDI data most often is note and velocity information from a keyboard or other MIDI instrument. After MIDI has been recorded, the data can be used to trigger samplers, sound modules, and synthesizers.

MIDI Continuous Controller (CC) Data: Not all MIDI data is about notes. MIDI can also be used to control parameters in synthesizers and effects units. For example, it might be advantageous to record changes made to knobs and buttons on the front panel of a synth. In this case, the changes made on the front panel will be recorded as Continuous Controller data. CC data is edited and can be created manually in Cubase SX using the Project window, the Key editor, or the List editor.

MIDI Interface: The hardware used to move MIDI data in and out of the computer is a MIDI interface. Most current MIDI interfaces connect to the computer via USB.

MIDI Part: (see *Part*)

MIDI Sysex Data: Sysex stands for System Exclusive. The MIDI specification defines certain commonly used parameters to particular CC numbers, and leaves many CC channels undefined to apply as users and manufacturers see fit. Even this flexibility, however, is not always enough, and sysex data fills the gaps where MIDI is deficient. A manufacturer can use sysex to control any parameters they can dream up, essentially allowing proprietary uses of the open MIDI spec. Sysex is often used to back up and restore the entire state of a synth, effect unit, or studio.

Monitoring: Listening to the playback of a project is called monitoring. The best way to monitor in Cubase will depend on how your audio hardware is configured and what you are doing with Cubase.

Multitimbral: A synth (hardware or software) is said to be multitimbral if it can play different sounds when triggered by different MIDI channels. MIDI channel 1 might trigger a synth bass sound, while MIDI channel 10 triggers drums.

Mute: A track, part, event, note, or mixer channel can be muted. Once muted, it is silenced and will not play back in the project.

Part: A part in the Project window can contain MIDI or audio events. Parts are containers for events, and make it easier to work with more than one event.

Plug-in: Plug-ins are used to process audio and MIDI in the Cubase mixer. Cubase includes some plug-ins and additional, third party plug-ins can be added to the program. A plug-in lets you add sonic options to your palette without having to learn a whole new application.

Polyphonic: A synth is called polyphonic if it can play more than one note at a time. Many of the classic analog synths of the '70s were monophonic, meaning they could play only one note at a time.

Project Tempo: Each Cubase project has an assigned tempo, expressed as beats per minute (BPM). The higher the BPM, the faster the tempo of the project. Cubase has a special track, called the tempo track, for creating and editing changes in project tempo.

Punch Recording: Cubase can automatically start and stop recording at any point in a project. The points where Cubase starts and stops recording (called *punching in* and *punching out)* are set in the project window before starting playback, hence the term punch recording.

Quantize: Quantizing modifies the timing of a MIDI note or notes, usually to bring the MIDI notes closer to a tempo grid. Most often quantizing is applied after creating a MIDI part to tighten the timing of the performance.

Record Enable: When the red Record Enable button is pressed, a track is ready to record. When the Record button on the Transport is activated, whether manually or automatically, all tracks with the Record Enable buttons selected will start recording.

ReWire: Steinberg and Propellerheads jointly developed ReWire, a protocol that allows multiple applications to transfer audio, MIDI, and tempo data. ReWire is used to slave one piece of software to another on the same computer.

Semitone: Western music divides each octave into twelve notes that are all pretty much the same distance from each other. A semitone is the distance in pitch from one note to the adjacent note above or below it. An easy way to visualize a semitone is the piano keyboard: each key is a semitone apart from the next key.

GLOSSARY

Sample Rate: Digital audio is created by taking a specific number of snapshots (or samples) of an analog audio signal over time. The number of times the analog signal is sampled is called the sample rate. Common sample rates supported by Cubase include 44.1 kHz, 48 kHz, 88.2 kHz, and 96 kHz. At 44.1 kHz (the sample rate for CDs) the signal is sampled 44,100 times each second.

Send Effect: A send effect is an effect that runs parallel to the main path of the audio channel. When using a send effect, a copy of the original signal is split off and sent to the effect, leaving the rest of the audio path for the channel untouched. The audio processed by the send effect is mixed back with the non-effects signal, usually at the master fader.

Solo: When the Solo button is clicked, only that track will be played back. More than one track can be soloed to hear only a few tracks.

Sysex: (see *MIDI Sysex Data*)

Template: A Cubase template is a project that can be opened with the File > New command. You can create customized projects for your various needs, and save them as templates.

Tempo Track: The tempo track is an audible, but usually invisible, track in every Cubase project. The tempo of the project will be governed by the tempo track if the Master button on the transport is clicked on. The tempo track can be graphically edited in the Tempo Track editor.

Track: Cubase tracks are where MIDI and audio data are placed in the Project window. Think of each track like a clothesline: audio and MIDI parts and events are hung on the clothesline as they are recorded, and are rearranged when audio and MIDI are edited.

Transient: The initial part of a sound, particularly on an instrument that is plucked or struck, is called the transient. The transient is the short, loud, initial onset of the sound.

Velocity: Every MIDI note comes with data to represent how hard the MIDI controller was struck. This parameter is called velocity, and usually controls the overall output that results from the MIDI note.

VSTi: VSTi is short for VST (virtual) instrument, and is the general term for software-based sound generators. Most VSTis are synthesizers or samplers that generate sounds when triggered by MIDI.

Word Length: The sample taken when creating digital audio (see *sample rate*) can be of varying resolution. Often the samples are referred to as "words" and the resolution of the sample is called the word length. A project might be recorded with a sample rate of 96 kHz with a word length of 24 bits.

GLOSSARY

INDEX

INDEX

INDEX

INDEX